This book is the first in-depth analysis of the interaction between the British and Irish governments and the role they have played in seeking to resolve the conflict in Northern Ireland since 1980.

Eamonn O'Kane examines Britain and Ireland's objectives in relation to the Northern Ireland conflict, focusing on the influential factors that persuaded these two governments to co-operate at a closer level and those which made this co-operation difficult to achieve and at times sustain. Drawing on extensive primary research, consisting of interviews with leading British and Irish politicians and civil servants, the book questions many of the most widely accepted arguments regarding the conflict. The arguments questioned include the objectives of the two states in Northern Ireland, the origins of the peace process, the role of the international dimension and the reasons that the conflict appeared so intractable for so long. These interviews, instrumental in shaping the policies of both states, help to place events in context as they offer a more convincing explanation for many of the advances and disappointments in Northern Ireland in recent years than is currently available.

This volume offers a different approach to issues which Northern Ireland has faced and is an invaluable resource for students and researchers of British politics, Irish studies and conflict studies.

Eamonn O'Kane is Senior Lecturer in Politics at The University of Wolverhampton, UK. His main research interests are the Northern Ireland conflict and Anglo-Irish relations. He has published several articles on the Northern Ireland peace process and conflict resolution theory.

Routledge Advances in European Politics

Britain, Ireland and Northern Ireland Since 1980

The totality of relationships

Eamonn O'Kane

Routledge
Taylor & Francis Group

LONDON AND NEW YORK

First published 2007
by Routledge
2 Park Square, Milton Park, Abingdon, Oxon OX14 4RN

Simultaneously published in the USA and Canada
by Routledge
270 Madison Ave, New York, NY 10016

Routledge is an imprint of the Taylor & Francis Group,
an informa business

Transferred to Digital Printing 2010

© 2007 Eamonn O'Kane

Typeset in Times by
Integra Software Services Pvt. Ltd, Pondicherry, India.

British Library Cataloguing in Publication Data
A catalogue record for this book is available from the British Library

Library of Congress Cataloging in Publication Data
O'Kane, Eamonn.
Britain, Ireland and Northern Ireland since 1980 : the totality of
relationships / by Eamonn O'Kane.
p. cm. -- (Routledge advances in European politics)
Includes bibliographical references.
ISBN 978-0-415-36545-1 (hardback : alk. paper) --
ISBN 978-0-203-01683-1 (e-book : alk. paper)
1. Northern Ireland--Politics and government. 2. Great Britain--Foreign
relations--Ireland. 3. Ireland--Foreign relations--Great Britain. 4. Irish
question. I. Title.
DA990.U46O15 2007
941.085′8--dc22
2007001628

ISBN10: 0–415–36545–7 (hbk)
ISBN10: 0–415–60258–0 (pbk)
ISBN10: 0–203–01683–1 (ebk)

ISBN13: 978–0–415–36545–1 (hbk)
ISBN13: 978–0–415–60258–7 (pbk)
ISBN13: 978–0–203–01683–1 (ebk)

In memory of Peter O'Kane

Contents

Acknowledgements

This book emerged from an idea of Christopher Norton's and has benefited immensely from the innumerable conversations I have had with him over the years. Paul Dixon has long been a great source of support, advice and encouragement. Michael Cunningham made very helpful observations on earlier drafts. Peter Anthony waded through the manuscript in its various guises without complaining and provided a very helpful, non-subject obsessed perspective. The themes of the book have been road-tested at numerous PSA and PSAI conferences over the years and I am grateful to the 'usual suspects' for their comments and suggestions. The normal disclaimer applies.

I would like to thank the University of Wolverhampton for the research fellowship that was instrumental in enabling me to complete the book.

Perhaps my greatest debt is to the British and Irish politicians and civil servants who agreed to be interviewed. I hope they feel I have reflected their views fairly, even if they disagree with the conclusions I have come to.

I would like to annoy Bridget by publicly acknowledging the debt I owe her and thanking her for the companionship, patience and encouragement. Thanks to my mother, and sisters, Siobhain and Jackie, for having the good grace not to ask me too often when the book would be finished, and to Thea, Niall and Dylan for just being great.

Finally the book would never have got to this stage without the unorthodox independent financial advice of Chris Broom and Paul Maguire, which kept me from having to get a proper job for many years. Stay lucky boys.

1   Introduction

Anglo-Irish relations: A brief historical overview

Modern Anglo-Irish relations can be dated from the Government of Ireland Act of 1920. The 1920 Act created two new governments in Ireland, one in Belfast governing six counties of the northeast of the country and one in Dublin governing the remaining 26 counties. This situation pleased no group. Nationalists in Ireland had wanted one government to exercise control over the whole of Ireland (though disagreement existed as to whether this should be over an independent state or one exercising powers devolved from Westminster under Home Rule). Unionists in the North wanted to maintain the situation that existed between 1800 and 1920 with Ireland governed directly from Westminster. British politicians wanted to end the ability of the Irish issue to dominate the wider British political scene and felt this would be best served by Irish unity of some description. This tripartite separation of power between London, Dublin and Belfast was widely believed to be a temporary situation. The 1920 government of Ireland Act called for the creation of a Council of Ireland, which would help to pave the path to the eventual unity of the island. Yet events conspired to make such unity less rather than more likely.

The South and North 1920–69: Waiting for the inevitable?

The newly installed government in Dublin had to deal with a civil war and the acrimony that followed it for most of the early part of the post-settlement period. The border was left unchanged in 1925 at the conclusion of the work of the Boundary Commission, which had been created to review the situation. The Irish government had hoped to make substantial territorial gains as a result of the Commission's findings (Kennedy, 2000, p. 7). It became increasingly apparent that division was not to be a temporary situation. The election of Fianna Fáil in 1932, led by the man who dominated Irish politics for the best part of half a century, Eamonn de Valera, also reduced the chances of unity. Whilst de Valera claimed, 'until I die partition will be the first thing in my mind', the priorities of his government were to create a Catholic Gaelic Ireland rather than to implement policies that would secure unity. For de Valera the obstacle to unity was Britain, not the Ulster Unionists. The key to ending partition was to get Britain to break its link with the Unionists, not attempting to persuade the Unionists of the desirability of Irish unity. De Valera believed that unity was inevitable and a corollary of this was that the South did not really need to do anything to bring unity about (Bowman, 1989, pp. 300–338). De Valera's other priority was, as far as possible, to negate the conditions that the 1920 Government of Ireland Act and the 1921 Anglo-Irish Treaty imposed, and to govern as if Ireland was an independent sovereign country. Relations between Eire and Britain were poor for much of the 1930s as a result of an 'economic war' between the two states. Ireland refused to pay land annuities to Britain and followed a policy of economic protectionism. Relations with the Northern state also deteriorated as a result of de Valera's new constitution, enacted in 1937. The constitution enshrined the special position of the Catholic Church and claimed, in articles 2 and 3, jurisdiction over the six counties that constituted Northern Ireland.

De Valera left active politics in the 1950s (though he served as President, 1959–73) with little progress towards unity to show for his years in office. The combination of his belief in the inevitability of unity, the desire to reshape the culture of the South and redefine its relationship with Britain arguably militated against his adoption of a policy that could have increased the likelihood of unity. (Though it is questionable whether any policy adopted by de Valera during the period could have secured such an end.) Whilst de Valera may have been committed to the ideal of unity, he would not sacrifice his quest for increased sovereignty in pursuit of Irish unity.

De Valera's view appears to have been widely shared by the population in the South. Indeed the proclamation of the Republic by the Fine Gael-led government in 1948 (whilst de Valera's Fianna Fáil were in opposition) arguably further decreased the chances of unity (Fanning, 1983, p. 119). By at least the late 1950s, nationalism within the South was 26-county nationalism where the issue of sovereignty and economic advancement within the 26 counties was more important than the issue of the unity of the 32 counties (Mair, 1987, p. 87). Although all parties and leaders in the South continued to state their devotion to the ideal of unity and pledge themselves to furthering this aim, in terms of practical politics the preoccupation was with the economic problems faced by the South. De Valera's successor as Fianna Fáil leader and Taoiseach, Sean Lemass, pursued a more open economic policy towards both Britain and Northern Ireland. The meeting between Lemass and the Northern Ireland Prime Minister, Terence O'Neill, in 1965 was a hopeful sign, the first meeting between Irish and Northern Irish prime ministers since 1925. Lemass also appeared to be reviewing the traditional belief that Britain not the Unionists was the obstacle to Irish unity (Dixon, 2001, pp. 60–64; Patterson, 1999). Yet any hope of rapprochement between North and South and the normalisation of relations were to be dashed by the growth of the civil rights movement in Northern Ireland and the reaction of the Unionist establishment and population to it. The spiralling disorder within Northern Ireland and the outbreak of the Troubles in the late 1960s made attempts to improve North–South relations impossible. The Southern government came under increasing pressure to act to protect the nationalists in the North and the salience of the issue to the Republic's politics increased to levels not seen since partition. Pressure increased in the South to move from rhetorical republicanism to practical action. Unionists in the North saw increased interest by the South as a symptom of their traditional irredentism and looked to more hard-line leaders to protect them from the combined threat of nationalist militancy and Southern interference.

Britain's Irish policy 1920–68: Insulation not participation

Between partition and the Troubles 'the predominant disposition on the part of the British political elite was to insulate this last vestige of the Irish problem from the rest of the British political system' (Bew, Patterson and Teague, 1997, p. 14). The Irish question had dominated and at times defined the British political scene for much of the late nineteenth and early twentieth centuries. After partition British politicians were keen to see a line drawn under the issue. To this end an attempt was made to quarantine British politics from events in Ireland, both North and South. Although Northern Ireland was still nominally under the jurisdiction of Westminster, a convention developed whereby it was deemed out of order to raise any issue at Westminster that was the responsibility of the devolved Northern Ireland government at Stormont (known as the Speaker's Convention).

Anglo-Irish relations in the inter-war years were dominated by the economic war and strategic considerations. In 1938, as part of the negotiations that concluded the economic war, Neville Chamberlain's government agreed to return control to the Irish government of three ports Britain had retained for strategic purposes in the South of Ireland. This was to be an issue of concern for Britain during the war, as it was feared that loss of the ports left them potentially exposed to attack via the Atlantic and Ireland. The participation of Northern Ireland in the war greatly raised the stock of Ulster Unionism amongst British political establishment. Churchill praised 'the loyalty and friendship of Northern Ireland' in his victory speech and suggested if it had not been for Northern Ireland, 'we should have been forced to come to close quarters with Mr de Valera [over the ports] or perish for ever from the earth' (Carroll, 1975, p. 163). Ireland's international standing was damaged by the country's neutrality during the Second World War (Salmon, 1989).

The apparent improvement in Anglo-Irish and North–South relations under Lemass in the mid-1960s was welcomed by Britain. The focus of Anglo-Irish activity during this period was primarily economic co-operation rather than concern with the border and partition. Although Lemass may have believed that better North–South relations could be instrumental in undermining partition, the British sought to encourage O'Neill to improve relations with Dublin for its own sake rather than as part of a policy to bring about Irish unity (Bew, Patterson and Teague, 1997, pp. 24–25). Britain's policy towards Northern Ireland in the Lemass period had echoes of British policy throughout the post-1920 period, insulation rather than participation. Such a policy of keeping Irish issues at arm's length could not though survive the outbreak of the Troubles in the late 1960s.

The Sunningdale initiative, the advent of an intergovernmental approach?

The outbreak of violence in Northern Ireland took both London and Dublin by surprise. For all its rhetorical republicanism the South was unprepared for, and deeply disconcerted by, events in Northern Ireland post-1968 (Fanning, 2001). Similarly Britain, which had for so long sought disengagement from the Irish question, found itself forced to re-engage with the issue and ultimately, in 1972, to suspend the Stormont government and once again govern Northern Ireland directly from Westminster. Yet the desire to disengage remained prevalent in British politics and direct rule was seen as a temporary measure. The belief remained that some form of devolved government was the best solution for Northern Ireland. Nationalists would not countenance a return to the Stormont model under which one party, the Ulster Unionists, had ruled since partition. Whilst both London and Dublin may have been shocked by events on the ground in Northern Ireland, this shared shock did not translate into a shared analysis of the problem or the solution. The British government originally denied that the Republic had any right of input on the issue, whilst in the early days the Irish sought to criticise the British in international forums and relied on traditional anti-partionist rhetoric. But the desire by the British to return to a system of devolved government in Northern Ireland forced the two governments to work together. It became apparent that nationalists would not enter any talks that did not allow for a formal recognition of the 'Irish dimension' via an institutionalised role for the government of the Republic in Northern Ireland's affairs. The Irish for their part mirrored the British concern that events in Northern Ireland would destabilise the political situation in their own jurisdiction and moved from a position of anti-partionism to co-operating with the British government on how to best stabilise the situation within the North.

The result was laid out in a British White Paper of March 1973. In June 1973, an election was held for a new 78-seat Assembly under proportional representation. The election returned a majority of 52–26 in favour of the White Paper proposals, but such figures masked the deep division within Unionism that were becoming evident. The pro-White Paper Ulster Unionist Party (UUP), the nationalist Social Democratic and Labour Party (SDLP) and the Alliance Party of Northern Ireland (APNI) agreed to form a power-sharing Executive in line with the White Paper proposals (Cunningham, 1991, pp. 50–56). The idea of power-sharing was seen by many Unionists as a betrayal but it was the provision of an institutionalised Irish dimension via a Council of Ireland that inflamed rank and file Unionism within Northern Ireland. The Irish dimension had been agreed at a conference of the two governments and the UUP, SDLP and APNI in December 1973 at Sunningdale in Berkshire. The Sunningdale Conference was important for several reasons. It can be seen as the first attempt by the British and Irish governments to broker an agreement between the two traditions in Northern Ireland (an approach that, as we will see, was to become far more prevalent in the post-1980 period). It also appeared to mark an acknowledgement by the British government that Dublin had an interest in the affairs of Northern Ireland and concede a co-sponsor role to the Republic. The Conference also saw the acknowledgement by the Irish government that the consent of the majority in Northern Ireland was necessary for any change in Northern Ireland's status (although the Irish refused to amend their constitution to remove Articles 2 and 3).

The Council of Ireland never came to fruition as the Executive and the Assembly collapsed as a result of Unionist opposition. The 1974 Ulster Workers Council Strike brought Northern Ireland to a standstill. The end of the power-sharing Executive also marked the end of Anglo-Irish co-operation designed to broker agreement between the two traditions in Northern Ireland in this period. Anglo-Irish relations have been described as entering a 'black hole' between 1974 and 1979 (Arthur, 1996a, p. 116). Although attempts were made by the British government during the rest of the 1970s to restart inter-party talks between Unionists and nationalists in Northern Ireland, these were slanted towards a more internal settlement model and had no direct input from the Irish government or any comparable Irish dimension. The opposition of Unionists in Northern Ireland not only to power-sharing but also to an institutionalised role for the Irish government ensured that no British government attempted to resurrect the Sunningdale model for many years. Yet nationalists saw the abolition of Stormont as a victory and were unwilling to participate in any devolved structure that did not allow for both power-sharing and an Irish dimension.

The chances of a British government taking steps in the late 1970s likely to antagonise Ulster Unionists were further negated by Westminster arithmetic. Both the Labour government and the Conservative opposition courted UUP MPs at Westminster due to the slender Labour majority and the possibility of a hung parliament after the next election. The role apparently ceded to Dublin at Sunningdale was subsequently rescinded. The British government retreated from close Anglo-Irish co-operation to the position of Northern Ireland being an internal British problem. The Irish for their part also returned to a more traditional stance. Fianna Fáil, who whilst in opposition in 1975 had called for a statement by the British government of intent to withdraw from Northern Ireland, were returned to office in 1977 with a landslide. As a result the hope that Sunningdale marked the start of a close and productive Anglo-Irish co-operation turned out to be short-lived. Normal service appeared to have been restored with the collapse of Sunningdale.

Problems with existing interpretations

Although the existing literature on Northern Ireland is far from sparse, there has been relatively little work dealing in-depth with Anglo-Irish relations and the impact that the interaction between the two governments has had on the Northern Ireland situation. There has been a presumption in some quarters that the fact that the two governments have managed to co-sponsor several initiatives and agreements since the 1970s meant that the differences between the two states are negligible; unity rather than division has been taken as the hallmark of intergovernmental interaction. This analysis was most clearly articulated by the former Irish Taoiseach, John Bruton, in 1997. According to Bruton, 'When historians look back on this period, they will notice a remarkable consistency of purpose in British and Irish Government policy from 1972 onwards.' Whilst Bruton acknowledged, 'there have been concrete developments and changes' since the White Paper of 1972, he stated, 'the key elements in the approach of the two Governments has evolved in a consistent, organic way over the entire period' (Address to the Oxford Union, 7 May 1997). Yet as this study will show, the development of Anglo-Irish relations from 1980 has been far from consistent or organic. What united the two governments was an agreement that steps must be taken to end the violence in Northern Ireland. What divided the two states was disagreement over *how* to end the violence. Another former Irish Taoiseach, Garret FitzGerald, has argued that the only positive achievement of IRA violence was that it 'transformed the Anglo-Irish relationship'. According to FitzGerald in the 1970s the focus was on Irish unity versus Northern Ireland remaining part of the United Kingdom, but this divergence of interest between the two states 'has been subordinated to the common concern, the restoration of peace' (Mallie and McKittrick, 1996, pp. 27–28). Yet it is important not to conflate agreement on the need to end violence with agreement on how to end violence.

Even writers who have dealt directly with Anglo-Irish relations have a tendency to overstate the level of co-operation and underplay the tensions that have marked the relationship. Paul Arthur, who has written extensively on the subject, has highlighted some of the strains that have been evident in the relationship but gives the impression that development of intergovernmental co-operation has been relatively linear. Writing in 1996, Arthur claimed, 'Relations between Dublin and London have never been more purposeful or consistent than they have been for the past decade'. Yet, as Paul Bew has argued, Arthur 'fails to suggest the tensions which frequently characterized the meetings of the Anglo-Irish liaison committee of senior officials, the intergovernmental conferences or the daily exchanges at Maryfield secretariat at County Down" (*Times Literary Supplement*, 20 September 1996).

As well as a tendency to overstate the level of intergovernmental unity some of the existing literature has placed too much emphasis on the role of external agents. Arthur has also been prominent amongst those who have stressed the impact of the international dimension, especially the role of the United States, in shaping Anglo-Irish co-operation. One of the main arguments in Arthur's *Special Relationships* (Arthur, 2000) is the importance of the impact of international actors and opinion on Anglo-Irish activity. The problem with such works is they fail to give sufficient weight to more important domestic factors.

The constraints and considerations that impacted upon Anglo-Irish intergovernmental co-operation were primarily domestic in origin. Undoubtedly both London and Dublin were sensitive to international opinion and at times sought to use international opinion to their own ends. There is though little evidence that either state shaped its Northern Ireland policy primarily, or even markedly, in response to international considerations. The international dimension is a variable that needs to be considered in any attempt to explain Anglo-Irish interaction over Northern Ireland, but much of the recent work gives the variable more weight than the evidence warrants (see, for example Part V of Cox, Guelke and Stephen, 2006).

A similar criticism can be levied at work that places too much emphasis upon the actions of one government without giving sufficient weight to the role of the other. Arguments that rest on an imperialist interpretation have been widely discredited. These interpretations rest on the presumption that the British held onto Northern Ireland for economic or geo-strategic reasons and portrayed the Irish government as a 'puppet' of the British. Such accounts fail to explain either why the British were so keen to hold onto Northern Ireland (especially given the financial cost) or why the Irish government would allow their Northern Irish policy to be dictated by London (O'Leary and McGarry, 1993, p. 223). Yet influential recent work on Anglo-Irish relations and the origins of the peace process has to some extent reversed the traditional interpretation of the diplomatic asymmetry that was usually taken to be in favour of London over Dublin. It has long been correctly noted, 'Britain looms larger in the Irish consciousness than Ireland in the British' (Fanning, 1984, p. 42). Yet it is not the case that Ireland's alleged historical pre-occupation with Britain and Britain's historical tiring of Ireland created a situation whereby Irish policymakers effectively set the intergovernmental agenda and as a result dictated the shape that the co-operation took. Mallie and McKittrick in their analysis portray Irish policymakers as driving the process and their British counterparts as being at best reluctant participants whose impact upon the negotiations and shape of agreements was either negligible or negative (Mallie and McKittrick, 1996). The reality is far more complex. The differences between London and Dublin over the purpose, form, speed and depth of intergovernmental co-operation were certainly shaped by the views and actions of key individuals on the Irish *and* British sides. However, to fully explain Anglo-Irish co-operation in the period it is also necessary to examine the factors constraining the two governments and the resulting different priorities and analyses they held. Whilst factually a rich source of information, Mallie and McKittrick's work fails to engage with the British perspective to a sufficient extent.

The activities of the British government have been studied in-depth, which has gone a long way to explaining London's policy (Cunningham, 1991, 2001). But some such accounts can be similarly problematic. In the most recent study on British policy on Northern Ireland, Peter Neumann over-states the extent to which the British created and dictated the peace process. The account's assertion that the peace process effectively saw the other parties to the conflict adopting the 'British agenda' and 'compelled the IRA to declare an indefinite cessation of violence without having obtained any privileges, assurances or concessions' underestimates the extent to which the British were reviewing their own policy by the early 1990s (Neumann, 2003, p. 186). To explain and understand the peace process it is necessary to examine the extent to which all parties were willing to review long-held positions. Although providing something of an antidote to the Irish nationalist explanation offered by writers like Mallie and McKittrick, and serving to put the role of the British government back at the centre of analyses of the peace process, Neumann's account also overstates the influence of one of the parties.

This failure to examine and contextualise the constraints which the two governments faced has also led some writers to portray British and/or Irish policy-makers as having a remarkable level of decision-making autonomy with regard to Northern Ireland. It is the case that the lack of electoral salience of the issue of Northern Ireland in Britain has given British policymakers a degree of decision-making autonomy (Cunningham, 2001, p. 55) (and similar, if less pronounced claims can be made for the Irish government's position). Yet care must be taken. There is a danger if one fails to sufficiently appreciate the constraints faced by policymakers, then it becomes tempting to simply 'blame' the British and the Irish governments for the failure to secure a 'solution' to the problem sooner. An underlying theme of this work is that the ability of the two states to secure the outcomes that they desire in Northern Ireland is severely limited. In her evaluation of Anglo-Irish relations, Etain Tannam makes much of the shifts she claims have taken place in Anglo-Irish policy between 1973 and 1998. According to Tannam these shifts are largely as a result of 'policy learning' by the two states (Tannam, 2001). Yet Tannam fails to examine the changes that have taken place within nationalist, Unionist, Republican and loyalist thought in the period. As a result there is the implication that if only the British and Irish policymakers had learnt from their mistakes sooner, we could have arrived at a Good Friday type agreement long before 1998.

Similarly Brendan O'Leary's analysis of Conservative governments' Northern Ireland policy since 1979 argues that the apparent contradictions he identifies in British policy towards Northern Ireland are a result of 'ethno-national policy learning'. O'Leary seems to believe that the British basically had understood the true nature of the problem in 1973 with Sunningdale, and the Conservative Party moved away from this model after returning to power in 1979. The Conservative policymakers then undertook 'painfully slow learning' and 'took two decades to learn what Edward Heath mostly understood in 1973'. O'Leary is correct in his assertion that the reason for the apparent contradictions in British government policy in the period is not simply that the British government has responded to the inevitable pressures at work in a pluralist state, 'like a weathervane to the relevant political pressures' (O'Leary, 1997, pp. 636–676). Yet to understand Anglo-Irish relations it is necessary to evaluate the pressures at work at various times, as although these do not dictate the Anglo-Irish relationship they do have a pronounced influence upon it.

Whilst some accounts of specific Anglo-Irish initiatives offer rich and rewarding explanations of particular intergovernmental initiatives such as the 1985 Anglo-Irish Agreement, no convincing analysis examining and explaining the development and complexity of Anglo-Irish relations in the post-1980 period has been written. This work seeks to fill that gap.

This study deals with the period since 1980. The year 1980 represents what can be seen as the beginning of the latest phase of Anglo-Irish co-operation on Northern Ireland. The early 1980s saw the idea of an intergovernmental approach to Northern Ireland back on the agenda and two new leaders, Margaret Thatcher and Charles Haughey (both of whom came to power in 1979) dealing with the issue. Yet the development of the intergovernmental approach since 1980 has been far from harmonious or inevitable. This study seeks to explore and trace the development of the intergovernmental relationship since 1980. Why was it that two governments nominally in dispute over a territory could work closely to try and bring about a situation that arguably would not fulfil their traditional stated aims? Why, despite this apparent willingness to co-operate on the issue, were disputes between the two states still so prevalent? To what extent can the developments in Anglo-Irish relations over the period be attributed to the actions of individuals (agents) or to the structural constraints that the agents found themselves working within? Were the policies of the two governments over the period driven by ideology or pragmatism? Did the changes of governments in the Republic and Britain fundamentally alter government policy in London and Dublin and intergovernmental co-operation? To what extent is the peace process a result of intergovernmental co-operation or did intergovernmental disputes retard the peace process in the mid-1990s? This work contextualises intergovernmental co-operation. It examines and explains the vagaries and contradiction of the relationship and assesses the contribution of intergovernmental co-operation to the search for a resolution of the Northern Ireland conflict.

The importance of context

The task of attempting to contextualise developments in Anglo-Irish relations in order to understand the constraints that the two governments faced, and therefore why they took the decisions they did, is a difficult one. If too much emphasis is placed on the autonomous activities of individual agents, then the two governments can appear as Machiavellian masters choreographing developments in Northern Ireland to suit their own aims and objectives. Conversely placing too much emphasis on the structural constraints facing actors risks portraying the input and influence of the governments as negligible with London and Dublin appearing purely reactive and simply engaged in crisis management. The problem for any analyst is what weight to place on the various factors? This work argues that it is vital to examine the interaction between the structural constraints and the actions of the agents to fully appreciate the intergovernmental relationship and how it impacted on the Northern Ireland conflict during the period. The actions and motivations of the main agents have heavily influenced the arguments of this study, not least because the work draws on interviews carried out with many of them. Yet as far as possible the structural constraints impacting on the agents have been included and examined. The underlying thesis of the work is that the conflict in Northern Ireland, and as a result the actions of the two governments acting both unilaterally and intergovernmentally, was shaped by the constraints imposed by the interaction of numerous variables. The British and Irish governments did not have complete autonomy but were constrained by the necessity to shape policy in pursuit of what was possible rather than what was necessarily their desired outcome. Yet caution is needed. It is not the case that the constraints impacting upon the two governments were so great as to completely limit their ability to influence, and at times shape, the events on the ground in Northern Ireland. By examining the interaction of the structural constraints and the actions of agents a more complex and convincing portrait of Anglo-Irish relations emerges than that which has tended to be traditionally portrayed.

This study is not a comprehensive history of the Northern Ireland conflict. Others have provided such works (Bardon, 2001; Hennessey, 1997). Whilst important events in Northern Ireland during the period are dealt with they are done so from the perspective of the Anglo-Irish relationship. Nor is it an attempt to examine every facet of Anglo-Irish relations in the period. The focus is on the interaction of Britain and Ireland at governmental level. Although the Northern Ireland conflict has at times been influenced by wider elements of the British–Irish relationship and non-governmental Anglo-Irish bodies, such instances are only dealt with in so far as they had implications for governmental co-operation. Given the complexities of the Northern Ireland conflict no work can explain every facet of the issue. The best an author can hope to do is offer a convincing analysis of an aspect of the problem and challenge existing misconceptions. This work seeks to do both in its examination of Britain and Ireland's approach to the Northern Ireland question during the period.

Finally a justification is needed for the use of the term 'Anglo-Irish' rather than 'British–Irish' throughout most of the book. A strong case can be made that the latter term is the more accurate (Gillespie, 2006). This would centre upon claims that 'British–Irish' better reflects the decreased English domination of British policy, the impact that wider British devolution has had on the relationship and Ireland's decreasing economic and political dependence on Britain. Indeed the Irish Taoiseach made such a case in speech in 1999 (Ahern, 1999). There is weight in such an argument. (It should be noted though that much of the responsibility for formulating Ireland's policy on Northern Ireland remains with the 'Anglo-Irish division' of the Department of Foreign Affairs.) The significance of wider British devolution was acknowledged with the creation of the British–Irish Council as part of the Belfast Agreement in 1998 (more commonly referred to as the Good Friday Agreement (GFA)). Wider British devolution did perhaps assuage Unionist concerns regarding Northern Ireland's exceptionalism. But at another level there is little to indicate that such considerations have significantly altered the policies of either Britain or Ireland towards Northern Ireland. The term 'Anglo-Irish' is used for most of the book as it was the one most commonly invoked to describe the relationship for most of the period under consideration. Although 'British–Irish' is employed at times in the later chapters, reflecting its wider usage since the late 1990s, the term 'Anglo-Irish' is also used in these chapters for reasons of convenience and consistency.

2 The growing pains of an intergovernmental approach?

The year 1980 saw the newly installed Irish Taoiseach, Charles Haughey, attempting to shift the direction of Northern Ireland policymaking from initiatives in the North to an intergovernmental focus on the North. Yet the hope that was evident in late 1980 of a closer and more productive intergovernmental relationship soon waned, the relationship deteriorated sharply in 1981–82. This chapter examines the early 1980s and examines why Haughey sought to pursue the intergovernmental avenue with such apparent zeal, and why in December 1980, Mrs Thatcher, seen as the most Unionist of British prime ministers of modern times, led the highest profile British delegation to the Republic since the formation of the Irish state. It demonstrates that these events were not the result of a shift in the analysis of the two governments to a shared evaluation of the problem. The actions of both the Haughey and the Thatcher governments can be explained in terms of domestic considerations and the perceived self-interest of the two states. The problem that was to become evident in the years following 1980 was that the perceived self-interest of the two states did not coincide to a large enough extent. The two governments did not manage to agree to what ends they were co-operating in 1980. This disagreement over ends led the two states to question the means of co-operation in the aftermath of the 'high' of 1980.

The period 1981–82 highlights the fact that the intergovernmental relationship is subject to a multitude of pressures. The two governments face contradictory demands and expectations, which can make pursuing a co-ordinated approach to the Northern Ireland issue extremely difficult. The fault-lines that emerged in the 2 years following the Dublin summit illustrated well the opportunities for the Anglo-Irish relationship to be undermined by happenings within Northern Ireland, on the wider international stage, and by domestic events within one or other jurisdiction.

Charles Haughey's 'new' policy for Northern Ireland

In his first address to the Fianna Fáil Ard Fheis as Taoiseach, Haughey set out what was to be the basis of his Northern Ireland policy. According to Haughey, 'The time has surely come for the two sovereign Governments to work together to find a formula and lift the situation onto a new plane, that will bring permanent peace and stability to the people of these islands.' The speech contained three proposals: the way to solve the problem was by the two sovereign governments working together; Ireland would seek to internationalise the issue; and for the British to declare 'their interest in encouraging the unity of Ireland' (*Irish Times*, 18 February 1980). Of these the first proposal was the most important. Talk of 'enlisting the aid of all our friends in support of our interests' according to diplomats actually meant 'very little in practical terms' (*Irish Times*, 23 February 1980). (In this respect Haughey's policy was not that different to his predecessors as Ireland had often in the past sought to harness international support to pressurise Britain to alter policy over Northern Ireland, with little success. Though the British were concerned to limit international criticism of their policy) (O'Kane, 2002). Similarly the call for the British to declare in favour of a united Ireland was little more than a rhetorical flourish. What was interesting was that Haughey did not repeat the demand that had been made by Fianna Fáil in 1975 for the British to withdraw from Northern Ireland (Arnold, 1993, pp. 136–137). Haughey's energies during his first term were spent on seeking to persuade the British to consult and co-operate with Dublin over Northern Ireland. He placed a far greater importance on intergovernmental co-operation than on seeking to reach an accommodation within Northern Ireland between Unionism and nationalism. This was seen as a break with the previous Irish view, held since the outbreak of the Troubles, that reconciliation within Northern Ireland itself was a more pressing goal than unity (see Dennis Kennedy's series of articles in *Irish Times*, 19–21 February 1980). According to Haughey, 'We must face the reality that Northern Ireland, as a political entity, has failed and that a new beginning is needed . . . . This Government sees Northern Ireland as the major national issue, and its peaceful solution as our first political priority' (*Irish Times*, 18February 1980).

Margaret Thatcher's policy

The Conservative Party's 1979 election manifesto had contained a commitment to a broadly integrationist approach to Northern Ireland. This integrationist approach was dropped, however, after the election. Instead the early policy of Thatcher's government was to launch a round of talks between the Northern Ireland Secretary of State (NISS), Humphrey Atkins, and the constitutional parties in Northern Ireland (Atkins Talks). These were aimed at securing agreement between the Northern Irish political leaders that would allow the British to devolve government back to Northern Ireland. The November 1979 White Paper outlining the approach contained no reference to an Irish dimension. (Though Atkins subsequently allowed discussion of the Irish dimension to be held in parallel talks to ensure the SDLP's participation.) Haughey's invitation notwithstanding there was a marked reluctance on the part of the Thatcher government to seek 'new planes' for considering Northern Ireland throughout 1980. Thatcher told the Commons in May 1980 that 'The future of the constitutional affairs of Northern Ireland is a matter for the people of Northern Ireland, this Government and this Parliament, and no one else' (House of Commons, vol. 985, col. 250, 20 May 1980). It was against this back-drop of a professed desire by the Irish to seek an inter-governmental approach to Northern Ireland, and an attempt by the British government to achieve an internal solution to the problem, that the first Thatcher–Haughey summit took place in May 1980 (Thatcher, 1993, pp. 385–386).

The teapot summit

In the run up to the summit hopes of a breakthrough on the Irish side centred upon Haughey's ability to convince Thatcher that the Atkins Talks were based upon too narrow a remit. For the Haughey government the problem was three-dimensional: the internal affairs of Northern Ireland, North–South, and Anglo-Irish relations (*Irish Times*, 21 May 1980). However, the British for their part played down the significance of the meeting. On the eve of the summit Humphrey Atkins repeated the British assertion that Northern Ireland was not a subject for anyone other than the people of Northern Ireland, Britain and the British Parliament (*Irish Times*, 10 May 1980).

The impact of the summit itself was relatively slight. Although the two leaders agreed to institutionalise twice yearly meetings, there was little to suggest that Haughey had convinced Thatcher of the need for his three-pronged approach. The two issued a joint communiqué stating, 'The Prime Minister and the Taoiseach each agreed that they wished to develop new and closer political co-operation between their two Governments'. In one respect though the summit was a success. By all accounts Haughey charmed Thatcher in London – he had presented her with a silver Georgian teapot. It was as a result of this summit that Thatcher developed her 'initial – and surprising . . . – if short lived – affection for Charles Haughey' (Howe, 1994, p. 413). Haughey himself described his private conver-sation with Thatcher as 'one of the friendliest and most open of my political career' (*Irish Times*, 22 May 1980). However, whilst the two leaders may have got on well at a personal level this on its own would not be enough to improve Anglo-Irish relations. It was important for Haughey to secure some tangible gains in regard to Northern Ireland to appease his own Republican flank. As the commentator, Mary Holland, noted, 'Mr Haughey has embarked upon a court-ship of Mrs Thatcher but he is by nature a man who expects some return for his courting' (*New Statesman*, 30 May 1980).

The Irish put a very positive interpretation on the summit; it was even claimed that Haughey 'left Downing Street . . . convinced that the British Prime Minister, Mrs Thatcher, is now prepared to give the problem of Northern Ireland the kind of attention once devoted to reaching a settlement in Zimbabwe' (*Irish Times*, 22 May 1980). Haughey refused to give any details of the talks though, claiming that he had agreed with Thatcher that the talks would remain confidential. As a result it is impossible to know what was discussed regarding Northern Ireland between the two leaders, but Bruce Arnold has claimed that actually very little conversation regarding Northern Ireland took place. Thatcher was apparently unwilling to discuss the issue and steered the conversation to wider international issues. Arnold maintains that Haughey's statements at the press conference afterwards 'had little to do with the actual content of their talks and a great deal to do with his imaginative perception of what they might have implied or suggested' (Arnold, 1993, p. 168). What is clear, however, is that Thatcher was not convinced of the need for his three-dimensional consideration of the Northern Ireland issue as evidenced by her government's discussion paper, *The Government of Northern Ireland. Proposals for Further Discussions*, published on the 2 July 1980, barely 6 weeks after the London summit.

Continuing the search for internal agreement

The first round of the Atkins Talks were adjourned indefinitely on the 24 March 1980 after making little progress. Atkins attempted to relaunch the initiative in July proposing two different models, neither of which contained any reference to an Irish dimension. The proposals illustrate that the British Government did not agree at that stage that the problem needed to be approached intergovernmentally. Haughey and the SDLP leader, John Hume had both impressed on Thatcher the importance of considering Northern Ireland in a wider context than just internal governmental arrangements. The Taoiseach had had a high-profile summit with Thatcher and had publicly pledged himself to harnessing international opinion to promote an intergovernmental approach. The Irish Government had let their disquiet at the July proposals be known before they were published and the Taoiseach had appeared on the influential British television programme, *Panorama*, to explain his position. Yet the July proposals contained no Irish dimension. In August, Humphrey Atkins specifically stated that whilst 'the South has as keen an interest as anybody else outside the United Kingdom' in the government of Northern Ireland, 'it is our responsibility and nobody else's' (*Irish Times*, 19 August 1980). Yet less than 4 months later there was to be talk of 'historic' breakthroughs and pledges by Haughey and Thatcher to consider 'the totality of relationships within these islands' and developing 'the unique relationship between the two countries'.

The Dublin summit

The discussions held between the Irish and the British Governments at Dublin Castle on the 8 December 1980 were, according to *The Irish Times*, 'the most extensive to have been held by Irish and British Ministers on Irish soil since the foundation of the State' (*Irish Times*, 8 December 1980). The British delegation included the Prime Minister; the Secretary of State for Northern Ireland, Humphrey Atkins; the Foreign Secretary, Lord Carrington; and The Chancellor of the Exchequer, Geoffrey Howe. The joint communiqué, which was issued at the end of the conference, noted that 'the peoples of the United Kingdom of Great Britain and Northern Ireland are inextricably linked' but this was put under strain by the situation in Northern Ireland. To this end 'they accepted the need to bring forward policies and proposals to achieve peace, reconciliation and stability; and to improve relations between the peoples of the two countries'. The paragraph that was subsequently debated and contested noted the governments would

> devote their next meeting in London during the coming year to special consideration of the totality of relationships within these islands. For this purpose they have commissioned joint studies, covering a range of issues including possible new institutional structures, citizenship rights, security matters, economic co-operation and measures to encourage mutual understanding.
>
> (*Irish Times* 9 December 1980)

The key phrases here are 'totality of relationships' and 'new institutional structures'. These rather ambiguous words were to provoke a great deal of debate as to what was actually envisaged by the two governments and, ultimately, to be a source of disagreement between the two governments on what had been agreed.

From May to December

Why then was there this apparent change in attitude by the British government between the middle and the end of 1980? And why was the Irish Government so keen to move consideration of Northern Ireland onto the intergovernmental level? The reasons for the change in emphasis are, like so much in Anglo-Irish relations, multifaceted and different factors can be identified that influenced the two governments.

It is debatable just how much a 'break' with the past Haughey instituted with the Northern Ireland policy he outlined in February 1980. At one level the idea of seeking to co-operate with the British government over the Northern Irish issue was a return to the policies of Sunningdale. Yet Haughey's plans placed a far greater emphasis on co-operating to bring about Irish unity rather than on seeking to stabilise the North as an end in itself. As such his approach had echoes of the traditional de Valerian policy of an earlier period, but with a greater emphasis on co-operating with Britain. What is clear though is that the vocal advocacy by Haughey of an intergovernmental approach was a departure from the Irish government's policy since the collapse of Sunningdale. (An avenue that was arguably closed to Haughey given his unacceptability to Unionists as a result of his connection to the arms crisis of 1970.) Haughey's stance was primarily motivated by domestic considerations. A 'success' in the Northern field would be a welcome distraction from the poor state of the Irish economy, although the chances of such a success were highly questionable. Such an approach also had the advantage that it could appease the important Republican wing of his parliamentary party. Such considerations, when coupled with Haughey's ideological view of the Northern Ireland issue, his belief that the British rather than the Unionists were the key to the issue, offer the most convincing explanation for the Fianna Fail leader's pursuit of intergovernmental co-operation.

Thatcher's attitude to the possibility of an intergovernmental approach to Northern Ireland is more ambiguous and hesitant than the enthusiasm of Haughey. In the period between the May and the December summits, Thatcher appeared to soften her stance on co-operating with the Irish. This can in part be explained by an increasing exasperation with Northern Ireland politicians. The failure of the Atkins Talks had led the British to despair of finding an agreement amongst the Northern Ireland parties and as a consequence of this exasperation the British were more inclined to respond positively to Haughey's overtures (*Irish Times*, 19 November 1980 and 13 December 1980). An intergovernmental approach would have the advantage of not requiring the agreement of the parties within Northern Ireland. It would also send a message to the Unionists that the British were determined to make progress and so may force them into a more accommodating stance (*New Statesman* 20 February 1981).

Whilst there was frustration with the lack of progress in the North this did not, of itself, necessitate the search for a different approach. The failure of previous initiatives, such as the 1975 Convention, had not caused Britain to pursue increased co-operation with Dublin. Other factors contributed to the apparent decision by the British to review Anglo-Irish relations by December 1980 not least security considerations. Thatcher viewed Anglo-Irish relations primarily in security terms. As she noted, 'I started from the need for greater security, which was imperative. If this meant making limited political concession to the South, much as I disliked this kind of bargaining I had to contemplate it. But the results in terms of security must come through' (Thatcher, 1993, p. 385). It was often unclear what level of security co-operation Thatcher was expecting or what political concessions she was willing to offer (an issue that was much debated during the later Anglo-Irish Agreement negotiations). In 1980, there was some speculation that Haughey was considering offering a British–Irish defence pact in return for a federal Ireland (*Irish Times*, 19 May 1980; FitzGerald, 1991, p. 351). Nothing came of this speculation, which was highly unrealistic on many levels, though it led to a heated debate in the Dáil on Irish neutrality. The primary concern for Thatcher, however, was security co-operation in relation to Northern Ireland (Thatcher herself ruled out a defence pact citing Britain's NATO membership and asserting 'it is not a bilateral matter'.) (*Irish Times*, 7 March 1981). Although Thatcher had stated in May that 'we are getting very good co-operation on security matters from across the border' (House of Common, vol. 985, col. 712, 22 May 1980), security remained a prime motivation for her and seems to have been a key consideration for her decision to go to Dublin in December 1980.

In October 1980, Republican prisoners in the Maze prison began a hunger strike. The British were concerned that the Irish government might adopt a critical stance in relation to the British handling of the protest or come out in favour of the hunger strikers' demands. If Thatcher were seen to be working with Haughey, it would be more difficult for him to criticise her handling of the hunger strike. As Padraig O'Malley noted, 'The more extravagant his claims of their mutual agreements, the more trouble he would have in repudiating her intransigence should the prisoners die' (O'Malley, 1983, p. 26). It was even claimed that British ministers considered it an extraordinary achievement that Haughey had not issued a statement favouring the IRA hunger strikers (*The Times*, 13 December 1980). This would have been difficult given that the policy of the South when faced with hunger strikes was markedly similar to that being pursued by the British government: a refusal to negotiate and allowing prisoners to die if they persisted with the strike. As a result the failure of Haughey to support the hunger strike was hardly surprising, let alone extraordinary. But the possibility for ambiguity in such matters was illustrated by an editorial in the *Irish Times* in the run up to the summit, which argued, 'To be sure, Irish Governments themselves will not be blackmailed by hunger-strikers. But the Government concerned today is not an Irish Government. Britain hardly needs support from our own people' (*The Irish Times*, 27 November 1980). (This particular hunger strike was called off before any of the prisoners died.)

It is the combination of the frustration with the lack of progress towards reaching agreement with Northern Ireland's parties, a desire to pursue possible ways of improving security co-operation and the desire to reduce the impact of the hunger strikes that led Thatcher to Dublin in 1980. However, this action should not be interpreted as an indication of Britain's acceptance of an intergovernmental approach. Indeed the attempts by the Irish to portray it as such were instrumental in damaging relations between the two states over the following months.

The effect of the Dublin summit

The outcome of the summit was portrayed in strikingly different ways. A commentator in the *Irish Times* claimed, the communiqué, strength of the British delegation and 'the British abandonment of any further attempts at an "internal settlement" in the North' meant it 'would be perverse to interpret the Dublin Castle meeting as anything but a significant new departure. The context has been changed and with a vengeance' (*Irish Times*, 23 February 1981). Yet according to the *Daily Telegraph* the summit was actually an attempt by Thatcher, 'to graft an Irish dimension on to the policy of full integration for Ulster in the United Kingdom' (*Daily Telegraph*, 10 December 1980). It was possible to draw such diverse interpretations due to the contradictory statements issued by British and Irish ministers in the days following the summit.

Haughey spoke of being 'in the middle of an historic breakthrough' and argued that the problems facing the two governments had been placed 'firmly on a new plane' (*Irish Times*, 9 December 1980). When asked whether the study of possible institutional structures referred to in the communiqué would concern direct arrangements between Ireland and Britain or a North/South arrangement, Haughey stated, 'A combination . . . both are possible . . . we set no limit on what institutions might be brought forward, might be considered, might be designed, might be conceived . . . '. In an off-the-record briefing for Dublin political correspondents, Haughey apparently went further and anticipated a future united Ireland. 'In order to achieve this, the "institutional structures" . . . were elevated by implication and innuendo, to "constitutional" ones' (Arnold, 1993, p. 155). The Minister for Foreign Affairs, Brian Lenihan, stated a few days later, 'as far as we are concerned everything is on the table' (*Irish Times*, 13 December 1980). When FitzGerald inferred from Haughey's statement to the Dáil that the constitutional position of Northern Ireland was not under consideration, the Taoiseach retorted, 'I am not accepting what Deputy FitzGerald said' (*Irish Times*, 12 December 1980).

The British on the other hand suggested far less had been agreed. At her own press conference after the summit Thatcher stated that she was committed to exploring whether the 'unique relationships' between the two states should be given 'institutional expression'. She did though, in answer to a specific question, state, 'I see absolutely no possibility of a confederation'. She also explicitly stated that the British guarantee to the Unionists would remain and 'There is nothing for the Unionists to worry about' (*Irish Times*, 9 December 1980). But worry they did, with the UUP leader, James Molyneaux, describing the summit as 'deplorable' (*Irish Times*, 9 December 1980), his colleague, Enoch Powell, calling the summit 'a mini Munich' (*Irish Times*, 11 December 1980), and Ian Paisley setting off on the 'Carson Trail' (*Irish Times*, 10 February 1981). The reason for this persistent difference in interpretation was the reluctance of both sides to clarify exactly what had been discussed at the summit.

Thatcher refused to make a statement in the House of Commons regarding the summit and placed it in the context of a routine meeting with a fellow European government, a stance that caused concern for Unionists (House of Commons, vol. 95, col. 1182, 9 December 1980). Thatcher did state in the House of Commons the following week that 'We were not considering any specific constitutional measures' (House of Commons, vol. 96, col. 210, 16 December 1980) but her refusal to make a statement on the summit was taken by some as 'confirmation that something is up' (*The Times*, 13 December 1980). Indeed it was not until the following March, when specifically asked if Thatcher and Atkins were lying that Lenihan acknowledged that it was institutional and not constitutional matters that were under consideration in the joint studies (*Irish Times*, 19 March 1981).

Despite the unsustainably inflated claims the Irish government attempted to make for the Dublin summit, the meeting was not without significance. Padraig O'Malley rightly argued the concept of an Anglo-Irish dialogue meant something different to all those who were involved in it (O'Malley, 1983, p. 19). What is clear though is that the summit did help to put intergovernmental co-operation back on the agenda in both London and Dublin. As a result of the Dublin summit, joint studies were carried out and institutional changes to how Anglo-Irish relations were conducted occurred. The Dublin summit did not herald the start of an unbridled intergovernmental approach to Northern Ireland, but it does mark the movement of the two governments towards greater, and institutionalised, co-operation on the issue.

Conflict and recrimination: A return to normality?

Within a few months of the summit intergovernmental relations were on a downward trajectory and whatever hopes there had been for improved inter-governmental co-operation seemed misplaced. Co-operation was problematic as a result of the 1981 Republican hunger strikes and the British government's latest plan to devolve government back to Northern Ireland. The international climate was dominated by the Argentine invasion of the Falklands, which, as if to demonstrate the fact that there is little in the Anglo-Irish relation-ship that cannot be viewed through the prism of Northern Ireland, further undermined the ability of London and Dublin to co-operate on the issue. Co-operation was also increasingly difficult due to the relative instability of the Irish governments with three being elected in 18 months. Whilst these epis-odes are at one level separate, each one had an impact on the Anglo-Irish relationship.

The 1981 hunger strike: Dealing the IRA a whole new deck

The hunger strike by IRA and INLA prisoners in the Maze prison in 1981 was to be one of the most destabilising events of the Troubles. Whilst its immediate effect was to increase tension and violence within Northern Ireland, its longer-term effects were far more important.

The 1980 hunger strikes had ended in confusion in December 1980 with the prisoners believing the British government had agreed to change prison conditions but ended the fast before the 'deal' had been formalised to save the life of one of the hunger strikers. The British government subsequently failed to make the changes Republicans demanded and denied any deal had been done. The 1981 hunger strike was a far more bitter and intense affair. The prisoners were again protesting for what was in effect the restoration of political status, which had been removed in 1976 – though as the protest developed the emphasis shifted away from political status and centred upon five demands, which in essence would have been the reintroduction of special category status. (The five were the right to wear their own clothes; to free association; increased recreational facilities; more visits and letters; and the restoration of lost remission.) What transformed the situation in 1981 was the election of the first hunger striker, Bobby Sands, to Westminster during his fast. After Sands died his agent, Owen Carron, was elected in his place. The electoral successes of Bobby Sands and Owen Carron were to lead to the adoption of the 'ballot box and armallite' strategy of Sinn Féin. The reaction of the nationalist community to the deaths during the hunger strikes served to increase the mistrust between the two communities in Northern Ireland.

In terms of the effect the hunger strike had on the Anglo-Irish relationship, in the short-term the hunger strikes, and more specifically the British handling of the dispute, led to a worsening of relations between the two states. In the longer-term, however, the result of the strike, and, more importantly the subsequent electoral rise of Sinn Féin, was to be a key factor in forcing the two governments to review their relationship. This review would contribute significantly to the decision to sign the 1985 Anglo-Irish Agreement.

The British government's handling of the hunger strike

The British government, at relatively little cost, could have avoided the 1981 hunger strike. If the British had introduced the changes to the prison regime after the 1980 hunger strike that they eventually introduced after the 1981 strike the subsequent history of Northern Ireland and Anglo-Irish relations may well have been very different. The 1980 hunger strike had ended with no deaths and relatively little impact on the political life of Northern Ireland. By contrast the 1981 hunger strike saw ten hunger strikers die; Republican prisoners and their supporters elected to the British and Irish parliaments; huge international coverage of the dispute and an increase in the levels of street violence in both the north and the south of Ireland. Most importantly of all the 1981 hunger strike set Sinn Féin on the path to entering the electoral arena, which was to have a profound impact on British and Irish policy formation.

Once the 1981 hunger strike began it was highly unlikely the British government would make changes to the prison regime whilst the strike continued. Thatcher was adamant that there was no question of conceding special category status to Republican prisoners. According to Thatcher 'Crime is crime is crime, it is not political' (*Irish Times*, 22 April 1981). Elements within the British government appear to have failed to appreciate the implications that the hunger strike could have. Thatcher spoke of 'the men of violence' who 'faced with the failure of their discredited cause' chose 'to play what may well be their last card' (*The Guardian*, 29 May 1981). The observation of Sinn Féin's Joe Austin that the British were actually 'dealing the IRA a whole new deck' was the more accurate comment (Clarke, 1987, p. 166).

Even the significance of Sands' election as a Westminster MP appears to have been underestimated by some. Atkins, discussing the subsequent decision to change the law to prohibit prisoners standing for election, remarked several years later:

> It's a fearful waste of time doing that, isn't it? As the chap can't serve anyway . . . . It's a negation of the whole democratic process to say, 'go on, you can elect anybody you like even if he can't sit there'. All that happens is that your choice is immediately disqualified and you knew that he was going to be before you started, so don't waste everybody's time.
>
> (Atkins, 26 October 1993)

The British government could afford to take such a publicly hard-line stance on the hunger strike as there was little pressure on them at either Westminster or from amongst the wider British public to pursue a different policy. The British Labour, Liberal and SDP parties all supported the stance of the Thatcher government. It had been a Labour government that removed special category in 1976. In 1981, Labour's Northern Ireland spokesman, Don Concannon (who had been an NIO minister in 1976) stated, 'the Opposition agree that the Maze prison is the newest and most modern prison in the United Kingdom and . . . for conforming prisoners the regime is the most liberal in the United Kingdom' (House of Commons, 3 March 1981). Although the Labour Leader, Michael Foot, privately urged Thatcher to make some concessions at a later stage of the hunger strikes, publicly Labour never deviated from this stance (Thatcher, 1993, p. 391).

Similarly public opinion in Britain was far from sympathetic to the plight of the hunger strikers. An opinion poll in England and Wales conducted after Bobby Sands' death showed 89per cent of people had no sympathy whatsoever for the hunger strikes and only 4 per cent backed the prisoners' demands (O'Malley, 1990a, p. 201).

It is, however, by no means clear that the British government never contemplated making concessions to end the hunger strikes. The NIO minister, Michael Alison, had a series of meetings with the Dublin-based Irish Commission for Justice and Peace (ICJP) and there was hope that a deal might be reached. Reports at the time suggested that Thatcher over-ruled Alison and refused to agree to prisoners being allowed to wear their own clothes as of right. The ICJP later stated that Alison 'acted in good faith' but there had been 'a clawing back on the part of the British government' on the day the NIO official was due in the Maze to confirm the details (*Irish Times*, 9 July 1981). Alison later made reference to the 'lady behind the veil', a comment that the ICJP took as a reference to Thatcher (O'Malley, 1990a, p. 90). The account offered in 2005 by one of the IRA leaders inside the Maze during the hunger strikes, Richard O'Rawe, claims that an offer was made by the British via an MI5 agent (known as the 'Mountain Climber') that was acceptable to the prisoners. The IRA's external leadership subsequently rejected this offer. O'Rawe suggests that the reason for this rejection may have been because they believed a better deal could be negotiated with the British. However, he is also deeply critical of Gerry Adams on the issue and notes that it may have served the external leadership's purpose to prolong the strike to ensure Owen Carron was elected (O'Rawe, 2005, pp. 181, 184–190, 221–223). The account is contentious from a Republican perspective as it suggests that the external leadership may have prolonged a strike that the prisoners themselves were willing to end and the deaths of 6 of the 10 hunger strikers could have been avoided. Other Republicans involved have vehemently rejected the account (*Irish News*, 12 October 2006; *An Phoblacht*, 3 March 2006 and 8June 2006). The account is also contentious from a British perspective as it seems to confirm the suspicion of the suggestion that they were liasing with the IRA over how the dispute could be ended. Whether the government had sanctioned this 'deal' remains unclear.

By the end of July the British publicly let it be known that changes would be made to the prison regime when the strike ended. As a British official put it, 'We haven't exactly said they can have their own clothes but we've made it pretty bloody clear they'll get them. And there are other things we can do, the gates are open. We haven't said it, nor will we say it, but we're giving them essentially what they want' (*Irish Times*, 25 July 1981). The problem was that this was the position that Republicans thought they were in at the end of the 1980 strike and the concessions had failed to materialise. The greater mistrust in 1981 accounts for the longevity of the strike.

It is hard to conclude that the British government handled the 1981 hunger strike anything but poorly. Although it may have appeared an important precedent that they would not make concessions under the duress of a hunger strike, as argued above, questions need to be raised regarding why they allowed themselves to become embroiled in the 1981 situation. If changes had been made after the 1980 dispute ended, the situation could have been defused. Ironically these changes could, perhaps, have been less extensive than the British eventually made after the 1981 strike. If this had been done, then Republicans could have been denied the increased validity and support within the nationalist community that the 1981 events provided. The 1981 hunger strike was one of the turning points in the history of the Troubles and Thatcher must surely be in a very small minority with her opinion that it 'was a significant defeat for the IRA' (Thatcher, 1993, p. 393).

The hunger strike and Dublin: A nudge and wink to secure a fudge?

The 1981 hunger strike also illustrated important aspects of the true state of Anglo-Irish relations in the early 1980s and of the attitude of the South towards the North. The hunger strike showed that Dublin was relatively powerless to alter British policy in Northern Ireland, and claims of a newly institutionalised role for the Republic after the 1980 Dublin summit were premature. The strikes also demonstrated that Dublin's residual fear that events within Northern Ireland could have a destabilising impact on the politics of the South was perhaps not misplaced.

The hunger strikes posed a particular problem for the Irish government. It was the long established policy in the South not to negotiate with hunger strikers or grant political status within their own jurisdiction. There could be no question of the Irish government attempting to pressurise the British to secure for the IRA a status that they themselves denied that organisation. However, there was the ever-present fear that events within the North could spill over and destabilise the Southern state. This concern was to lead the Irish to publicly refuse to support the demands of the prisoners whilst at the same time attempt to play a role in brokering an end to the dispute. Most of the five demands of the prisoners were available to similar prisoners held in the South, without being termed political status. The Irish government believed that a compromise might be possible whereby prison conditions were changed, perhaps for all prisoners, without conceding that this conferred political, or even special, category status. As the Irish political commentator, Joe Joyce noted,

Few people [in the South] want IRA men to be treated as prisoners of war, but most accept that they are not 'criminals' in the conventional sense. The difficulty in resolving the prison status of such people has been solved in the Republic by nods, winks and flexibility. Why it is asked, time and time again, cannot Britain fudge the issue too? Why does it seem intent on confrontation?

(*The Guardian*, 4 May 1981)

The hunger strike came at an inconvenient time for Haughey, who wanted to call an election for May 1981 and was understandably keen that the hunger strike was over before the Irish electorate voted. To this end Haughey reversed his previous stance of not meeting the families of the hunger strikers and contacted Bobby Sands' sister, Marcella Sands, on 22 April, in an attempt to get her to make a formal complaint to the European Commission on Human Rights. Marcella Sands made the complaint but the initiative collapsed when Bobby Sands refused to meet the Commission members without the external Republican leadership of Gerry Adams and Danny Morrison present.

Within a few weeks of Sands launching his fast, pressure was growing on Haughey from elements of his own party. Sile de Valera, a Fianna Fáil TD and two other TDs, who were also MEPs, Neil Blaney and John O'Connell, went to meet Bobby Sands and then called for an urgent meeting with either Thatcher or the Home Secretary, Willie Whitelaw, to discuss the issue. Thatcher dismissed this noting, 'It is not my habit or custom to meet MPs from a foreign country about a citizen of the UK, resident in the UK' (quoted in Clarke, 1987, p. 146). Not for the first or last time, Thatcher's tone inflamed Irish sensibilities. Mary Holland argued the, 'public snub to Sile de Valera, one of Mr Haughey's most critical supporters within his own party will not be forgotten. The claim to have a special relationship with Thatcher would not be something any Irish politician would want to boast about in the event of Bobby Sands' death' (*New Statesman*, 1 May 1981).

The increased violence and disruption in the South (though not on the scale of that in the North) signalled a worrying potential for the hunger strike to destabilise the Republic. The Irish government urged a resolution to the issue on 'humanitarian' grounds but was careful to neither endorse the Republicans' demands nor be seen to criticise the hunger strikers. To this end Haughey offered 'deepest sympathies' to the families of the hunger strikers who died stressing, 'I have constantly made known to the British Government the deep concern and anxiety felt by the Irish Government at the developing and highly dangerous situation as we saw it . . . ' (quoted in Mansergh, 1986).

Haughey's unease over the hunger strike and his fears that it could damage Fianna Fáil in the election were warranted. The decision by the H-Block campaign to field candidates in nine constituencies in the Republic was to be a deciding factor in the election. Whilst the hunger strike itself never became the primary issue in the election – again illustrating that Southern voters, whilst concerned with Northern Ireland, vote primarily on 'domestic' issues such as the economy – the H-Block candidates secured enough votes to capture two seats, both from Fianna Fáil. Fianna Fáil secured 78 seats in the new Dáil as opposed to the combined 80 seats of Fine Gael and Labour. The two H-Block victories almost certainly cost Haughey the Taoiseach's office.

The H-Block supporters had been successful in their stated aim: to punish Haughey for what they perceived was his lack of support over the hunger strikes. The result enabled FitzGerald, someone who had traditionally shown less sympathy with Republicanism than Haughey, to become Taoiseach. At first FitzGerald appeared to be even more interventionist on the issue than Haughey. As soon as he took office FitzGerald pledged to make the settling of the hunger strike the first political priority of his administration (*Irish Times*, 1 July 1981). This stance was dictated more by domestic political concerns than any sympathy with the plight of the hunger strikers. The election had demonstrated the ability of events in the North to have repercussions on Southern politics. FitzGerald was now faced with the situation where an elected member of the Dáil, Kieran Doherty, was starving himself to death in a British prison. However, FitzGerald did not move away from the Haughey stance of not supporting the demands of the hunger strikers. He was also careful not to take steps which could be perceived as bestowing legitimacy on those connected with the H-Block campaign (For example, he refused to meet Owen Carron to discuss the hunger strike after Carron was elected as MP. Haughey was not as restrained in opposition though and did meet Carron and explicitly pledged support for the hunger strikers' five demands) (*Irish Times*, 2 September 1981).

FitzGerald was aided in his attempt to get a solution based on a compromise over prison conditions by a statement issued by the hunger strikers on 4 July 1981. The statement refuted the allegation that they were seeking special treatment. It noted they 'would warmly welcome the introduction of the five demands for all prisoners' (O'Rawe, 2005, p. 168). This appeared to the Irish Government to provide a possible framework for solution. If the British announced changes to the general prison system in Northern Ireland, then it could be argued they had not conceded a special status to Republican prisoners and the dispute could end. FitzGerald is clear on this point:

> If it had been a net issue that the only way of ending it would be to give in to the IRA, then we would have stuck it out. But when it became evident in the first few days in government that it could be ended by arrangements that would not have given in to the IRA ... well then it seemed reasonable to press the British on those things.
>
> (FitzGerald, 13 November 1993)

There followed intense discussions between the two governments over the issue. The breakdown of the ICJP initiative, discussed above, caused particular annoyance to the FitzGerald government who believed the initiative was undermined by the secret communication between the British government and the IRA. FitzGerald wrote to Thatcher arguing that 'a rising tide of sympathy for the hunger strikers was threatening the stability of the Republic'. He urged Thatcher to use the apparent agreement negotiated by the ICJP as a basis for a settlement. FitzGerald specifically linked the hunger strike issue with wider Anglo-Irish co-operation. He informed Thatcher that ending the hunger strikes 'would restore a climate in which our efforts could again be directed to more positive and constructive endeavours in pursuance of the process initiated by her and my predecessor in December 1980'. (The obvious implication being that it would not be possible to improve the relationship whilst the hunger strike continued.) He also appears to have threatened actions that the British would have viewed far more seriously: calling into question Irish maintenance of the present levels of cross-border security co-operation. The only effect this appears to have had, however, was to antagonise Thatcher. In her reply Thatcher 'repudiated any suggestion of [British] bad faith' and, FitzGerald recalled, 'responding to my remarks . . . about the problems of ensuring security co-operation in these circumstances, she remarked that the British reaction to any suggestion of less than full co-operation in security matters would be "sharp and bitter" ' (FitzGerald, 1991, pp. 372–373).

FitzGerald also wrote to Ronald Reagan

> to ask him, in view of the increased support accruing to the IRA as a result of the situation, which was threatening our security, to use his influence with the British Prime Minister to secure the implementation of what I described as 'an already existing understanding' mediated by the Commission for Justice and Peace.
>
> (FitzGerald, 1991, p. 372)

The move served only to highlight the traditional reluctance of American presidents to jeopardise Anglo-American relations over Northern Irish issues. FitzGerald acknowledges the approach to the Americans was counterproductive. 'It was an abortive approach, which must have made the British more irritated but produced no positive result. In retrospect it was a mistake' (FitzGerald, 13 November 1993). Similarly FitzGerald's attempts to enlist the help of EC states to pressure the British government bore little fruit (*Irish Times*, 18 July 1981).

FitzGerald reduced his government's involvement in the affair at the end of July. By this time it was clear that the lobbying of the British by Dublin was having little effect and the violence in Dublin on 18 July 1981 when 10,000 people attempted to march on the British embassy outraged the Irish government. This spill over of violence onto the streets of Dublin was seen as instrumental in reducing the support for the hunger strikers cause in the Republic (Clarke, 1987, p. 182; O'Malley, 1990a, p. 150).

The effect of the hunger strikes on the Anglo-Irish relationship

The hunger strikes illustrated the relative powerlessness of Dublin to influence the British government to change its policy. Whilst Haughey may have boasted of a special relationship and being conceded a new partnership status in relation to Northern Ireland, the hunger strikes were to demonstrate a very different reality. From the British point of view, internal Northern Ireland matters were clearly and simply that: internal matters. Attempts by the Irish government under Haughey and FitzGerald to try and persuade the British to deflate the issue by making changes to the prison regime were to no avail. The Irish input into how the British government conducted its policy was purely dictated by the prevailing attitude of the British government itself. During the hunger strike period the Irish government invoked almost all of their 'tools' to influence the British: private representation and intergovernmental contact, international opinion and threatening to reduce security co-operation. Yet there is little evidence that any of these made an impression on Thatcher or her policy.

Eventually the Irish government accepted that they could not persuade Britain to alter their policy on the issue. As FitzGerald noted, 'There was simply nothing to be gained by pressing the British government any further; we should just have to live with the consequences of the way they had handled the situation . . . ' (FitzGerald, 1991, p. 375). The Irish were not willing to escalate the dispute with Britain not least because the issues of concern to Dublin in the context of Anglo-Irish relations were much broader than a dispute over how prisoners were detained in the Maze. There was a growing concern amongst policymakers in Dublin that the deteriorating situation in Northern Ireland could have implications for their own stability. The hunger strikes and the resultant rise of Sinn Féin exacerbated these fears during the early 1980s. As a concomitant of this Dublin felt that improved Anglo-Irish relations were more important than ever if the apparent increase in support for militant Republicanism was to be addressed. Dublin was faced with the ironic reality that the hunger strikes, which had led to deterioration in Anglo-Irish relations, illustrated why Anglo-Irish relations had to be improved. This explains why, even at the height of the hunger strikes, efforts were taken to ensure the issue would not derail wider Anglo-Irish relations. During the protest the two Cabinet Secretaries Dermot Nally (Irish) and Sir Robert Armstrong (British) met to prepare the ground for a future summit – eventually held in November 1981 (FitzGerald, 1991, p. 375).

This is not to say that the hunger strike issue had no lasting influence on Anglo-Irish relations. The irritation felt by Haughey over Britain's handling of the hunger strike may have been a contributory factor in the Irish stance over the Falklands conflict. Irish exasperation with the British over the hunger strike was to be mirrored the following year by British exasperation with the Irish over the Falklands.

The Falklands: Tweaking the British lion's tail?

Haughey returned to office as head of a minority government in February 1982. This meant that another election in the relatively near future was likely. It is against this background of leading a minority government that the actions of the Haughey government in relation to the Falklands conflict must be set.

Although the Irish government initially agreed with the imposition of EEC sanctions in April 1982, a month later the Irish were to call for the ending of economic sanctions and used their position as a member of the UN Security Council to call for an 'immediate' meeting of that body to review the situation. (Ireland had been elected to the Security Council for a 2-year term in 1981.)

The immediate catalyst for this change in stance was the sinking of the Argentine ship *The Belgrano* by the British, on 2 May. The Minister of Defence, Paddy Power, stated 'We felt that Argentina were the first aggressors. Obviously Britain themselves are very much the aggressors now'. The Minister went on to explicitly link the issue to the situation in Northern Ireland stating only a withdrawal of British troops 'from the little island of ours' would bring peace to Ireland (*Irish Times*, 4 May 1982). Whilst Haughey claimed that 'it was a personal statement by the Minister for Defence and does not represent Government policy,' he pointedly did not rebuke Power for the comments and refused calls for his dismissal (Dáil Éireann, vol. 334, cols. 36–37, 4 May 1982).

Such anti-British rhetoric led to expressions of anger by some members of the House of Commons. The British government was, however, very careful not to have a public spat with the Irish. A spokesman for the British Foreign Office when asked about the Irish stance after Power's comments and the call for an end to sanctions stated, 'It would be much better if we did not comment' (*Irish Times*, 6 May 1982). The strongest public statement from the British side was the assertion of the NISS, Jim Prior, to the House that 'We have been disappointed by the Irish Government's attitude in recent weeks . . . ' (House of Commons, vol. 26, col. 1026). Privately though it was reported that Thatcher was furious. One British government source claimed if Haughey 'was to turn up tomorrow with a silver coffee-pot she's likely to crown him with it' (*Irish Times*, 18 May 1982).

Why then did the Irish government's stance on the Falklands alter? The Irish Government claimed that the escalation of the dispute into a military conflict meant that, due to their neutral status, Ireland could no longer support sanctions. Haughey informed the Dáil that

> As a neutral country, we are not prepared to back military action. Nothing in our EEC obligations requires us to give such a backing. We consider that it would be inappropriate for these measures to remain in force if they were being applied or seen to be operating so as to reinforce a military solution to the crisis rather than to promote a diplomatic and negotiated settlement.
>
> (Dáil Éireann, vol. 334, col. 802, 11 May 1982)

The accuracy of Haughey's interpretation of the obligations and necessities of Irish neutrality was questionable on two counts. First Ireland had in the past supported sanctions after military conflicts had arisen and indeed Ireland had actually endorsed the EEC sanctions after hostilities started on 2 April (Salmon, 1989, p. 272). Secondly the claim that it became impossible to continue to support the sanctions after the British launched military action is hard to accept given that the sanctions were imposed after the British Task Force had set sail for the Falklands. Haughey did attempt, rather unconvincingly, to get around this point by claiming that when it was dispatched 'the British Task Force was on what appeared to be a blockade mission' (*Irish Times*, 7 May 1982) an interpretation of the Task Force's role that few commentators seemed to have shared when it departed.

Whether the sanctions did compromise Irish neutrality or not, it is difficult to refute FitzGerald's other accusation that the Haughey government's actions over the Falklands was 'riddled . . . with inconsistencies and contradictions' (Dáil Éireann, vol. 334, col. 806, 11 May 1982). Dublin's Falklands policy appeared to be constructed on the hoof, or as the leader of the Irish Labour Party, Michael O'Leary, put it in the Dáil, 'an excessive reliance on improvisation' (quoted in MacQueen, 1985, p. 48). Confusion surrounded when the Irish Government were seeking an end to the sanctions, at one time apparently calling for the sanctions to be ended immediately, and later calling for them to end after the original sanctions elapsed on 17 May (see Dáil Éireann, 4 May 1982 and 11 May 1982). Haughey's government was also criticised for the 'extraordinary omission' of a call for Argentine withdrawal from the Falklands in the Irish proposal to the UN (*Irish Times*, 5 May 1982). In the end the machinations of the Irish at the UN and EEC was to have little effect other than to strain relations with Britain. There was no UN resolution calling for a cease-fire and the EEC did renew the sanctions, though Italy and Ireland refused to agree – a somewhat symbolic stance as both countries did agree not to violate the EEC sanctions.

Why would the Irish take actions that were bound to antagonise their relationship with Britain? Economic explanations cannot account for the stance. As Austin Deasey of Fine Gael told the Dáil: 'Economically our stance is suicidal'. Ireland's trade with Argentina amounted to only £15.5 million per annum (£9.5 million exported to Argentina, £6 million imports) as opposed to the £4,500 million of trade between Britain and Ireland per annum (*Irish Times*, 1 June 1982). (Indeed statements from Haughey that Ireland would not break the sanctions and would 'go along with whatever our Community partners decide' (Dáil Éireann, vol. 334, col. 39, 4 May 1982) were somewhat superfluous as all Irish exports to Argentina went via Britain (Dwyer, 1987, pp. 163–164).) Once again domestic considerations and the Northern Ireland issue offer the most persuasive explanations of the Irish stance.

Given Fianna Fáil's lack of a majority, Haughey was reliant on the support of independent TDs to retain power. One theory in this regard is that Haughey's more anti-British stance can be accounted for by his need to retain the support of independent TDs with Republican sympathies, such as Neil Blaney (Arnold, 1993, p. 192). Another suggested reason was that Haughey took the more critical anti-British stance in order to protect himself from a leadership challenge from within Fianna Fáil (Coughlan, 1986, p. 62). The fact that the Haughey government was a minority administration undoubtedly limited its room for manoeuvre. To suggest, however, that the Irish government's foreign policy was entirely dictated by the party's Republican wing over-simplifies the interaction of the three events that shaped the Anglo-Irish relationship at this time: the hunger strikes, Rolling Devolution plan (discussed below) and the Falklands crisis. By 1982, Haughey appears to have become increasingly frustrated with the reneging by the British government on the agreement he believed he had secured in December 1980 to be of consulted over Northern Ireland. The Falklands spat can be seen as an expression of this frustration rather than an unavoidable consequence of Ireland's neutrality (an example of Fanning's observation that at times the Irish succumb to the 'temptation to tweak the British lion's tail') (Fanning, 1984). If Mary Holland was right when she claimed Haughey 'is by nature a man who expects some return for his courting', his perceived rejection by Thatcher over both the hunger-strike and the Prior plan may well account for his more vociferous anti-British stance. This is not to suggest that Haughey was behaving as a petulant thwarted suitor; rather he appears to have made a judgement that 'if the special relationship is not going to pay any dividends, he would do better to exploit the strong anti-British sentiments among Fianna Fáil's supporters' (*Economist*, 29 May 1982). The Falklands stance had, from Haughey's point of view, the advantage that it 'provided Ireland with the opportunity to demonstrate to Britain the value of a special relationship in the two forums in which she has international influence, the UN Security Council and the EEC' (*The Guardian*, 19 May 1982). Whilst it may not be the case that elections were won by 'Brit-bashing', there is also little to suggest that any Fianna Fáil leader was damaged by being seen to take a tough line in relation to the British.

Rolling Devolution: Conceivably the last variant of a devolutionist strategy (Bew and Patterson, 1985, p. 123)

James Prior, who replaced Humphrey Atkins as NISS on 13 September 1981, decided 'within a few weeks of arriving in Northern Ireland . . . a fresh political initiative was urgently needed to bridge the gap between Catholic and Protestants' (Prior, 1986, p. 189). The Prior plan centred upon the idea of 'Rolling Devolution', a concept first suggested by Brian Mawhinney in July 1980 (Cunningham, 1991, p. 147). Prior proposed a new 78-member Assembly elected by proportional representation that in the first instance was to simply shadow the work of the NIO departments. Prior hoped that as the members from the various parties co-operated in this monitoring role they would 'gradually get used to the idea that they could work together' (Prior, 1986, p. 195). In this respect Prior's plan was based on the hopeful premise that, unlike in the old adage, familiarity would breed consent. As a level of understanding and agreement emerged the Assembly could apply to the NISS for certain powers to be devolved to an executive. The pre-requisite for this was the support of 70 per cent of the Assembly. This was a device aimed at protecting the position of the minority and ensuring that the Assembly would not exercise power on the basis of simple majority rule. Prior also allowed for the provision that the Secretary of State could recommend to

Parliament the transfer of power even if the 70 per cent hurdle was not reached as long as the NISS was happy that the proposals had general cross-community support.

Contrary to what is sometimes claimed, the Prior plan did not theoretically necessitate a power-sharing executive. Prior told the House of Commons that the only criteria was cross-community support, 'that does not have to be achieved by a power-sharing executive' (House of Commons, vol. 21, col. 700, 5 May 1982). The White Paper stated clearly that 'It will be for the Assembly to consider and report on how powers should be exercised'. In reality though the SDLP would never have countenanced such an arrangement and the need for cross-community support effectively gave that party a veto on the creation of an executive.

The White Paper outlining Rolling Devolution was published on 5 April 1982, 3 days after the Argentine invasion of the Falklands. Whilst the timing was far from ideal (the Home Secretary, William Whitelaw, had urged him to delay the proposals) it was the content, or lack of it, that was to prove contentious. The Prior plan, like any proposal for Northern Ireland, came up against the problem of conflicting expectations and priorities between the two traditions in Northern Ireland and, perhaps even more problematic for Prior, divisions within the British Government and between the British and the Irish governments. Whilst Prior may have had the advantage of being a heavyweight on the British political scene and the highest profile NISS since Willie Whitelaw, he was handicapped by his poor relationship with the Prime Minister. He acknowledged that there was a belief that Thatcher posted him to Northern Ireland 'to get rid of me from the centre of government'. Though other senior members of the Cabinet, notably Whitelaw, the Defence Secretary, Francis Pym and Humphrey Atkins were supportive of Prior's proposals, Thatcher and the Lord Chancellor, Quintin Hailsham, were far from convinced. Prior claims that in Cabinet discussion Thatcher 'made her views abundantly clear, saying that she thought it was a rotten Bill . . . ' (Prior, 1986, pp. 171–199). Thatcher noted in her memoirs, 'Ian Gow, my PPS, was against the whole idea and I shared a number of his reservations' (Thatcher, 1993, p. 394).

The reluctance of the Unionists to embrace a plan that seemed to be designed to force them to co-operate in government with the SDLP was unsurprising. Since the failure of the Sunningdale plan in 1974, Unionists had, in general, opposed power-sharing in any guise. Whilst the DUP welcomed the plan on the grounds that it was a step towards devolved government, the UUP, divided as it was between integrationists and devolutionists, were very half-hearted in their attitude to the proposals and their participation in the subsequent Assembly was marked by periodic boycotts. The attitude of the Prime Minister, the SDLP and the Irish Government, however, can all be explained in relation to the other issue which was a legacy of Sunningdale: the Irish dimension.

For Thatcher the legacy of Haughey's 'over-selling' of the December 1980 summit had made her reluctant to grant too high a profile to the Irish government in relation to Northern Ireland. The Irish Government claimed that there had been a lack of consultation by Prior with Dublin over the plans. The forthright criticism of the Prior plans and the complaints about the lack of consultation led the British to take the very public step of calling in the Irish Ambassador to inform him that Britain did not consider itself obliged to consult Dublin on matters relating to Northern Ireland (*Irish Times*, 28 July 1982). Thatcher underlined this very publicly in the House of Commons 2 days later stating, 'no commitment exists for Her Majesty's Government to consult the Irish Government on matters affecting Northern Ireland. That has always been our position. We reiterate and emphasise it, so that everyone is clear about it' (House of Commons, vol. 28, col. 1225, 29 July 1982).

The Irish for their part continued to claim that a right of consultation had been granted at Dublin Castle. In a statement the Irish referred to the Dublin communiqué and claimed, 'In the light of this agreed statement and many other similar ones it is difficult to find any justification for the recent British claims that there was no commitment on the part of the UK Government to consult with the Irish Government on matters affecting Northern Ireland' (*Irish Times*, 30 July 1982).

The deterioration in the personal relationship between Thatcher and Haughey cannot, on its own, account for the apparent lack of consultation between London and Dublin over the rolling devolution plans. For most of the period when the plans were being drawn up it was FitzGerald, not Haughey, who occupied the Taoiseach's office. FitzGerald had had a relatively harmonious summit with Thatcher in November 1981 (see below) and had launched a 'constitutional crusade' to make the South more secular and so less threatening to Ulster Unionists. Such considerations did not result in the inclusion of an Irish dimension or to Prior consulting the FitzGerald's administration to any great degree. Whilst he was less vociferous in his opposition to the Prior plans, it is the case that FitzGerald was concerned about the proposals. To this end he wrote 'privately' to Jim Prior weeks before the White Paper was published urging him to give greater consideration to the Irish dimension (*Irish Times*, 1 March 1982). Given that this took place after the election but before the Dáil vote on who would be Taoiseach, it may again be at least in part a play for votes in the Dáil but both FitzGerald and Haughey were frustrated with the lack of consultation and absence of what they regarded as an effective Irish dimension.

The White Paper itself had very little to say on the Irish dimension. It merely 'welcomes the significant improvement in relations between the two countries in recent years' and stated, 'Relations between the United Kingdom and the Republic will in general continue to be conducted within the ambit of the Council'. There had been speculation since the 1980 summit that a parliamentary tier would be added to the Anglo-Irish Intergovernmental Council, formally created in 1981. This was one of the main objections of the UUP who claimed that the Assembly was simply a mechanism to provide a body from which the Northern Ireland representatives to the parliamentary tier could be drawn. There is no doubt that such a proposal was contained in the earlier drafts of the White Paper, which Prior had shown the UUP in mid-March. By the time the White

Paper was published the parliamentary tier was once again a matter 'for the parliaments concerned to consider'.

The official British line was that the Irish dimension was not being watered-down since it was now dealt with through the mechanism of the Intergovernmental Council. Prior claimed the White Paper was concerned with trying to bring about internal devolution to Northern Ireland, a separate issue.

> [T]he reason why the Bill does not deal with the Anglo-Irish Intergovernmental Council is that these are not matters on which any further legislation is required. The Anglo-Irish Intergovernmental Council is already established. There is already statutory provision in the 1973 Act enabling a Northern Ireland Administration to reach bilateral agreements with the Government of the Republic on transferred functions if they so wish. Hon. Members interested in the proposed interparliamentary body will appreciate that an elected Northern Ireland Assembly would provide an opportunity for a valuable Northern Ireland input to any such body on which this House and the Dáil may agree. In that respect the proposals are complimentary and not alternatives to the Government's policy of maintaining sensible, and indeed, close arrangements for co-operation with the Republic.
>
> (House of Commons, vol. 23, col. 474, 10 May 1982)

This idea that there was now a formal 'delinking' of the two traditional elements seen as comprising the basis of any solution, a devolved (presumably power-sharing) administration in Northern Ireland and an Irish dimension, has a logical appeal. Discussion of an Irish dimension alienated Unionists and made them less likely to agree to work with the SDLP to find an acceptable form of devolved government. At the same time the SDLP would not accept any purely 'internal' settlement that ignored the Irish dimension. If the two issues could be separated progress on both fronts was more likely. In his review of the various attempts to broker a solution for the Northern Ireland problem David Bloomfield claims under the plan:

> the Irish dimension was now a matter for the two governments to consider through the Anglo-Irish Intergovernmental framework, and was no longer directly on the local agenda. . . . The new strategy was now based on the assumption that the Unionist veto might remain uninvoked in a straight-forward discussion of power-sharing, while any nationalist veto might also be avoided if they knew, via Dublin, that the Irish dimension was being addressed in a different arena.
>
> (Bloomfield, 1997, p. 36)

However, this argument is flawed for three reasons. First, on a purely practical point, it would be virtually impossible to 'separate' the two issues to the extent that would be necessary to create the situation Bloomfield envisaged. The Unionists would not discuss power-sharing if it were obvious that an increased Irish dimension was being discussed on a separate parallel track. If the SDLP were to be reassured that the Irish dimension was on the agenda, they would have to know about it so it would have to be evident that an Irish dimension was being given serious consideration, which in turn would alienate the Unionists. The two spheres could not be separated to a satisfactory extent; there would inevitably be 'leakage' between the two forums.

Secondly, for this to be a coherent policy it required that both the British and the Irish Governments be party to the arrangement. The Irish had to feel that the intergovernmental plane was being fruitfully and seriously utilised by the two governments. This was clearly not the case in respect to the Prior plan. The Irish complained about the lack of an Irish dimension in the White Paper. The Irish Government evidently did not agree that the intergovernmental relationship was adequately catered for in the Intergovernmental Council. Bloomfield claims the separation was effective in so far as it allowed the Irish Government to reassure the SDLP that the Irish dimension was being addressed in a different arena; hardly the case in this instance. A joint statement issued by the Irish Government and the SDLP damningly noted, 'Both sides considered that the proposals as they were emerging were unworkable. They found them deficient in that they concentrated on the details of an administration in Northern Ireland without due regard for the broader dimension of the problem' (*Irish Times*, 23 March 1982).

The third and more fundamental reason why the delinking thesis is unconvincing is because, by his own admission, Prior wanted to address the Irish dimension in the White Paper but was forced to remove proposals for a much stronger Irish dimension by Thatcher:

> although the suggestions which I had made for greater co-operation with the Republic of Ireland fell well short of the arrangements which had been agreed at Sunningdale between the British and Irish Governments in 1973, they were far too much for her. She insisted that a separate chapter on Anglo-Irish relations in my draft should be scrapped, and a less positive version incorporated at the end of the chapter on 'The Two Identities' in Northern Ireland.
>
> (Prior, 1986, p. 197)

Thatcher later wrote, 'before publication, I had the text of the White Paper substantially changed in order to cut out a chapter dealing with relations with the Irish Republic' (Thatcher, 1993, p. 394). Whilst it is unknown exactly what Jim Prior had wanted to include in regard to the Irish dimension it is clear that by failing to address the Irish dimension in any recognisable form, the plan was unlikely to achieve its goal of achieving devolved government for Northern Ireland.

Thatcher's opposition to the Irish dimension was not surprising given her apparent Unionist instincts, the influence of Ian Gow and Enoch Powell, and her mistrust of Haughey; but it was counter-productive. Due to the exclusion of the Irish dimension the plan was unworkable. It did not even have the advantage of being welcomed by the Unionists. Enoch Powell claimed it was 'a deliberate conspiracy to keep the Province in turmoil until it can be disposed of' and Molyneaux questioned why a devolved system of government was necessary at all (House of Commons, vol. 22, cols. 874–875, 28 April 1982). Prior acknowledged that the divisions within the British Government undermined the Assembly from the outset. It would, he claims, have been better to have 'taken on the Unionists' and been 'more generous to the Nationalists' (Prior, 1986, p. 199). It also worsened Anglo-Irish relations with the Irish effectively breaking off negotiations with the British when Haughey refused Prior's request for a meeting in September (*Irish Times*, 10 September 1982).

Ironically the only group who benefited, at least in the short term, from the creation of the Assembly were Sinn Féin. In the elections for the Assembly in October 1982, Sinn Féin contested a Northern Ireland-wide election for the first time and secured 10.1 per cent of the vote, against 18.8 per cent for the SDLP, leading to fears that Sinn Féin may ultimately replace the SDLP as the voice of Northern Nationalists and decreasing any likelihood that the SDLP would participate in the Assembly. The Assembly limped on, never attended by the SDLP, and was finally wound up in June 1986 when it became a forum for Unionist protest against the Anglo-Irish Agreement.

Hope amongst the gloom?

The 2 years following the December 1980 summit were fractious times in the Anglo-Irish relationship but nestled between the lows of the hunger strike and the Prior plan/Falklands problems was a relatively successful summit in November 1981. It was at this summit that the joint studies set up after the Dublin summit in December 1980 were discussed. In the meantime FitzGerald had replaced Haughey as Taoiseach. The studies themselves were divided into five areas: possible new institutional structures; citizenship rights; economic co-operation; measures to encourage mutual understanding and security issues. It was decided at the summit that all the reports, with the exception of the security study, should be published. The main reason for this was to try and deflate some of the more excessive speculation that had surrounded the run up to the studies in the post-Dublin summit days. The studies themselves were a relatively workmanlike exercise that contained nothing especially controversial. *The Times* leader went so far as to claim the result of the studies 'looked rather meagre' (*The Times*, 7 November 1981). The most 'political' of the studies was the one dealing with possible new institutional structures. It was this area that had caused the most concern for Unionists when it was announced. The main proposal in the study was for the two governments to establish an Anglo-Irish Intergovernmental Council. The study suggested that the Council should 'have flexible characteristics permitting it to subsume many of the existing patterns of contact between the executive branches of Government . . .' and advised that the Council should meet at Heads of Government level 'once or twice a year'. The study also suggested that a secretariat be created, though this was to be a loose arrangement only necessitating that 'each Government should designate an official to act as Secretary of the Council and each of the two Secretaries would be responsible for ensuring the provision of a secretariat for the activities of the Council'. (These nominated secretaries were later confirmed at the first meeting of the Anglo-Irish Council, 20 January 1982, as the two Cabinet Secretaries, Sir Robert Armstrong and Dermot Nally. This mechanism and these two individuals were later to play a vital role in the negotiating of the 1985 Anglo-Irish Agreement.)

The studies also examined the institutionalising of two other tiers to the Anglo-Irish Council, an inter-parliamentary body and an Advisory Committee to deal with 'economic, social and cultural co-operation' – which would be institutionalised as Anglo-Irish Encounter in July 1983. The studies revealed a difference of opinion over the creation of the inter-parliamentary tier. Whilst both sides agreed it would be 'a natural and desirable development', the British seemed to prefer to leave it as a matter for the consideration of the two parliaments, whilst the Irish wanted the studies to draw up proposals for the 'composition, ambit and purposes' of such a body. (The inter-parliamentary body was not in fact to be created until 1990, and was of questionable worth in terms of securing a Northern input to the intergovernmental process as Ulster Unionists never took up their seats.)

Taken as a whole the studies were a serious attempt to address areas of confusion between the two states and highlight areas where relations could be improved (such as voting rights and economic co-operation). They were judged by some – not least Haughey – to be disappointing and empty, though this rested on the unrealistic expectations which had been built up around them – primarily by Haughey himself once he had left office. The joint studies were undertaken by British and Irish officials to review the relationship between Britain and Ireland under specific headings. These civil servants were never going to propose radical changes that would fundamentally alter the way the two states dealt with Northern Ireland. Haughey's claim that the joint studies had been altered between his leaving office in July and the publication in November has not been substantiated. David McKittrick noted at the time of the November summit, 'Viewed from the London perspective . . . it has to be said that nobody can be found here who believes that Mr Haughey would have gone home with more than Dr FitzGerald did' (*Irish Times*, 14 November 1981).

Conclusion

After the hope of late 1980, the 1981–82 period was a particularly difficult and comparatively unproductive one in Anglo-Irish relations. But whilst the individual events examined above undermined the ability of the two governments to co-operate, and collectively soured the Anglo-Irish relationship, a sense of perspective must be retained. Writing in 1982, Patrick Keatinge warned of the 'danger of giving excessive weight to the 'fever chart' interpretation of Anglo-Irish relations'. Whilst the 'fever chart' 'reflects the immediate and dramatic event, conflicts of personality, and explanations of behaviour in terms of parochial, party or sectional interests . . . they rarely reflect either the whole range of issues at stake or the continuity of contact and purpose at the bureaucratic level' (Keatinge, 1982). This point was to some extent endorsed by the Irish Minister for Foreign Affairs, Peter Barry. Speaking at the end of 1982 he noted, 'there are daily contacts at all levels and my experience is that no matter what shouting some people do at one level the ordinary people recognise the common interest we both have in good relations' (*Irish Times*, 28 December 1982). The joint studies and the fledgling Intergovernmental Council that it created did indeed increase the level of bureaucratic contacts between London and Dublin and do appear to have gone some way to offset the disputes that occurred in the period (though the Anglo-Irish Intergovernmental Council did not meet at Heads of Government level after November 1981 until November 1983).

What makes the 2-year period 1981–82 comparatively unusual is the number of 'fevers' the Anglo-Irish relationship was subjected to. The fevers of the hunger strike, Falklands and Rolling Devolution were harder to shake off given their proximity to one another and the instability within Ireland's political system during the period. The NIO minister, Lord Gowrie, acknowledged that Anglo-Irish relations were not as good as they should be but concluded 'of course they will improve . . . . We have too many interests and ties in common for things not to improve' (*Irish Times*, 17 July 1982). However, things do not simply improve of their own volition. Although the issue of Northern Ireland, the shared land border, membership of the EEC and historical and cultural ties dictated that there must be an Anglo-Irish relationship, these alone did not ensure it must be harmonious. British and Irish officials did continue to work together throughout 1981–82 but their efforts were undermined by the variety of fevers and considerations that made it difficult for Thatcher and Haughey to build on the apparent success of the 1980 summit. By 1982 the British appeared to have given up hope of working with Haughey to improve relations. Prior wrote that the fall of the FitzGerald government in January 1982 was 'something of a disaster' (Prior, 1986, p. 236). In Haughey's defence it can be argued that he was constrained by the lack of a working majority during the period. But whilst his stance on issues such as the Falklands and Rolling Devolution can be explained in terms of the domestic constraints he faced, such constraints meant little to British policymakers when considering British interests and the Anglo-Irish relationship. The return of FitzGerald as head of a stable coalition government in November 1982 created the opportunity for London and Dublin to re-evaluate and re-formulate Anglo-Irish relations. Jim Prior noted in October 1982 that 'good relations between London and Dublin make nothing but sense and the Government much regrets the way our paths have diverged recently. We shall seek to mend relations in the coming months' (*Irish Times*, 8 October 1982). A few weeks later FitzGerald pledged to restore Anglo-Irish relations to the state they were in at the time of the 1981 summit and urged that the two governments 'turn away from this unhappy year of 1982...' (*Irish Times*, 18 November 1982). Over the 3 years that followed, the climate within Northern Ireland and, as a result, the relationship between London and Dublin were altered by the spectre of a politically resurgent Sinn Féin.

3 Institutionalising the intergovernmental approach

The Anglo-Irish Agreement

After the tumultuous preceding 2 years the Anglo-Irish relationship was placed on a firmer, institutionalised footing as a result of the inter and intra-governmental negotiations in the run up to the Anglo-Irish Agreement (AIA) of November 1985. This period witnessed a re-examination and articulation of the Republic's view of Northern Ireland in the New Ireland Forum (NIF), which in turn caused a re-evaluation and restatement by Unionists of their objectives in Northern Ireland with the UUP's *The Way Forward* and the DUP's *Ulster: The Future Assured*. The British Government also came under pressure from the Irish Government, the United States and European Parliament to engage in a review of its own Northern Ireland policy.

The NIF needs to be examined in respect of how it impacted upon Anglo-Irish relations. The AIA was not a direct result of the NIF but the NIF served to increase pressure upon the British to further intergovernmental co-operation. The AIA was contentious and a seemingly surprising departure for the British (and particularly for Thatcher given her Unionist principles). The reasons for this departure are analysed and the content and purpose of the AIA evaluated.

The New Ireland Forum: In the hope of being overheard?

The Irish general election in November 1982 resulted in a Fine Gael/Labour coalition government, led by FitzGerald, with a six-seat majority. In June 1983, Thatcher's Government was returned to office with a majority of 140. This meant that both states had comparatively secure governments which could expect to remain in office for several years. This was felt by members of both governments to be an important factor in enabling London and Dublin to pursue the possibility of greater intergovernmental co-operation (Prior, 1986, p. 237; *Irish Times*, 8 October 1982). For the British the size of the majority meant, as Jim Prior noted, 'we were in no way beholden to the Unionists' (Prior, 1986, p. 237). Sir David Goodall, one of the key British negotiators of the Anglo-Irish Agreement, also claims that the fact that it was FitzGerald rather than Haughey in the Taoiseach's office was an important factor. Haughey's 'over-selling' of the Dublin summit in 1980 and his stance on the Falklands conflict 'put the whole relationship into cold storage and Margaret Thatcher never trusted Haughey again, and indeed as long as Haughey was there, there wasn't any real chance of things resuming where they had been broken off after the joint studies' (Goodall, 24 June 1999).

Whilst Northern Ireland and specifically Anglo-Irish relations did not feature prominently in the British election campaign, the Conservative Party's manifesto in 1983 contained a reference to the importance of the intergovernmental relationship. 'We believe that a close practical working relationship between the United Kingdom and the Government of the Republic can contribute to peace and stability in Northern Ireland without threatening in anyway the position of the majority community in the province.' Although this was hardly an undertaking to consult the Irish over the governing of Northern Ireland, it was at least an implicit acknowledgement that the intergovernmental relationship had moved up the agenda of the Conservative Government. The previous Conservative manifesto had made no mention of the intergovernmental relationship and had advocated a more integrationist approach. For all the problems that had gone before (and were indeed to come) Thatcher's government seemed to be considering whether a better relationship with the Republic's government may be advantageous to their Northern Ireland policy.

The Irish announced the creation of the NIF on 11 March 1983. It was ostensibly an intra-nationalist dialogue between the three major Southern parties, Fianna Fáil, Fine Gael and the Labour Party, and the major nationalist party from the North, the SDLP. The stated aim of the Forum was 'consultation on the manner in which lasting peace and stability can be achieved in a New Ireland through the democratic process' (*Irish Times*, 12 March 1983). The extent to which the Forum marked a fundamental re-evaluation by Irish nationalists of the Northern Ireland issue has been questioned. Clare O'Halloran has argued the exercise 'merely clothed traditional values and aspirations in a new language of pluralism and deferred the question of fundamental change' (O'Halloran, 1987, p. 194). The Forum was 'a monument to the evasion and ambiguities which have been a hallmark of Irish nationalism to date' (O'Halloran, 1987, p. xviii). Whilst O'Halloran may be correct in her belief that the Forum report did not mark a shift away from the traditional Irish commitment to the goal of unity, in terms of the attempts to increase Anglo-Irish co-operation, the Forum was of more significance. Subsequent developments suggested that there was a growing awareness in the South of a need to move away from stressing the traditional belief in the inevitability of Irish unity, to looking at how the situation within the North could be stabilised. The NIF was a part of this process.

Although there was no British Government involvement in the Forum, and the Ulster Unionist parties refused to take part, the Forum was not an isolated Irish event that had no bearing on Anglo-Irish relations. Ronan Fanning recounts,

> a conversation between an eminent Irishman and a no less eminent Englishman – a conversation which occurred very late at night during [an] . . . Anglo-Irish conference. 'Are you', interrupted the Irishman, 'are

you addressing your remarks to me, or are you merely talking to yourself?'
'I am talking to myself' replied the Englishman, 'in the hope that I may be
overheard. It seems to be the only way of conducting Anglo-Irish relations.
(Fanning, 1984, p. 151)

The New Ireland Forum was the inverse of this scenario – a dialogue between
the Irish parties which had the intention of not only establishing a common
nationalist view on the form a new Ireland should take but also of engaging the
interest of the British government or at least forcing a response to its report.

The purpose of the New Ireland Forum

One of the main, though unstated, purposes of the NIF was to bolster the position
of constitutional nationalism in Northern Ireland. In March 1983, Mary Holland
claimed the growth of Sinn Féin 'is now a source of major concern to the
Irish government, which sees it, quite rightly, as a threat to the stability and
institutions of its own state' (*New Statesman*, 1 April 1983). Sinn Féin had
already demonstrated during the hunger strikes that in times of crisis it was
possible for them to make electoral inroads in the Republic. If they were to
become the major nationalist party in the North, it would make it far more
difficult to construct a power-sharing devolved government in Northern Ireland.
The SDLP needed some demonstration that constitutional politics still had a
role and could achieve results. They were still boycotting the Northern Ireland
Assembly; primarily as to enter it would further erode their position vis-à-vis
Sinn Féin. Their protests over the construction of the Assembly had achieved
little and there seemed no chance of a British initiative that would provide them
with a tangible 'success' in the near future.

The New Ireland Forum and Anglo-Irish relations

The NIF report was published on 2 May 1984. The report contained three
options: a unitary state, a federal/confederal state and joint authority. It stated
the 'particular structure of political unity which the Forum would wish to see
established is a unitary state'. However, in a section that was to be the basis
claimed by FitzGerald for negotiating the AIA, the report stated, 'The Parties
to the Forum also remain open to discuss other views which may contribute to
political development.'
    However, the importance of the NIF lay not in the options that it proposed but
in the fact that it provoked responses. The British could not ignore the NIF report
even though much of the report was understandably unacceptable to the British.
The 'Origins of the Problem' section (Chapter 3) was particularly unpalatable
from the British point of view given its strongly nationalist interpretation of
the causes of the conflict in Northern Ireland and overt criticism of the British.
Many in the Forum itself were unhappy with the tone of the chapter and there
was a feeling within FitzGerald's own party that he was giving in too much to

Fianna Fáil demands (Hussey, 1990, p. 99). FitzGerald felt that the nationalist interpretation of history had to be included to secure an agreed report and provide him with what was 'needed to initiate open-ended negotiations with the British Government' (FitzGerald, 1991, p. 489).

The immediate response from the British was a strong rejection of the historical account of the problem. Prior issued a statement noting, 'The Forum's account of the British position is one-sided and unacceptable.' The British were careful, however, not to be seen to reject the work of the Forum out of hand. The same statement went on, 'Nevertheless the Government welcomes important positive elements of the report', particularly the commitment to peaceful persuasion and the rejection of violence. In a sentence that must have pleased FitzGerald, Prior asserted, "The United Kingdom Government welcomes the statement in the report that the parties in the Forum remain fully open to discuss other views" (*Irish Times*, 3 May 1984).

The British response to the Forum continued to follow this pattern, rejecting the historical interpretation and the main 'solutions' of the report whilst welcoming the tone of the comments regarding Unionist identity and commitment to consent and non-violence. Prior acknowledged parts 'of the Forum report go further than any nationalists have gone before, in showing a much greater understanding of the Unionists' position in Northern Ireland' (House of Commons, vol. 60, col. 1237, 24 May 1984).

FitzGerald's government sought to pressurise the British government into taking the report seriously by using the American platform to promote the Irish agenda. Two months before FitzGerald had told a joint session of Congress of the work of the NIF and his 'hope that it will find a response in Britain' (*Irish Times*, 8 March 1984). In a speech on St Patrick's Day, President Reagan had praised the work of the NIF and welcomed the fact that 'the high level dialogue between Ireland and Britain has been renewed . . .' (*Irish Times*, 17 March 1984). The British press also gave widespread coverage to the report. Whilst the coverage was far from uncritical of the report the document was deemed important enough to warrant front-page articles in *The Times*, *The Guardian* and *The Daily Telegraph*.

The seriousness with which the British treated the NIF report is illustrated by the fact that a Commons debate was held to discuss it. According to Prior the three models proposed in the document

> is where the report's difficulties begin to show . . . . Inasmuch as any of the models significantly alters the sovereignty of Northern Ireland; it is a dangerous fallacy to imagine that the Unionists would agree. It is equally false to imagine that the Government or anyone else can engineer or induce such an agreement.

But Prior argued 'it would be unfair to the tone of the report and to the way in which it has been presented by the Irish government to concentrate only on those detailed points' (House of Commons, vol. 63, cols. 23–26, 2 July 1984).

Prior's comments during the debate were a long way short of a ringing endorsement of the NIF Report. He restated the traditional British position that the government of Northern Ireland was a matter for the British Parliament – though interestingly Prior did not state it was *only* a matter for the British Parliament. He also restated his comment to devolution, and by implication to his Rolling Devolution plan. Prior did though note that geography and the allegiance felt by nationalists in Northern Ireland called for a 'close relationship between the United Kingdom Government and the Republic'. He concluded by appealing to all sides in Northern Ireland to enter into detailed discussions over the situation in the North. He argued that the Unionists could do this with the assurance that their position in the Union was safe. The nationalists "can do so knowing that we want to find an acceptable way to involve them and that we are concerned about the views that the Irish Government have expressed on their behalf" (House of Commons, vol. 63, cols. 26–29, 2 July 1984). This is a significant phrase as it implied that it was an acceptable function of the Irish government to act as spokesperson to the British government on behalf of Northern nationalists. Too much should not be read into this statement though, as the week before Prior had stressed in the House that the way forward was not via an exclusively intergovernmental approach. 'It would be no good the British Government and the Government of the Republic discussing these matters unless there was a degree of consultation and acceptance by the political parties within Northern Ireland itself. That is where any solution must come from' (House of Commons, vol. 62, col. 142, 28 June June 1984). Yet within 18 months the two governments had signed an agreement that was the result of intergovernmental discussion, had been negotiated without consultation with the representatives of the majority community in Northern Ireland and was rejected by all the parties representing that community.

The NIF was an important exercise, which did have an impact on Anglo-Irish relations. On its own it did not force the British to engage in the discussions with the Irish that led to the AIA, but it did help focus attention on the Northern Ireland problem. The British had indeed overheard the Irish talking to themselves and were about to join the discussion. For much of the conversation, however, the two governments were not necessarily having an integrated discussion, at times it resembled concurrent monologues, but it led to the AIA.

Negotiating the Anglo-Irish Agreement

The process of negotiating the AIA was long and complicated, with over 50 negotiating meetings. These included 2 prime-ministerial summits; at least 4 prime-ministerial meetings on the fringes of EC summits; 3 meetings of the Irish Tánaiste (deputy prime minister) and Irish Minister of Foreign Affairs with the British NISS and Foreign Secretary; 10 meetings between the Irish Minster of Foreign Affairs and the British Foreign Secretary or NISS; and over 30 meetings of the officials of the two governments negotiating groups, led by the Cabinet Secretaries (Sir Robert Armstrong and Dermot Nally) (Dáil Éireann, cols. 2573–2573, 19 November 1985). 'For practical purposes' Armstrong and Nally's deputies, Goodall and Lillis, carried out most of the discussions (Goodall, 24 June 1999).

On 7 November 1983, FitzGerald and Thatcher held a summit meeting at Chequers. This was the first summit for 2 years and was perhaps of more symbolic than practical importance, indicating an improvement in Anglo-Irish relations. Due to the continuation of the NIF no real breakthrough was possible but FitzGerald used the meeting to try and impress on Thatcher his fear that nationalist alienation from the Northern Ireland state was undermining the SDLP and leading to the rise of Sinn Féin. FitzGerald argued this alienation needed to be addressed by the two governments. At this stage Thatcher does not appear to have been convinced of FitzGerald's alienation thesis. She reported to the House of Commons 'we have not found an increase in alienation, but . . . we are worried about the apparent increase in support for Sinn Fein' (House of Commons, vol. 48, col. 150, 8 November 1983). But Thatcher records that after the Chequers summit 'I felt that we must now come up with our own proposals and I asked Robert Armstrong to draw up an internal paper setting out the options . . . . This meeting, from our side, was the origin of the later Anglo-Irish Agreement' (Thatcher, 1993, p. 396).

The result of the British review was a proposal that was delivered to Dublin on 1 March 1984 (as the NIF was drawing to a close). According to Dermot Nally 'That is the crucial date' (ICBH, 1997, p. 32). The proposal was for a security band along the border to be overseen by a Joint Security Commission and policed by joint crime squads (which could eventually evolve into a common police force or crime squad). The British also suggested the possibility of an all-Ireland court and changes to the Northern Ireland franchise rules along with symbolic changes such as movement on the Flags and Emblems Act. Much of the British proposal was unacceptable to the Irish but the importance of the document is that it marked the formal start of the AIA negotiations.

The AIA negotiations took on a distinct pattern. The Irish government attempted to achieve an agreement that would give them a status approximating joint authority; the British sought an agreement that would improve security but not compromise sovereignty. The negotiations illustrate that the agreement was the result of compromises on their original position from both sides. Neither side seems to have had a clear idea when entering into the negotiations what the specific outcome of the agreement would be. The Irish in essence were looking for a way of decreasing nationalist alienation in the North and halting the rise of Sinn Féin, whilst the British wanted improved security co-operation from the South. Neither side's objectives were acceptable to the other and 18 months were spent edging towards the middle ground.

Head versus heart: Thatcher and the AIA

Thatcher's attitude towards the intergovernmental negotiations is interesting and at times contradictory. There is little doubt that Thatcher had strong Unionist views. Indeed a former head of the Northern Ireland Civil Service went so far as to state 'She was in sentiment the most deeply Unionist of British prime ministers for a very, very long time' (Bloomfield, 19 May 2000). Yet Thatcher was also a pragmatic politician (perhaps more pragmatic than she is often presented). Douglas Hurd explained that Thatcher 'always starts with first principles' and will examine whatever seems to be potentially a logical solution to a problem (This at times led her to contemplate repartition as a possible solution though it was never seriously considered as government policy) (Hurd, 25 July 1999, and 2003, p. 306). By late 1983, Thatcher appears to have become convinced that something needed to be done about Northern Ireland and that that something may well have to involve an input for Dublin. However, this acceptance of the intellectual rationale behind an intergovernmental approach waxed and waned during the negotiations as her instinctive Unionism reasserted itself. Goodall claims,

> People have rightly said, I think, that for her, her head took her in one direction and her heart in another. So the thing tended to waver a bit depending upon if she had been listening to Enoch [Powell] and Ian Gow. All her doubts would be sort of reinforced and then we'd work away at it again and then she'd come to see that even if she didn't like it, it would be a good thing, so it was a bit of a yo-yo really.
>
> (Goodall, 24 June 1999)

The Irish side were also well aware of the struggle that Thatcher was having with the institutionalising of an intergovernmental approach. FitzGerald actually claims that the main thrust of the negotiations was on how to bring Thatcher along. 'The whole problem was how to persuade her'. Whilst FitzGerald notes that there were other problems during the negotiations – he is particularly critical of the role of the NIO during the negotiations (discussed below) – the basic problem 'was to persuade Margaret Thatcher'. FitzGerald claims that British officials and ministers accepted this as the major problem at an early stage. 'Within weeks, the entire system of government was reorganised to how do you get round the prime minister? So the negotiation was not between Ireland and Britain, it was between Margaret Thatcher and the Irish and British ministers and Irish and British civil servants, effectively' (FitzGerald, 6 June 2000) (not an analysis that was shared by the British participants). Thatcher never though resolved her conflicting views over the necessity of an intergovernmental approach and ultimately came to regret the AIA (Thatcher, 1993, p. 412, and see Thatcher's obituary for Enoch Powell, *Daily telegraph*, 23 November 1998).

The 1984 summit: Disabusing the Irish/gratuitously offensive

The good relationship between FitzGerald and Thatcher was a contributory factor in advancing the negotiations. Although she was less than flattering of FitzGerald in her memoirs, those who worked with the two leaders at the time stress the importance of the good relationship and the respect that they had for each other. However, this relationship was severely strained on occasions, as at the Chequers summit in November 1984. FitzGerald saw the summit as an opportunity to push for a greater institutionalised role for Dublin to counter nationalist alienation in the North. Thatcher noted that in the run up to the summit the British were 'alarmed by the lack of realism which still seemed evident in the Irish proposals' and she went into the summit 'determined to disabuse him [FitzGerald] in no uncertain terms of the possibility of joint authority' (Thatcher, 1993, p. 400). Not surprisingly the summit itself was, according to an Irish official, 'a very difficult meeting' (*Irish Times*, 20 November 1985) during which, according to Hurd, 'The Prime Minister began to compare the Nationalists with the Sudeten Germans in 1938; the Taoiseach looked grey and sad' (Hurd, 2003, p. 306). The problem centred on the governments' differing interpretations of what was an acceptable agreement. Thatcher was determined to scale down Irish expectations of what could be achieved in the negotiations. The British proposed a far more exclusively security-orientated agenda. Whilst the differences between the two sides were evident, the leaders did agree to allow the 'close and continuing dialogue' to continue.

The Irish appeared to believe that the summit had furthered the negotiations with FitzGerald stating 'we have got down to discussions in earnest, to brass tacks. We are talking about realities in a way that has not been done before . . . we have had realistic discussions on the basic, but complex, issues of security and politics in Northern Ireland' (*Irish Times*, 20 November 1984). This appearance of unity was though destroyed in Thatcher's post-summit press conference (*The Economist* headlined its article on the summit 'Softly, softly, squelch'). The Prime Minister started by describing the summit as 'the fullest, frankest and most realistic bilateral meeting I have ever had with the Taoiseach' but in reply to a question on the NIF she replied, 'A united Ireland is one solution. That is out. A second solution was confederation of the two states. That is out. A third solution was joint authority. That is out' (*Irish Times*, 20 November 1984). At one level Thatcher was simply restating what Jim Prior had said in July. But the tone of her comments caused deep offence in Dublin and problems for FitzGerald. Her remarks were seized upon by the Irish opposition leader, Haughey, who attacked FitzGerald for 'abject capitulation to a new British intransigence and a craven desertion of the principles of the Forum Report'. He accused the Taoiseach of 'incompetence,' 'ineffectiveness,' 'pathetic behaviour' and asserted, 'it's a wonder you had the nerve to come home at all' (*Irish Times*, 20 November 1984). While such attacks may be expected from the opposition, Thatcher's comments also caused problems within FitzGerald's coalition government. Gemma Hussey, a member of FitzGerald's Cabinet, wrote in her diary of the 'Political chaos and depression about last week's unrolling of events after the Anglo-Irish summit'. Hussey noted there were 'hard feelings against Garret' in the Fine Gael ranks and concluded 'It is difficult to defend Garret's handling of it . . . it is all quite appalling' (Hussey, 1990). FitzGerald noted that Dick Spring, the Labour Party

Leader and Tánaiste, told him he 'had never seen such anger and frustration as had been visible at his party meeting; the security of the state had been put at risk' (FitzGerald, 1991, p. 525). FitzGerald was very restrained in his reaction, which Howe described as 'a measure of his statesmanship' (Howe, 1994, p. 422) though he did tell a meeting of the Fine Gael party that he found the remarks 'gratuitously offensive' (FitzGerald, 1991, p. 525).

Explaining Britain's hardening position: Departmental objectives and the entry of the NIO

The fact that the proposals of the NIF were unacceptable to the British was neither surprising, nor by that stage in the negotiations, particularly relevant. By 1984 the negotiations were in line with the NIF only in so far as they could be accommodated under paragraph 5.10 of the NIF (the willingness to discuss other views). What was more concerning from the Irish point of view was an apparent hardening of position by the British negotiating team. This was the result of two related factors, the inclusion of the NIO into the British negotiations and the appointment of Douglas Hurd as the new NISS.

The main motor for the negotiations had been the Cabinet Office with strong support from Geoffrey Howe at the Foreign Office. Around the time of Hurd becoming NISS in September 1984, Thatcher 'widened the circle of those involved on our side of the talks to include senior officials in the Northern Ireland Office' (Thatcher, 1993, p. 399). FitzGerald claims that at a meeting on 25 October the British scaled down their proposals. The British were negative towards the proposals for changes in the policing and court structures in Northern Ireland. FitzGerald attributes this to the 'involvement of the NIO for the first time' which he felt was 'having a very negative effect'. At the meeting Hurd ruled out a power-sharing executive and 'wanted only to concentrate on security co-operation' (FitzGerald, 1991, pp. 510–511).

There were differences between the various British departments during the negotiation of the AIA. These differences are widely acknowledged by British officials and politicians. The former Head of the Northern Ireland Civil Servant, Kenneth Bloomfield, notes 'People talk about "the British government" as if the British government is a monolith. The British government is never a monolith, there are different influences working there, particularly in relation to Northern Ireland' (Bloomfield, 19 May 2000). The three main departments that were involved in the AIA negotiation were the Cabinet Office, Foreign Office and the NIO, and their focus was slightly different. The head of the NIO at the time, Sir Robert Andrew, argues,

> The Cabinet Office, having been asked by the Prime Minister to try and sort out an agreement, wanted to get an agreement and move onto other business as it were, as the Cabinet Office has many other things to do apart from Northern Ireland. The Foreign Office wanted an agreement for overseas political reasons: good relations with Dublin, good relations particularly with

the United States. I certainly wouldn't say they wanted an agreement at all costs but they wanted an agreement and to reach an agreement was in itself an objective for them for these overseas political reasons. The Northern Ireland Office . . . did want an agreement. . . . But we were conscious that whatever agreement was signed we had got to live with and work it whereas the other departments would be moving on to other business.

(Andrew, 21 November 2000)

Hurd makes a similar point; 'there were differences in emphasis . . . . The Foreign Office . . . would have gone further in meeting different Dublin points and I had often to say, "Look, this isn't going to run, it's not going to move like that, we must take into account this or that Unionist feeling". . . ' (Hurd, 25 July 1999). Goodall, who was seconded to the Cabinet Office for most of the negotiations from the Foreign Office, saw the role of the NIO in a similar light. Goodall noted that the NIO

were always more cautious about what they would agree to and acted therefore, I mean perfectly legitimately, as a sort of brake on the thing, because they had responsibility for actually running the Province and they, I think rightly, thought that too many bright ideas by people who weren't responsible for running it would land them in a mess which they would then have to deal with.

(Goodall, 24 June 1999)

These differences of emphases evidently frustrated the Irish and the inclusion of the NIO does appear to have caused a re-evaluation of the British position. However, the negotiations show that in a complex series of discussions there is an element of what O'Leary and McGarry term the 'organisational process' having a bearing on the shape of what is agreed. According to the organisational process argument, unitary actors do not take the decisions but decisions bear the 'hallmarks of the state agencies involved' (O'Leary and McGarry, 1993, p. 235). It is clear that whilst the NIO may have been able to act as a brake on the AIA, they were not able to wrest control of the steering wheel. This is evident by the fact that when Hurd was replaced as NISS a few weeks before the AIA was signed, the new NISS, Tom King, who by his own admission had 'not been deeply versed in Northern Irish matters before' (ICBH, 1997, p. 35), immediately raised objections to the AIA. The fact that King raised concerns may illustrate that the NIO was not entirely happy with the shape the AIA had taken and were, even at that late stage, seeking to change its composition.

Given the nature of Cabinet government such differences between departments are both inevitable and necessary. What was fortunate in the negotiating of the AIA was that the original discussion took place between the two Cabinet Offices, and the NIO were included only after a momentum of sorts had been established. The Irish believed that the key to getting an agreement was to reduce the role of the NIO as far as possible. According to Dermot Nally, once the Cabinet and Foreign Offices were committed to the project it would have been difficult for the NIO to undermine the process. The Northern Ireland Office was

> a small department with a very limited outlook. The Foreign Office had a far broader perspective and the Cabinet Office naturally had the same type of broad perspective. So with the Cabinet Office and the Foreign Office involved we could hope to negotiate something that was not a narrow type of agreement, if the NIO alone had been doing the negotiations it just wouldn't have happened.
>
> (Nally, 2 November 2000)

Kenneth Bloomfield who acknowledged the 'NIO is at anytime a fairly modest player on the big Whitehall pitch, it is not a heavyweight department, it is not one of the big beasts of the jungle' echoes this point from the British side (Bloomfield, 19 May 2000). Indeed Hurd suggested that Northern Ireland was of little interest to the rest of the cabinet and 'the less the colleagues heard from me the better' (Hurd, 2003, p. 297).

The NIO were more cautious given that they were more concerned with the events on the ground in Northern Ireland. What is more difficult to ascertain is whether this was the only criterion used by the NIO in considering what, if any, should be Dublin's input in Northern Ireland affairs? To some extent the NIO might, like any government department or indeed any section of any large organisation, be concerned that sharing its role meant reducing its power. Andrew accepts that the NIO had reservations about a role for Dublin in the affairs of Northern Ireland on the grounds that 'if you're trying to run Northern Ireland you'll have some reluctance about bringing somebody else in' (Andrew, 21 November 2000).

There is also, however, another implicit reason why the NIO, or elements of the NIO, might have been reluctant to accede a role to Dublin: their own Unionist beliefs. The distrust by London of the 'locals' in the NIO highlights a belief in British policymaking circles that ideological considerations of some in Belfast's NIO may colour their judgement towards the Anglo-Irish relationship (Needham, 1998, p. 69). As a result the NIO input into the negotiations was by the Englishman, Robert Andrew, and other senior 'locals' in the NIO, such as Kenneth Bloomfield, were kept in the dark until the final weeks. This exclusion was resented by some of the 'locals'. Bloomfield recalls that not only was his boss, Andrew, involved in the negotiations, but 'there were people below me who also were directly involved in it'. He found this exclusion 'very distressing'. As it meant, 'they misunderstood and misjudged, in personal terms, my own loyalty to constitutional government' (Bloomfield, 19 May 2000). Andrew admits to being worried about the exclusion of senior members of the NIO. The decision was not, however, Andrew's, who recalls 'I had instructions not to brief my staff in Belfast about it' (Andrew, 21 November 2000).

Whatever the rationale behind who was to be in and who was to be out of the negotiating loop the content of the AIA was largely shaped by the negotiating process that formed it. As the negotiations progressed the plans for a maximalist agreement that would combine a movement towards joint sovereignty with the removal of articles 2 and 3 from the Irish constitution were dropped. Instead a more minimalist agreement emerged that was more restrained in what it granted the Republic and in what it expected in return. The inclusion of senior English personnel from the NIO was largely responsible for this. However, questions must be raised regarding how likely it was that the more maximalist agreement could ever have been achieved? The intrinsic Unionism of Thatcher would have made it difficult to persuade her to agree to joint sovereignty/joint authority over Northern Ireland. Similarly at least some on the Irish side doubted whether it would have been possible to get a referendum passed to remove articles 2 and 3, even if there was joint authority. Dermot Nally believed that 'it would not have been possible to carry a referendum on 2 and 3 almost irrespective of what was in the agreement because Fianna Fáil were opposing what was happening' (Nally, 2 November 2000). The maximalist plan was though seriously considered at the earlier stages of the negotiations. Indeed Andrew recalls that although in his view 'this ambitious scheme was never a starter . . . in fact it was pressed for quite a long time' (Andrew, 21 November 2000). So the entrance of the NIO into the process did scale back the proposals for the agreement and resulted in a more muted package being agreed. It is understandable why the Irish may express regret for this outcome and blame the NIO (and Andrew in particular) for this reduction but it would have been practically impossible, and certainly of questionable efficacy, to exclude the NIO completely from the whole process. Given the Unionist reaction to the minimalist AIA it is likely that there would have been a far more virulent reaction if joint authority had been agreed. If a resultant referendum on articles 2 and 3 in the Republic had also been rejected, then the AIA may have led to a long-term deterioration in Northern Ireland far greater than the problems encountered after November 1985.

The content of the Anglo-Irish Agreement

Margaret Thatcher and Garret Fitzgerald signed the AIA on 15 November 1985 at Hillsborough Castle in Co Down. The AIA was a 13-article document that was subsequently registered at the United Nations. It was a very carefully worded document designed to achieve a variety of ends. Although the Agreement was an intergovernmental document, given the different interpretation that each government had of elements of the conflict and the different constituencies they sought to address, the imprint of London or Dublin is identifiable on each paragraph. The Agreement began by setting out the shared values of the two governments but the bulk of the text dealt with the attempts to address what each government saw as the main problem in Northern Ireland: alienation for Dublin, security problems for London. The AIA was the institutionalisation of intergovernmental co-operation through a newly created body, the Intergovernmental Conference

(IGC). The two governments created a unified mechanism to deal with what at times were diverging analyses. In order to try and ensure that there were no public differences in how the document was presented, Lillis and Goodall drew up a document that was known colloquially as the 'catechism'. This document contained agreed answers to 'every conceivable question' on the AIA that the officials could think of. Lillis and Goodall then 'went through the whole thing with both FitzGerald and Thatcher at Hillsborough' at least in part to avoid another 'out, out, out number' from Thatcher (Lillis, 20 October 2000). The written British version of this document was entitled *Index of Questions and Answers on Anglo-Irish Agreement* and was marked 'secret and personal' (obtained by the author under the Freedom of Information Act, 30 June 2006). Whilst the document demonstrates the areas of shared understanding between the governments and how, ideally, the agreement was intended to work, subsequent pressures on the governments and differences between them strained this attempt at unity.

Identifying shared values

The preamble to the agreement was an important and succinct summation of the goals of the two governments, containing the main objectives for each government – the importance and primacy of which had been debated over the preceding months. The goal of reducing violence was undoubtedly of great importance to both governments, but the issue of how to fulfil this goal was the area of contention. As will be discussed in more detail below, for the Irish in particular, nationalist alienation from the state in Northern Ireland was an important contributory factor to Republican violence and the rise of Sinn Féin. The pledging of the creation of a society free from discrimination, where each tradition was respected and nationalists had the right to work peacefully for a united Ireland, was an attempt to address the problems of nationalist alienation. For the British (and especially Thatcher) the problem was a security one, and so a pledge that each government would work towards ensuring those who pursued violence would not succeed was aimed at securing greater practical cooperation from Dublin in tackling Republican violence. These general points and the differences in the priorities of the two governments are well reflected in the AIA. To this end it is possible to identify which articles of the AIA are primarily addressing the concerns of each government.

Ascertaining the purpose of the articles of the AIA

In article 1 the two governments jointly pledged that the status of Northern Ireland could only be changed 'with the consent of a majority of the people of Northern Ireland'. The agreement recognised that the majority in Northern Ireland wished that there be no change in its status. The two governments declared that if in the future a majority in Northern Ireland wished to see a united Ireland established they would 'introduce and support' legislation 'to give effect to that wish' (a pledge that Hume subsequently cited in his talks with Adams to argue that the British were neutral in regard to Northern Ireland). The purpose of this article was an attempt to assure both sides in Northern Ireland that their position was valid. The desire for a united Ireland was an acceptable and attainable goal if a majority of the people in Northern Ireland could be persuaded of its value. Similarly the Unionist position was secure, as the status of Northern Ireland could not be changed without agreement of the majority (which, according to Hurd, was the most important British gain of the AIA, although he acknowledges that Thatcher believed the security issue was more important) (Hurd, 25 July 1999).

Articles addressing Dublin's analysis

THE SOUTH AS SPOKESPERSON FOR NORTHERN NATIONALISM

In terms of Anglo-Irish relations, article 2 was the most significant section of AIA as this concerned the creation of the IGC. Legally the Conference was under the auspices of the Intergovernmental Council set up at the November 1981 summit. However, practically the new IGC had a far more defined role than the previous Council. The governments agreed that the IGC would be acknowledged as a departure from the previous situation and was 'a framework, more systematic than anything that has hitherto existed . . . ' (*Index*). The IGC was specifically 'concerned with Northern Ireland and with relations between the two parts of Ireland . . . '. The IGC would act in four specified areas: political matters; security and related matters; legal matters and promoting cross-border cooperation.

Under article 2 the British 'accept that the Irish Government will put forward views and proposals on matters relating to Northern Ireland within the field of activity of the Conference in so far as those matters are not the responsibility of a devolved administration in Northern Ireland'. For the Irish this constituted an undertaking by the British to consult them over Northern Ireland affairs, an apparent reversal of Thatcher's statement in July 1982. During the negotiations much of the discussion had centred upon the Irish claims that they needed to have an executive role in order to address nationalist alienation, and the British assertion that a consultative role was all that could be offered as no derogation of sovereignty could be countenanced. The negotiations resulted in the compromise statement, which stipulated, 'In the interest of promoting peace and stability, determined efforts shall be made through the Conference to resolve any differences.' This pledge to attempt to resolve differences via the IGC was to enable the Irish Government to claim that the British had ceded to the Irish a real role in Northern Ireland. FitzGerald told the Dáil, the Irish position was 'beyond a consultative role but necessarily, because of the sovereignty issue, falling short of an executive role . . . ' (Dáil Éireann, cols. 2562–2563, 19 November 1995). The British agreed to this and the *Index* document states, 'It is accepted by both sides that the words 'consultative' or 'consultation' should *not* be used to describe the agreement' (emphasis in the original).

Article 2b also stated clearly that that there was no derogation of sovereignty. To this end there was no undertaking to comply with the concerns of the Irish Government regarding Northern Ireland, or even theoretically to consult them. The only right the Irish had was to put forward their views and proposals to the British. The tone of the agreed answers in the *Index* document is very conciliatory noting Britain would take 'full account of any views and proposals put forward by the Irish' and emphasised the 'the desire of both Governments to implement the agreement in a spirit of co-operation and goodwill'. (In reality though this proved difficult to achieve. The failure of the British to consult the Irish – for example, over the decision not to bring prosecutions as a result of the Stalker/Sampson report in 1988 – was to lead to accusations that the British were acting against the spirit, if not the letter, of the AIA).

Almost all the remaining articles of the agreement are concerned with the details of how the IGC would function and its powers and limitations. Article 3 asserted that the IGC would meet at Ministerial or official level and pledged the meetings would be regular and frequent with each side having the power to convene a special meeting by request. Membership of the IGC was not fixed but at Ministerial level it was to be jointly chaired by the NISS and 'the permanent Irish Ministerial representative' (the Minister of Foreign Affairs since its inception). Other ministers could attend depending on what was being discussed and by convention the heads of the RUC and Garda Síochána (Irish police force) were present for at least some of all meetings. Article 3 also provided for the IGC to have a permanent Secretariat – which was housed in Maryfield in Belfast. The permanent presence of Dublin civil servants in Northern Ireland was one of the most contentious parts of the AIA for the Unionists and one of the key demands of the Irish Government. In order to assuage fears on this point the *Index* noted the Secretariat 'will have no executive functions' and that it would be 'very small' (*Index* 3 (a) and (b)).

DEVOLUTION

Article 4 noted the desire of the British Government to secure devolution to Northern Ireland and noted the Irish government 'support that policy'. It was acknowledged, however, that devolution required the co-operation of the constitutional parties of both traditions. This effectively gave the SDLP a veto on devolution, as without them it would not be possible to secure the co-operation of both traditions. This was not in itself a new pledge. Prior's Rolling Devolution plan's need for a weighted majority and cross-community support for devolving powers ensured that no devolution was possible without the SDLP acquiescence.

NATIONALIST ALIENATION

Articles 5, 6 and 7 were directly concerned with the issues that the Irish argued contributed to nationalist alienation. Under article 5 the IGC would examine 'measures to recognise and accommodate the rights and identities of the two traditions in Northern Ireland, to protect human rights and to prevent discrimination'. The types of areas that the article cites as areas to be examined included some of the most high-profile issues, notably the Flags and Emblems Act and an examination of the case for a Bill of Rights. Under article 5 the Southern government were formally given the role of spokesperson for the nationalist community in the North in the absence of devolution. Through the IGC 'the Irish Government may, where the interests of the minority community are significantly or especially affected, put forward views on proposals for major legislation and on major policy issues . . .'. The purpose of this article was to provide the nationalist community with the sense that it had a channel to air its grievances in the hope that this would reduce the feelings of alienation. However, it also had the secondary purpose of attempting to persuade the Unionists to consider co-operating with nationalists towards devolution, as without devolution the role of the Irish government in Northern Irish affairs would be greater than if there was a devolved structure in the North.

Article 6 gave the South a right to express views regarding the role and personnel of various bodies dealing with the issues of human rights, fair employment and police complaints, all bodies dealing with areas of traditional nationalist grievances. Article 7 concerned attempting to address the alienation of the nationalists from the security services in Northern Ireland. The article noted the need to make 'the security forces more readily accepted by the nationalist community'. The IGC pledged to examine various ways of making the security services more acceptable to nationalists and increasing that community's participation in the services.

Articles addressing London's analysis

EXTRADITION

If many of the preceding articles were designed to reduce nationalist alienation, thus addressing concerns primarily associated with the Irish government, articles 8 and 9 addressed, to a greater extent, issues more traditionally associated with British government concerns. For the British, Republican violence was primarily seen as a security problem. To this end they wished to secure greater co-operation from the Irish government in security matters, especially in terms of extradition (long an issue of contention between the two states). The reluctance of Irish courts to extradite suspected terrorists to Northern Ireland had caused concern and annoyance over the years in Britain (though the successful extraditions of Dominic McGlinchey in December 1982, and Seamus Shannon in July 1984, were welcomed by the British government). The Irish defended their record on extradition claiming that of 116 requests for extradition from the South to the North between 1971 and 1985, the Irish authorities had endorsed 103 and 87 extraditions had occurred (*Financial Times*, 16 November 1985). Whatever the reality of the numbers, the perception at least remained that the Irish were reluctant to extradite terrorist suspects, thus providing a safe-haven for IRA gunmen. To this end article 8 pledged the Conference would consider 'policy aspects of extradition and extra-territorial jurisdiction as between North and South'.

Article 9 also addressed issues of concern to the British. Whilst publicly the British always claimed co-operation with the South was good in the pursuit and prevention of terrorists and terrorist activity, privately it was felt that poor RUC–Garda relations and inadequate training and intelligence in the South was hampering effectiveness. Thatcher claimed, 'The real area of difficulty lay in cross-border co-operation between the Garda and the RUC. In spite of our efforts to help, Garda training and use of information were unsatisfactory. These shortcomings were worsened by personal mistrust between Garda and RUC personnel' (Thatcher, 1993, p. 397). Although it is difficult to judge the 'effectiveness' of the Garda intelligence and training, what was evident at this time was a serious and visible rift in relations between the head of the Garda, Laurence Wren, and the RUC Chief Constable, John Hermon. The cause of this rift was a somewhat bizarre incident dating back to September 1982, known as the Dowra affair, which led Wren to refuse to meet Hermon in November 1983 (*Irish Times*, 30 November 1983; Hermon, 1997, pp. 137–149). Relations deteriorated further in May 1985 when Hermon claimed that materials and personnel for a bomb exploded in Newry had come from the South. It was later acknowledged that there was no evidence that this was the case (*Irish Times*, 22 May 1985).

Article 9 stated the Conference was to 'set in hand a programme of work to be undertaken by the Commissioner of the Garda Síochána and the Chief Constable of the RUC . . . in such areas as threat assessments, exchanges of information, liaison structures, technical co-operation, training of personnel and operational resources'. The IGC would not have 'operational responsibilities' with the heads of each force retaining complete control over its operations. This new structure and the regular IGC meetings did have the desired effect of forcing the two chiefs into more frequent contact. Hermon records that when he met Wren at the inaugural IGC in December 1985, their first meeting since February 1983, 'We shook hands and I found him at least as easy going as when I had first got to know him 9 years earlier; the Dowra affair appeared to have been forgotten. Clearly, the Agreement had already achieved something positive' (Hermon, 1997, p. 182).

The RUC and Garda subsequently created Joint Working Parties. Hermon himself records that 'relationships between the participants were excellent' but he claims that 'many of the positive proposals advanced were never approved at Conference level' due to an unwillingness by the Irish Government to restructure the Garda. Hermon does though praise an element of the AIA. According to the RUC Chief Constable, 'whatever else, it provided the impetus and vehicle for the Republic of Ireland to enhance its level of attrition against Republican terrorists' and records that he established 'cordial relations' with several of the Irish staff at the Joint Secretariat with whom 'we enjoyed open and frank discussions on many matters' (Hermon, p. 182).

A critical analysis of academic explanations of the purpose of the Anglo-Irish Agreement

It has already been noted that the wording of the AIA was ambiguous, but the purpose of the AIA was also unclear. Whilst at a surface level the purpose was, as the joint communiqué stated, the 'achieving (of) lasting peace and stability', this is not an adequate explanation. Various more specific goals have been attributed to the AIA by academics. As the AIA is the result of intergovernmental negotiation to be viable an explanation must have an identifiable advantage to one or both governments.

Security

Hurd notes that Thatcher's 'main aim in negotiation was to shame and galvanise Dublin into effective anti-terrorist action, making as few concessions on points of interest to them as was compatible with that objective' (Hurd, 2003, p. 301). Goodall argues Thatcher was 'prepared to pay a price' for increased security co-operation but she did not have 'any clear idea of what that price might be' (Goodall, 1993, p. 130). One of the difficulties in this respect was the fact that Thatcher felt the 'price' should be comparatively low, hence her reluctance to negotiate a 'maxiamlist' AIA. Periodically Thatcher would question the scope of the agreement and contemplate a purely security-based agreement with perhaps some element of repartition (Thatcher, 1993, p. 398; Howe, 1994, p. 420; FitzGerald, 1991, p. 517).

Mrs Thatcher's security concerns were also used by some on the British side as a tool to persuade her of the advantages of the exercise. Howe acknowledged the British negotiators used the issue of security to persuade Thatcher to pursue the AIA, which for them was at least partly directed to different ends.

> If we wanted more effective cross-border security co-operation from the Irish government – as we all did, and Margaret most of all – then [Dublin] had to be able to demonstrate an enhancement of their political role in the affairs of the Province. This less than heroic argument enabled us to keep both the Prime Minister and Cabinet sceptically in step and supportive of the continued search for a balanced package.
>
> (Howe, 1994, p. 417)

O'Leary and McGarry have pointed out that the security situation in the mid-1980s was better than in the mid-1970s and the security situation in Northern Ireland deteriorated after the AIA was signed (O'Leary and McGarry, 1993, p. 231). Statistically this is beyond question, for example in 1974 there had been 216 deaths and 1,113 bombs planted, in 1984 there were 64 deaths and 248 bombs planted. In 1987 the numbers had risen to 93 and 674 respectively (Bew and Gillespie, 1999, pp. 183, 196, 209). The numerical reduction in the level of violence alone does not invalidate the security as motivation argument. Although the level of the violence in the mid-1980s was far lower than in the mid-1970s (and was increasingly accounted for by Northern Irish members of the security forces rather than 'British' army personnel), this does not mean that such a level of violence was 'acceptable'. If the AIA would help reduce the level of violence as a result of better security co-operation it would have been a viable reason for the agreement. The *Index* document notes 'One of the main purposes of the agreement will be to enhance the co-operation against terrorism which already takes place between North and South.'

However, at least some of the main participants accepted that the AIA was likely to destabilise the situation in Northern Ireland due to the anticipated Unionist reaction. It has been claimed that the two governments underestimated the likely reaction of the Unionists (O'Leary, 1987, p. 21). Goodall questions this.

> It was pretty obvious that the Unionists were going to object to it . . . . I think a very hostile Unionist reaction was expected . . . it might have gone much further . . . it didn't bring the Province to a halt like the Workers Strike after Sunningdale. I think the depth of Unionist anger may have taken the Prime Minister by surprise, perhaps . . . .
>
> (Goodall, 24 June 1999)

Andrew has made a similar point rejecting the idea that the NIO underestimated the likely Unionist response (ICBH, 1997, p. 40). It is interesting that both Goodall and Armstrong, officials who were involved in the negotiating of the AIA, argue that the Unionist reaction was expected. Hurd notes that he and Howe told the Cabinet in July 1985 (at a time when he feared that the Cabinet might scupper the initiative due to its apparent lack of progress) that the Unionist reaction 'although strong, would be containable'. Hurd suggests though that there was more unease amongst NIO officials than the politicians (Hurd, 2003, p. 308). Hurd's successor Tom King later claimed, 'considering the amount of trouble it raised in Northern Ireland, I don't think I was adequately warned' (ICBH, 1997, p. 40). Such comments suggest that there were differences amongst British policymakers over the likely Unionist reaction but at least some people on the British side anticipated a likely hostile Unionist reaction. Such a reaction would at least increase the possibility of rising levels of violence and thus a deteriorating security situation in the short term. As a result factors other than security need to be examined to explain the signing of the AIA.

Nationalist alienation

This argument is closely associated with the Irish government and in partic-ular with FitzGerald. According to this theory the nationalist community in Northern Ireland was alienated from the institutions of the state. The reasons for this alienation are partly historic, about which little could be done, and partly structural, which could be addressed. As a result of the perceived bias of the institutions and agents of the state (especially the legal structure: judiciary and security forces) against the nationalists, that community was unwilling to involve itself in the governing or policing of Northern Ireland. It was in this vacuum that the IRA operated. Alienation did not mean every nationalist was a terrorist or terrorist supporter but dealing with the terrorists was greatly hampered by the scepticism and suspicion with which the minority community viewed the agents of the state. To this end if steps could be taken to address the issues that contributed to this alienation, the nationalist community would become more reconciled to the institutions of Northern Ireland and the support for/toleration of terrorist activity would be reduced. The nationalist alienation theory is important in explaining why the Irish pursued the path that led to the AIA. According to FitzGerald the aim of the Irish government in signing the AIA was not to secure a say in Northern Ireland for its own sake but as a necessity to reduce nationalist alienation. 'These were not things that we sought because we wanted to be more involved in the difficult situation there; on the contrary, it was with great reluctance that we were prepared to take on responsibility without power – always a dangerous thing to do' (FitzGerald, 1991, p. 543).

Whilst the desire to reduce alienation was undoubtedly a primary motive for FitzGerald it needs to be set in context. In 1981, FitzGerald had stated 'we have always understood that the future of Northern Ireland will not be shaped by politicians or civil servants in London and Dublin aiming mirrors at Belfast and Derry. Ultimately it will be decided by Irishmen and women acting together in Ireland' (*Irish Times*, 1 July 1981). This was a clear expression of his view that what was needed was dialogue within Northern Ireland between the two traditions. Yet the whole basis of the AIA was discussion between London and Dublin (whilst actually trying to shield the mirrors from Belfast if not Derry). The reason for this about-turn by FitzGerald was that although nationalist alienation was not a new phenomenon, it had a new avenue of expression after 1981: votes for Sinn Féin. The decision by Sinn Féin in the post hunger strikes period to contest elections was to have a concentrating effect on the Irish and British governments. In the 1983 Westminster election, Sinn Féin's vote increased to 13.4 per cent and Adams took the West Belfast seat from the veteran nationalist MP (and ex-SDLP leader) Gerry Fitt. The SDLP's vote slid to 17.9 per cent (Flackes and Elliot, 1989, pp. 339–345). Dublin was concerned that achieving an accommodation between the two traditions in Northern Ireland would be far more difficult if Sinn Féin became the largest nationalist party.

The idea of the electoral rise of Sinn Féin as the key to the Irish motivation for the AIA is though slightly undermined by FitzGerald himself. FitzGerald records that he asked Hume not to tell Thatcher that the SDLP would perform well in relation to Sinn Féin in the 1985 local election. The reason, according to FitzGerald, was because 'it was the perceived menace of the SDLP losing ground to Sinn Féin that had provided in the first instance the underlying logic of the agreement we were seeking with the British government'. The fear of

Sinn Féin's electoral success was then the spur that led FitzGerald to seek an Anglo-Irish agreement, based as it was on his theory regarding the dangers of nationalist alienation. Once it appeared that the rise of Sinn Féin may not have been the menace it had originally appeared, it did not undermine the negotiations to any great extent as by then they 'had gained a momentum of their own . . . ' (FitzGerald, 1991, pp. 529–532). But the rise of Sinn Féin was undoubtedly the vital original consideration for FitzGerald.

There is no doubt that the British were also worried by the rise of Sinn Féin. Not only did Thatcher acknowledge as much in the House of Commons after her 1984 meeting with FitzGerald, but in 1983 Jim Prior had told the Conservative Backbench Committee on Northern Ireland of his fear that the rise of Sinn Féin could lead to Ireland becoming 'a Cuba off our western coast' (*Irish Times*, 11 November 1983). However, this acceptance that the electoral advancement of Sinn Féin was undesirable did not mean that the British accepted the rest of the nationalist alienation thesis. Hurd questions whether nationalist alienation was as extensive as FitzGerald and Hume claimed,

> I don't think we ever accepted the phrase 'alienation' because there were a lot of Catholics, a lot of nationalists, who were actually co-operating perfectly well. But a lot of the things that direct rule tried to do in housing, education, labour laws and so on were really designed to bring the nationalist community more into the actual daily working of the Province. So there was a truth behind the phrase even though I think the phrase was rather over-used.
>
> (Hurd, 25 July 1999)

(Thatcher for her part disliked the word 'alienation' as she felt it had Marxist connotations and Goodall claims its use had 'a rebarbative effect' on her (Goodall, 24 June 1999).)

The alienation thesis is also not as acceptable an explanation of British motivation as it is for the Irish for the simple reason that the British doubted that nationalist alienation would be alleviated by institutionalising a role for Dublin as spokesperson for nationalist community. Hurd wrote in his diary in March 1985, 'the truth is that we want a minimalist agreement, because we don't accept their [the Irish government's] basic analysis, which is that their involvement will rally the minority in a few months' (quoted in Stuart, 1998).

Given this scepticism, how can we explain the fact that the Irish were given the role as spokesmen for the nationalist community under the AIA? The reason again seems to be that it was the price that Thatcher was persuaded she had to pay for what she wanted: increased security cooperation.

Coercive consociationalism

Brendan O'Leary and John McGarry have argued that the AIA can be seen as an exercise in coercive consociation (power-sharing). According to this theory the AIA was designed as a rational power game whose purpose was to coerce Unionists into accepting a new version of the Sunningdale agreement (O'Leary and McGarry, 1993, p. 234; O'Leary, 1987; O'Leary, 1997). This interpretation rests on the provision contained in the AIA that in the absence of a devolved government Dublin would take on the role as spokesperson for the nationalist community and have a wide-ranging (albeit consultative) role in Northern Irish affairs. Articles 1b and 5c clearly stated the South could only discuss matters not devolved to a Northern Ireland administration. The reduction in the role of the South if there was a devolved Assembly was seen as an incentive to Unionists to work for devolution. The most abhorrent part of the AIA for the Unionists was the idea of Dublin having an input into the affairs of Northern Ireland. As a result a mechanism was created by which the Unionists could reduce this role and the scope of IGC discussions (though the IGC would continue to function even if devolution was achieved, albeit with a reduced remit. Some, including Thatcher and Haughey, misrepresented the position by suggesting that devolution would result in the dissolution of the IGC). Whilst it is undoubtedly the case that in the event of devolution the role of the IGC would be reduced, what is a matter of debate is whether the securing of devolved government was one of the primary aims of the AIA?

Statements can certainly be found which appear to support the view that the British and Irish hoped the possibility of reducing the South's role would tempt the Unionists to pursue devolution. Goodall argued that the AIA 'offers the Unionists an inducement to come to an accommodation with the nationalists by providing that if both communities can agree on a system of devolved government for the Province, the role accorded to the Irish Government in the Province's affairs will to a large extent lapse' (Goodall, 1993, p. 131). Similarly the Irish Tánaiste, Dick Spring, told the Dáil 'The agreement provides a stimulus to efforts within the North to find effective structures for devolution which will have widespread acceptance. As we have made clear, our involvement in devolved matters will cease when those structures are agreed by both communities' (Dáil Éireann, vol. 361, col. 2713, 20 November 1985). The *Index* document reiterated the commitment of the governments to restoring devolution to Northern Ireland (Q.4 (a)) and notes 'Should it prove impossible to achieve and sustain devolution, the Irish Government would be able to put forward views on *major* legislation and *major* policy issues where the interests of the minority community are especially or significantly affected' (Q.2 (aii)).

However, although such statements show the two governments were in favour of a devolved government in Northern Ireland they do not support the view that securing devolution was *the* (or even one of the) primary purposes of the AIA. It is clear from the statement of the Northern Ireland Minister, Nick Scott, that by March 1985 the British believed that full power-sharing 'was ruled out by the opposition of some parties in the province' (Dixon, 2001, pp. 200–201). The idea of forcing Unionists into a devolved government does not appear to have had much influence upon Thatcher. The coercive consociation argument is also undermined by the evidence that Douglas Hurd appeared to be anticipating a trade-off between an Irish dimension and majority rule in the North. When he was first told of the Anglo-Irish discussions upon becoming NISS, Hurd wrote, 'my own mind clears. I think the answer may be an Irish dimension, as the SDLP want, plus majority rule as a safeguard, which is what the Unionists want' (quoted in Stuart, 1998, p. 138). The fact that Hurd felt the way forward may be to trade off an Irish dimension against majority rule undermines the argument that securing power-sharing was a primary aim in negotiating the AIA.

It is now clear that whilst many on the British side favoured power-sharing devolution they did not believe it was achievable. Goodall recalls, 'I remember saying to Robert Andrew 'are you arguing . . . that if we don't have an agreement that the Unionists are more likely to agree [to power-sharing devolution]?' and the answer to that was, of course, no, as they weren't likely to agree anyway to work with the SDLP' (Goodall, 24 June 1999). So the mechanism to reduce the role of the Irish if devolution was secured was not seen by the British as one of the key reasons for the AIA. Hurd argues devolution 'in principle was right and we should aim for it' but it was not the pressing concern of the negotiations. As Hurd put it 'it wasn't the sort of thing you got up in the morning and thought 'what can we do for devolution today'?' (Hurd, 25 July 1999) and in his memoirs he argues there 'was no scope for political initiatives in the short term to replace direct rule' (Hurd, 2003, p. 301).

Bew, Patterson and Teague have argued that the desire to secure devolved government in the North was more important for the Irish than the British. This was the reason the Irish pushed to have the right of consultation on matters that could be devolved to Northern Ireland (Bew, Patterson and Teague, 1997, pp. 59–60). The British were, according to FitzGerald, reticent about including the areas of possible devolution in the remit of the proposed IGC. The Irish saw this as a very important omission as 'this would remove an incentive to Unionists to agree to devolution in order to reduce the role of the proposed body. This was to become thenceforth a major issue between us' (FitzGerald, 1991, p. 531). The Irish believed that if there was an Irish dimension of substance the SDLP would participate in a power-sharing government and FitzGerald sought assurances from Hume on this point, which he passed on to Thatcher (FitzGerald, 1991, p. 540). So with this undertaking from the SDLP, and the mechanism for a declining Irish role in the IGC to persuade Unionists, it may be that the Irish were more inclined to view the AIA as a tool towards coercive consociationalism. However, even for the Irish this appears to be at best a secondary consideration. It is not the case that the Irish were unaware of problems that a consultative role being acceded to Dublin would cause to the task of persuading the Unionists to enter a power-sharing structure in Northern Ireland. One of the key Irish negotiators remembers the British making this point in no uncertain terms during the negotiations:

I have a strong memory of the British constantly saying to us, 'Look, if you get this consultative role, power-sharing must be deferred indefinitely because they both won't work together. Unionists won't come in on those terms'. So the structure was built in such a way, as there was an incentive for the Unionists to come in, which we thought would be attractive to them. But I suppose the emphasis was generally on the consultative role for Dublin, it was 'Dublin in' rather than 'Brits out' if you like.

(Dorr, 25 May 2000)

The Irish were primarily concerned with reducing nationalist alienation, if this could be coupled with a devolved power-sharing executive, all the better. This would further insulate the Irish political environment from Northern Irish affairs. FitzGerald has been explicit on this point arguing that the South's motivation for seeking a role in Northern Ireland is not the traditional Republican perceived ideal of seeking incremental movement towards unity.

The only reason is because all along it has been clear since Sunningdale that if there isn't *some* North–South relationship sufficient to engage the emotions of the nationalist community, they will not settle down in a Northern Ireland which will for an indefinite future be part of the UK. And our objective has to be to get the Nationalist population to settle down to that, because there isn't any other answer, Northern Ireland is part of the UK.

(ICBH, 1997, pp. 44–45, emphasis in the original)

The creation of a devolved government in which representatives of the nationalist community participated would obviously aid this process but the first step, for Dublin, had to be to reduce nationalist alienation.

Twin tracks

Whilst the coercive consociation argument sees the AIA as a conscious policy to create a power-sharing devolved government in Northern Ireland, a less Machiavellian interpretation has been proffered regarding the relationship between the AIA, devolution and the Irish dimension. O'Leary has also argued (a somewhat contradictory position to the coercive consociation argument) that the AIA can be seen as an attempt to separate the issues of the Irish dimension and devolution in Northern Ireland. The 'internal track' sought to encourage the broadest possible agreement within Northern Ireland for an internal settlement, whilst the 'external track' sought to pursue good relations with the Republic and limit the international embarrassment that Northern Ireland caused Britain. According to O'Leary the AIA has both tracks built in and so can be seen to be 'broadly consistent with the 'broad thrust' of British policy making in the Province' (O'Leary, 1987, pp. 24–26).

This view of the AIA as the continuation of the twin track policy of the British (and Irish) governments is partially validated by the records available. Hurd asked Northern Ireland Minister, Chris Patten, in 1984 to 'look at the possibility of the "twin track" strategy: developing not only the relationship between London,

Belfast and Dublin, but also an attempt to persuade the political parties to work together in some form of devolved institution in Northern Ireland' (Stuart, 1998, p. 137). This was confirmed by Nicholas Scott in March 1985 when he told the Conservative's Backbench Northern Ireland Committee that a twin-track policy was being pursued, 'designed on the one hand to involve Constitutional nationalists in the institutions of Northern Ireland, and on the other to make progress on the Anglo-Irish front'. To this end Scott told the Committee that Patten was acting as a 'shuttle diplomatist' (Northern Ireland Committee, Minutes, 28 March 1985). However, this is undermined by the fact that months before the AIA was signed the British had accepted that no progress was possible on the internal 'track' and so concentrated on the 'external' one. Patten told the Committee in June, 'The Government were pursuing a twin-track approach which had originally aimed to try to bring both the internal train and the Anglo-Irish train into the station at the same time. This would now be impossible'. It was clear that the British were, as a result, concentrating on the external element. Whilst he made hopeful noises that after the AIA was agreed progress may be made on the internal issues, he accurately and succinctly summed up the problems of the zero-sum nature of the SDLP/Unionist relationship when he accepted that an AIA might mean all sides

> had at least an idea what the second train might look like. If an Anglo-Irish deal were done then the SDLP might be prepared to get on the train, although there was a risk that this context might alienate the Unionists sufficiently for them to refuse to even talk about progress.
>
> (Northern Ireland Committee, Minutes, 13 June 1985)

This evidence of a belief by the British that progress was not possible on the internal track and that pursuing the external aspect may make devolution harder to secure in the future undermines the idea that the AIA was a continuation of the twin-track strategy. (The above also further undermines the coercive consociation as motivation argument.) These comments by Patten support the criticism of the twin track policy levelled by Bew, Patterson and Teague who claim that 'there was little faith in the 'internal track' at the highest levels of British calculation' (Bew, Patterson and Teague, 1997, p. 53).

International pressure

An underlying theme of the AIA negotiations was the consideration of the international dimension and international opinion. Thatcher's memoirs note in several places a concern at improving the international (primarily American) opinion of the British role in Northern Ireland. Indeed she goes so far as to cite the problems that it would have caused 'with broader international opinion' as a reason for not breaking the AIA when she subsequently became disillusioned with it (Thatcher, 1993, pp. 403–412). Enoch Powell argued that the AIA had 'been done because the United States insisted that it should be done' (Shepherd, 1997, p. 484).

Whilst the British have traditionally been concerned about the reaction of international opinion, to what extent can the AIA be seen as a result of this concern? In the most comprehensive study of the international dimension to the Northern Ireland question Adrian Guelke has argued that American pressure was probably a significant factor in why the AIA was signed (Guelke, 1988, p. 147). It is questionable though whether the British signing of the AIA was motivated by the desire to secure external legitimisation of their position in Northern Ireland. There is a danger that Guelke's analysis suggests that it was the desire to secure such international legitimacy that forced the British to enter into the AIA (Guelke, 1988, pp. 98–99).

The traditional desire of the British to limit international criticism alongside the desire of the Irish to harness international opinion for its own ends does not mean that international pressure was the motivation for the AIA. Whilst it is clear that it was a consideration for both sides, it was a secondary one which did not directly influence the negotiations. Howe, as Foreign Secretary, would have been particularly concerned about the international opinion. He notes though, 'Only rarely were we under direct pressure from the other side of the Atlantic specifically to change our policies' (Howe, 1994, p. 423). Goodall, who was involved in the day-to-day negotiating of the AIA, is even more explicit on failure of international opinion to directly influence the negotiations:

> It didn't particularly impinge upon me as one of the negotiators but I think it was very present in the Prime Minister's mind and the mind of ministers . . . One of the factors in keeping the negotiations going and bringing them to a successful conclusion was that it kept the Americans and President Reagan on board, so to speak. So as long as that was going on and seemed to produce a successful result the American administration was not going to put any pressure on the British over Northern Ireland. So it was a factor and an important factor, but . . . it was not a determinant factor but it was very present in the minds of ministers.
>
> (Goodall, 24 June 1999)

It is also noteworthy that Sir Robert Armstrong, who was Cabinet Secretary, does not mention international considerations amongst the nine "ambitions" of the AIA he identified (Armstrong, 1993).

This neatly summarises the role of international opinion in the negotiations. It was a factor but not a determining factor. It did have an underlying influence on the reasons for negotiating the AIA and was a consideration for Thatcher after she became disillusioned with the AIA, but it did not shape the AIA and nor is it the most persuasive suggested motivational factor for either government. It was a tool for the Irish and a consideration for the British but not a primary motivation for either.

A marker on the road to withdrawal

For many Unionists the motivation behind the AIA was another step towards British disengagement and the creation of a united Ireland. As the DUP's Peter Robinson told the House of Commons 'the agreement is intended to trundle Northern Ireland into an all-Ireland Republic' (Kenny, 1986, p. 114). Arthur Aughey claimed that the purpose of the AIA for Britain was 'for progress in security, containment and a framework for eventual disengagement' (by which Aughey appears to mean disengagement militarily from Northern Ireland). Aughey claims that during the negotiations the British conveyed to the Irish 'that they would do nothing to hinder progress towards Irish unity' (Aughey, 1989, p. 190). There is obviously a difference between these two positions – British neutrality on the Union is not the same as the British proactively attempting to bring about a united Ireland. Arguably since at least Sunningdale the British, due to their commitment to abide by the wishes of the majority in the North, have been neutral on the Union (assertions by individual British PMs and Secretaries of States that they favour the Union, not withstanding). The problem with the Unionists' assertions that AIA was a tool to force them from the Union is that there is no evidence for it. The British took great pains to ensure that, legally at least, there was no derogation from sovereignty. Thatcher herself was emotionally attached to Unionism as a concept (although she was not an Ulster Unionist). Whilst the British establishment were aware of the economic drain Northern Ireland placed on the British taxpayer and its potential to embarrass the government internationally, this does not mean the British were working to oust Northern Ireland from the Union (Howe, 1994, p. 411). The important distinction between accepting the democratic will of the majority in Northern Ireland and working to create a united Ireland is one that is often lost in the Unionist view. If every step towards improving relations with the South is seen as another incremental step towards forcing unity, then the Unionists become victims of their own complaint that a united Ireland is portrayed (by others) as inevitable. Evidence suggests this was not the case in respect to the AIA. Tom King has argued that there were 'some people I dealt with . . . who always actually inherently believed that the British wanted to get out of Northern Ireland, and whatever the British said it was always part of a play to go that way'. King argued this was especially believed in some Irish quarters. 'I never believed that is the case, I never believed that the British government, realistically, or the British parliament, would depart from the democratic principle of consent' (ICBH, 1997, p. 36).

Not only is the argument that the AIA was an attempt by the British to disengage from Northern Ireland not persuasive, there is also little evidence to suggest it was the Irish side's motivation. Mallie and McKittrick have claimed that for the Irish the AIA was, according to one Irish official, seen as giving the Irish 'a sort of long-term apprenticeship in how to run the place when they were going to go'. The official noted that the British never said they intended to leave and would have denied the suggestion, but they knew they would be going at some stage in the future (Mallie and McKittrick, 1996, pp. 30–31). This would appear to fit exactly what King was complaining about above. The presumption by some in the South was that the British knew they would go at some stage. For this to be a viable explanation the Irish would have had to desire British withdrawal. If the motivation for the Irish regarding the AIA was to secure British withdrawal, then obviously Dublin must have desired unity. However, a more persuasive argument is that the Irish were seeking to reduce the ability of the Northern question to disrupt the political stability in the South. The Irish only sought an input into Northern Ireland to try and reconcile Northern nationalists to the Northern Ireland state, not as a precursor to unity. As FitzGerald has stated, for any Irish government to say 'We don't want Irish unity' would be extraordinarily unhelpful and make things much worse in Northern Ireland. But I tell you, that's the reality, even if, because we don't want to make the situation worse for (the British government) in Northern Ireland, we don't say it (ICBH, 1997, p. 46).

So there is little evidence to support the view that the AIA was a step towards British withdrawal, for either side.

A departure or continuity in British policy?

In general the AIA is seen as in line with previous British policy (Dixon, 2001, p. 203; Cunningham, 1991, p. 242). Brendan O'Leary has portrayed the IGC as little more than the institutionalisation of the talks set up in 1980 (O'Leary, 1987, p. 14). Douglas Hurd certainly saw the IGC as merely recognising an existing situation. Hurd claimed that the AIA gave the Irish 'the formalisation of a right, not a veto, but a right to be consulted . . .'. Hurd argues the Irish:

> exercised this right anyway, they were constantly on the phone, [if] some-thing had happened at a checkpoint overnight the Foreign Minister was on the phone to me and there was no point in my saying to him before the Anglo-Irish Agreement 'I'm sorry you've got no right to ring me up and to tell me about this and give me your views about what happened last night at the back of some farm'. It was useless, I needed a good relationship with him and therefore there was no point in standing on the letter of the law. They exercised this right anyway, what the agreement gave them was a right, the right to do something that they were doing anyway, which we couldn't actually stop them doing.
>
> (Hurd, 25 July 1999)

This underestimates the significance of granting the Irish *de jure* a right they had been exercising *de facto* before the AIA. Although the British could not stop the Irish exercising the right to give their opinions, they had on numerous occasions publicly denied that this right existed. Indeed Lillis challenges Hurd's depiction of the relationship.

As somebody who did a lot of the phoning and badgering of the British before we got the Agreement I was told very formally, indeed in writing on several occasions, that I had no right to do so and they had no obligation to listen to me . . . it was handed to me on instruction by no less a man than my old friend David Goodall. 'You have no *locus standi*, absolutely no right whatsoever to make these observations'.

(Lillis, 20 October 2000)

From the AIA onwards this was no longer possible and the IGC provided an institutionalised forum for the discussions of matters relating to Northern Ireland and Anglo-Irish relations. The right of either side to call a meeting of the Conference provided a platform for the Irish (and British) to air their grievances and offered the opportunity to reduce tensions between the two sides before they escalated, thus reducing the need for 'megaphone diplomacy' (though, as we shall see, this was far from wholly successful).

Conclusion

The AIA is indeed an ambiguous document. This ambiguity has allowed various interpretations to be placed both on its purpose and on its meaning. With respect to the motivation of the two governments in negotiating the agreement it is clear that there were differences of emphasis, both between and within the governments. In evaluating the differences within the British side the separation made by Bew, Gibbon and Patterson between the maximalists and the minimalists is persuasive and is backed up by the accounts of those involved in the process (Bew, Gibbon and Patterson, 1995, p. 213). It is clear that Howe, Goodall and Armstrong may, due to different outlooks and priorities, have contemplated an agreement that acceded a greater role to Dublin. The minimalists of Thatcher, Andrew and Hurd wanted a fairly limited input for the South and were primarily concerned with the security situation (especially Thatcher). The AIA is to some extent a product of these divisions, but this in itself is not necessarily either surprising or damaging. Both Hurd and Goodall have stressed that whilst these differences were apparent they were natural and did not threaten to undermine British unity during negotiations. Hurd claims that Howe was 'operating at perhaps 10 or 15 degrees angle difference of approach to myself, not more than that and none of these discussions amounted to a row or a particularly huge difficulty or hold up . . . '(Hurd, 25 July 1999).

Divisions within the Irish side seem to have been less apparent, though whether this reflects a genuine unity between all in the Dublin team or the relative scarcity of first-hand accounts by those involved in negotiating the AIA for the Irish is hard to tell. FitzGerald does acknowledge four Irish ministers 'were fearful of a strong Unionist counter-reaction and . . . kept on inquiring were we sure the Unionists wouldn't go mad about the agreement?' FitzGerald believed that Molyneaux had been briefed by the British 'and so I wrongly reassured the Cabinet that the Unionists would be alright. That was the only issue that the cabinet took up, really' (FitzGerald, 6 June 2000). However, the future Taoiseach, John Bruton, who was a member of FitzGerald's cabinet, suggests that there may have been more division. Bruton states he 'and a number of other ministers . . . from both parties' were unhappy during the negotiations over the exclusion of Unionists and made this clear during discussions in cabinet (though he accepts that it may not have been able to negotiate the AIA without following this course and he fully supported the content of the AIA) (Bruton, 6 December 2006).

For the Irish the primary motivation in pursuing an Anglo-Irish agreement was the issue of nationalist alienation and the rise of Sinn Féin. The desire to improve security issues was a consideration for Dublin but one that meant something different for the Republic than it did to Britain. For the Irish, international opinion was a tool to be used to put pressure on the British rather than a motivating factor in its own right.

Given the differences evident within the British negotiating team the British motivating factor is less apparent. Certainly for Thatcher the security issue was the key. For others considerations such as the alienation of nationalists and international concerns were considerations, but without the motivation of improved security the British team would not have been able to persuade Thatcher to sign the AIA.

Bew, Gibbon and Patterson have described what the AIA resulted in as 'direct rule with a green tinge' (Bew, Gibbon and Patterson, 1995, p. 217). This is to a large extent an accurate description. The AIA did not give the Irish an executive say in the affairs of Northern Ireland, nor did it mark the start of British withdrawal, or prohibit the pursuit of a united Ireland by peaceful means. The motivation behind it for the two sides was both unifying and contradictory at different levels. It was though a vitally important document in the Anglo-Irish relationship. It did indeed mark the acceptance and institutionalisation of an Irish role in the affairs of Northern Ireland by Britain. Whilst it may be the case that this had previously been accepted at Sunningdale, the failure of the power-sharing executive and the collapse of almost all the facets of that agreement effectively removed the Irish dimension from the agenda for the rest of the 1970s. The AIA can be seen as the restoration of the Irish dimension, this time in an agreement that was not dependent on the acquiescence of the parties in Northern Ireland. The tinge may not have been as green as the Irish originally wanted (and far too colourful for the Unionists) but it represented, in an internationally registered agreement, an acceptance of their right to proffer opinions and suggestions regarding Northern Ireland. Whether the British should act on these opinions and suggestions and what the Irish should provide in return was though to lead to serious intergovernmental disputes in the coming years.

4   The Anglo-Irish Agreement in operation

It might have been expected that the period immediately following the AIA would be one of more harmonious intergovernmental relations. The two governments had formalised their relationship and their roles regarding Northern Ireland. An internationally registered treaty had been signed which acknowledged the right of the Irish government to act as a spokesperson for the nationalist community in the North. The British had undertaken to co-operate with the Irish and make 'determined efforts' through the IGC to 'resolve any differences'. The British concerns over cross-border security and extradition were to be addressed. In short the AIA was carefully constructed to cover, if not solve, the areas of tensions between the two governments. Yet anyone expecting that the AIA would usher in a more peaceful or less contentious period in either Anglo-Irish relations or Northern Ireland affairs was to be quickly and comprehensively disabused. By all visible indicators the three-and-a-half years between the signing of the AIA and its review were years of increased instability in Northern Ireland set against the backdrop of periodic public disputes between the two governments. To judge why this was the case it is necessary to briefly examine how the AIA was received in Northern Ireland, how it worked in practice, and what areas were still to be disputed between the two governments. Only then can an examination of the value and shortcomings of the Agreement be made.

Reactions to the AIA

The view from London and Dublin

The reaction to the AIA was largely favourable in both Britain and the Republic of Ireland. The British press took a generally supportive editorial line. *The Times* was critical of the failure to move towards setting up devolved government at the same time, arguing that 'the price [that] should have been exacted' from the SDLP was 'participation in provincial government on terms short of executive power sharing, which is quite unrealistic. The Agreement is unbalanced to the disfavour of the Unionists.' But it concluded that the AIA 'deserves to be supported . . .' (*The Times*, 16 November 1985). The *Sunday Telegraph* argued that 'this is a brave agreement, if also a gamble, and one which deserves general support' (*Sunday Telegraph*, 17 November 1985). The *Financial Times* was more enthusiastic arguing that it was 'a civilised acknowledgement that the two governments most affected by the Irish troubles should work together to resolve a common problem' (*Financial Times*, 18 November 1985). Even those papers that had been traditionally hostile to increased intergovernmental co-operation and very supportive of Unionism were reluctant to come out firmly against the AIA in the early stages. *The Daily Telegraph* argued that the AIA 'does not amount to treachery; but it is an extraordinarily dangerous document' and attacked the creation of the IGC over the lack of reciprocity given that Britain could not comment on events in the South. However, the AIA was not damned by the editorial line, which argued that the Agreement showed that both London and Dublin were equally opposed to the IRA. This is a 'worthy objective, for which some risks are justified' (*Daily Telegraph*, 16 November 1985). What is interesting in the reaction of the British press is that no paper, including *The Telegraph*, opposed the AIA on the general principle that it seemed to give the Irish government a say in the affairs of Northern Ireland. This general level of support for the AIA in the British press was mirrored in the House of Commons, which approved the AIA overwhelmingly by 473 votes to 47. The government did though lose one junior minister, Ian Gow, Minister of State at the Treasury, and Thatcher's former Parliamentary Private Secretary. Gow resigned in protest at the AIA arguing that it changed the status of Northern Ireland and would prolong Northern Ireland's problems.

In the Republic the reaction was also relatively favourable with 55 per cent approving of the AIA, and only 29 per cent disapproving of it shortly after it was signed (*Irish Times*, 23 November 1985) (increasing to 69 per cent approval and 20 per cent disapproving within three months (*Irish Times*, 12 February 1986).) The Agreement was not, however, greeted as warmly by all the political parties in the Dáil as it had been at Westminster. Fianna Fáil, under Haughey, opposed the Agreement claiming the FitzGerald government had acted 'in a manner repugnant to the Constitution of Ireland by fully accepting British sovereignty over a part of the national territory and purporting to give legitimacy to a British administration in Ireland' (Dáil Éireann, vol. 361, col. 2581, 19 November 1985). Haughey suggested that he would seek to renegotiate the AIA if he were returned to government stating, 'we will certainly not be prepared to accept it in its present form' (*Irish Times*, 16 November 1985). Fianna Fáil also criticised the AIA in America with Brian Lenihan, Fianna Fáil's Deputy Leader, taking a very critical line on the Agreement in the US in the run up to its signing. Barry, the Irish Minister of Foreign Affairs when the AIA was signed, called the move 'treachery' (*Irish Times*, 22 March 1986) arguing 'it was pure naked political opportunism for base reasons . . . . It was one of the most dishonourable things that was done in Irish politics in 80 years' (Barry, 23 May 2000). FitzGerald also claimed to have been surprised by this part of Fianna Fáil's campaign of opposition to the AIA. FitzGerald claimed that the move by Fianna Fáil broke the convention that Irish politicians do not criticise the actions of the Irish government abroad (FitzGerald, 6 June 2000).

The Dáil did approve the Agreement by 88 votes to 75, dividing straight down party lines on the issue with only Fianna Fáil opposing the AIA. (One Fianna Fáil Deputy, Mary Harney, voted in favour of the AIA and was subsequently expelled from the party. Two independent TDs, Neil Blaney and Tony Gregory, also opposed the Agreement.) The only notable exception to this non-Fianna Fáil approval of the AIA was the resignation of Senator Mary Robinson – who would become President of Ireland in 1990 – from the Irish Labour Party on the grounds that the Agreement was unacceptable to Unionism.

The view from Belfast

If the general reaction in the Republic and Britain was favourable, the reaction in Northern Ireland was quite different. Northern nationalists generally supported the Agreement with 72 per cent of Catholics in Northern Ireland in favour of the Agreement and only 12 per cent disapproving (*Irish Times*, 12 February 1986). This was an important factor, at least for the Irish government, as one of their stated aims in pursuing the AIA had been to reduce the alienation felt by Northern nationalists. Whilst support for the AIA at this early stage did not necessarily indicate a reduction in alienation, it was important that nationalists in the North saw the AIA in a favourable light. The main nationalist party in Northern Ireland, the SDLP, had been closely consulted during the negotiations by the FitzGerald government and so, unsurprisingly, warmly endorsed the AIA. Sinn Féin unsurprisingly condemned the deal which they argued was a cynical attempt by Britain to put a 'diplomatic veneer on British rule', isolate themselves from international criticism and shore up the SDLP (Patterson, 1997, p. 198). Republicans were also scathing about the Irish government and the SDLP, claiming they were lackeys to traditional British imperialist motives. However, Henry Patterson has shown that the Republican leadership 'were seriously concerned about the various possible effects of the Agreement' and the AIA contributed to a review within the Republican movement of its tactics and the need to forge some sort of pan-nationalist front (Patterson, 1997, pp. 196–209).

The Unionist reaction

The most marked short-term result of the AIA within Northern Ireland itself was the opposition it provoked throughout the Unionist community. The Agreement caused a mass movement of opposition to emerge within Unionism of a type not seen since the protests that led to the fall of the Sunningdale Agreement in 1974. The hostility and betrayal felt by Unionists as a result of the AIA manifested itself in mass demonstrations, days of action, strikes, attacks on the homes of RUC members, resignations from public office, boycotting of Westminster and an increase in the level of activity by loyalist paramilitaries.

For much of the period the leaders of the two main Unionist parties James Molyneaux and Ian Paisley appeared to be struggling to keep control of the protests. In the early stages of the opposition the two seemed to be more willing to compromise over the AIA than their followers. After meeting Thatcher in February 1986 Molyneaux and Paisley issued a joint statement with the government saying both sides would 'reflect on the various suggestions which had been made and would meet again shortly'. But after consulting with Unionist workers and party members on their return to Belfast a few hours later the two announced they were pulling out of further talks with the British government and a planned strike would go ahead the following week. Back in Belfast Ian Paisley could find 'no comfort' from the meeting with Thatcher (*Irish Times*, 26 February 1986).

The event illustrates the depth of opposition felt by rank and file Unionists to the AIA and the somewhat precarious leadership position of Molyneaux and Paisley at this time. The attempts by Paisley and Molyneaux to present a united front and co-ordinate Unionist opposition to the AIA were only partly successful. The one-day strike succeeded in bringing Northern Ireland to a standstill but the protest was also marred by violence, claims of intimidation and RUC unwillingness to confront the protesters. The actions of the day were to trouble Molyneaux who announced himself to be 'horrified, shocked and disgusted' at the violence (*Irish Times*, 4 March 1986). King was also critical of the activities of the actions during the strike, telling MPs there had been 'widespread obstruction, intimidation and some violence'. He also, whilst praising the actions of the RUC, noted there had been a number of complaints against the force for not intervening and announced the Chief Constable was preparing a report. But the NISS did not seem to have much sympathy for the struggle of the Unionist leaders to keep control of the protests stating that 'The House will have seen elected Members of this House making common cause with people in paramilitary dress' (House of Commons, vol. 93, col. 153, 3 March 1986).

Whilst intimidation may well have played a role in the strike there is no doubt that the opposition felt by Unionists to the AIA was genuine and widespread. By February 1986 only 8 per cent of Protestants were in favour of the AIA with 81 per cent opposing it (*Irish Times*, 12 February 1986). For many Unionists it was not the form of the AIA itself that was the problem but the principle of it. An increased say for Dublin in the affairs of Northern Ireland was anathema to them. This was further complicated by the fact that Unionists had been excluded from the negotiations. Kenneth Bloomfield who had been excluded from the negotiations of the AIA emphasises this point:

What was so invidious, I think, what really incensed the Unionists . . . was the reality that you had the two sovereign governments negotiating, but patently, from beginning to end, the SDLP were kept very well informed by the Irish Government. They were told exactly what was going on and the Unionist Party, like me, were held at arms-length. This is a two-community country, albeit not by a huge amount, the Unionist community are the majority here and that seemed to me wrong both in principle and in practice and likely to lead to greater alienation, greater trouble . . . .

(Bloomfield, 19 May 2000)

For Bloomfield the way the AIA was negotiated as well as the new role it gave to Dublin meant that a Unionist backlash and rejection of the AIA was almost inevitable.

The logistics of the AIA

What then was the system that the AIA created to which the Unionists took such offence? The Agreement did provide a formalised mechanism for the two governments to co-operate in respect of Northern Irish issues. The main mechanism for this was the creation of the Anglo-Irish Intergovernmental Conference (IGC).

The Intergovernmental Conference

The IGC has rightly been described as 'the centre-piece of the Agreement' (Hadden and Boyle, 1989, p. 22). However, the IGC is a rather loose term applicable to any meeting of the governments whether at ministerial level or official level – the frequency and length of IGC meetings varying markedly over the years meeting nine times at ministerial level in the first 13 months of its existence (December 1985–December 1986) but only on seven occasions in 1987. Meetings at official level took place regularly as officials were in constant contact via the work of the Secretariat.

The atmosphere of the meetings themselves depended to a large extent on the topic under discussion, the relationship between the British and Irish ministers at the time, and events on the ground in Northern Ireland. The presumption of the Unionists was that the IGC was an attempt to move towards joint stewardship of Northern Ireland by the two governments. The First Report of the Grand Committee of the Northern Ireland Assembly, set up by the main Unionist parties to consider their response to the AIA, claimed: 'The Intergovernmental Conference is a joint authority in embryo . . . ' (Hadden and Boyle, 1989, p. 70). However, there was little to suggest that the two governments ever envisaged this. The British had ruled out any movement towards joint authority in the negotiations of the AIA. The IGC was an arena whereby the Irish could put forward plans for Northern Ireland and raise issues of concern to nationalists. It was never an arena wherein the two sides jointly took decisions on running the North.

The IGC was often used by the Irish to express their frustration at what they felt was the lack of action by the British on the areas of concern they raised. Whilst it may well have been the case that the AIA's 'intellectual logic was joint authority' (Bew, Patterson and Teague, 1997, p. 66), the IGC never developed into, nor appeared to be developing into, a joint decision-making body. Although the Irish were successful in securing changes in some aspects of British policy, on fundamental issues the Irish were demonstrably unsuccessful in their attempts to change the way Northern Ireland was administered. It may well be argued that this does not negate the claim that, intellectually, the new role given to the Irish under the AIA, and most visibly exercised in the IGC, seemed to be a step towards joint authority. For this intellectual direction to become discernible movement towards joint authority it would be necessary to show that the IGC enabled the Irish to succeed in securing widespread changes in Northern Ireland on issues to which they attached great importance. This is not the case.

Part of the problem, which caused Unionists to be suspicious of the IGC, was that its workings were largely conducted in secret. Due in part to the nature of the issues under discussion, as well as the protests surrounding its operation, IGC meetings tended to not be announced in advance and little information was released afterwards other than short and bland joint statements. Although this may have been intended to avoid further antagonising Unionists by suggesting that the IGC was not taking fundamental decisions, the lack of detail led some Unionists to believe that such empty statements were actually masking the far more dynamic, decision-making role the Conference was playing. Kenneth Bloomfield, who attended these IGC meetings, argues that the reality of the Conference work was somewhat different. According to Bloomfield 'there was much more tedium than excitement' (Bloomfield, 19 May 2000).

It was not just the nature of the discussions taking place within the IGC but the very existence of the IGC that was the problem for Unionists. The Unionist anger at what they felt was the lack of an effective voice for Unionism in the running of Northern Ireland was increased by what they saw as the asymmetry of input for the voice of nationalism via Dublin's role in the IGC. Kenneth Bloomfield argues, 'It was something of a rum-do that British Ministers are discussing how Northern Ireland is being governed with someone elected from a constituency in Co. Cork when nobody elected from Northern Ireland has any input to this deliberation at all' (Bloomfield, 19 May 2000 – Barry was TD for Cork).

In an attempt to offset criticism over this perceived imbalance the argument was made that Unionists already had adequate access to the British government. According to the *Index* document the argument was that

> The unique arrangement we have made with the Irish Government reflects the position of a minority which looks to Dublin to express its aspirations. The unionists by definition identify with the United Kingdom; they have, and will continue to have, ready means of access to the British Government, including unionist Members of Parliament in Westminster; and the Government pays close attention to their views.
>
> (*Index* B1 c(iii))

However, Unionists viewed the situation in very different terms and their trust in the British government, as well as their willingness to access it, disappeared for several years after the AIA.

The Secretariat

The Secretariat was set up by the AIA to service the IGC. If the IGC was at the heart of the AIA, the role of the Secretariat was to ensure that the heart beat healthily and did not find its arteries becoming blocked. The role or composition of the Secretariat was not made explicit in the AIA itself. It merely stated that a 'Secretariat shall be established by the two Governments to service the Conference on a continuing basis in the discharge of its functions . . . '. The *Index* document claimed it would be 'very small' and 'It will have no executive functions' (*Index* A3(a&b)).

The Secretariat's role had been a bone of contention during the negotiations of the AIA. The British side, and especially the NIO, saw the Secretariat as merely 'note takers' who would act as a conduit for the Irish to the NIO. The Irish for their part wanted the Secretariat to be a channel between the two governments rather than to the NIO and be staffed by relatively high-ranking officials. According to FitzGerald's account, 'The Secretariat would not be note-takers: they would be applying their experience and rank to deal with problems and would have to represent themselves and each other in the decision making process' (FitzGerald, 1991, p. 575).

The Secretariat fulfilled at least three functions. First it carried out research, prepared reports and made suggestions for the IGC regarding matters on forth-coming IGC agendas (and discussed the agenda itself). The other two roles were, however, more contentious and were a result of the comparatively high status of officials staffing the Secretariat. It served 'as an important forum of discussion and channel of communication between the two governments' (Hadden and Boyle, 1989, p. 28). Whilst major decisions were taken at ministerial level much of the preliminary work on issues was to be carried out at the level of the Secretariat and less contentious issues were effectively settled at Secret-ariat level, enabling ministers to concentrate on more pressing issues. The third, and perhaps most important function of the Secretariat, was as a tool of crisis management.

Consideration was given to the structure of the Secretariat and its working patterns as Séan Donlon, Secretary of the Irish Department of Foreign Affairs, explained:

> We decided in setting up Maryfield that we should use the model that the oil companies used for offshore platforms. We decided, for example, to make sure food was of a very high quality; we sent in two or three very good chefs, we banned alcohol, except for formal dinners. We just created a situation generally where people who had to live and work closely together could get on and we adopted more or less the same system as the oil platforms, I think it was seven days on, five days off, that sort of thing. So a very close camaraderie and friendships developed.
>
> (Donlon, 12 April 2000)

As officials from both sides were posted to the Secretariat for an initial period of 2 years, later increased to 3 years, close working relationships developed. This structure ensured that there was always a British and Irish duty officer on hand, 24 hours a day.

The institutionalising of a mechanism to allow instant contact between the two governments within Northern Ireland itself enabled the Irish to utilise far more effectively a system of communication that had existed with the nationalist community in the North for many years. Since the early days of the Troubles the Irish had people on the ground in nationalist areas reporting to the Irish Government. Whilst the system of having contacts within the nationalist community in Northern Ireland pre-dated the Agreement it was 'intensified' after the Agreement (FitzGerald, 6 June 2000). According to Donlon:

> let's say there was a security incident in Belfast involving an allegation that British soldiers shot and killed somebody. The way the system worked was we had what we called 'travellers' on the ground in Northern Ireland who were officials from the Department of Foreign Affairs, who divided up Northern Ireland between them. [They] had a range of contacts in nationalist areas, somebody from the nationalist area, usually the local SDLP person, perhaps a priest, or a teacher, or a community leader; somebody would phone their Foreign Affairs contact immediately. The Foreign Affairs contact would immediately get on to the relevant government official based in the Maryfield Secretariat. The Maryfield Secretariat would immediately ask for a report on the incident and that then became the subject (of discussion). There might be a disputed version, but the problem tended to be, I won't say sorted out within a matters of hours, but tended to become a subject for discussion for the two governments almost immediately it happened. So you couldn't get the rabble-rousers on the streets saying nothing was happening because the community leader, or the SDLP person, or whoever it was, could go to his community and say: 'Look, this matter is receiving attention at a high level between the two governments who are seeing what can be done to resolve it.' We didn't always resolve episodes like that to people's satisfaction but at least they were able to be reassured that somebody was taking care of their problems . . . .
>
> (Donlon, 12 April 2000)

This was part of the Irish government's attempts to reduce the influence of Sinn Féin. By having the mechanism whereby the SDLP could contact the Irish government directly it was hoped that the community role that Sinn Féin liked to portray itself as fulfilling would be reduced. Barry, who was the first Irish co-Chair of the IGC, claims,

> it was hugely important, and it settled down nationalist opinion. It made them feel a Dublin government was interested, which they never believed, and it made them know that . . . [the SDLP's] Joe Hendron could achieve

things for West Belfast through a political circle, that Gerry Adams couldn't achieve through the gun. That was hugely important.

(Barry, 23 May 2000)

Even those who were sceptical of the AIA acknowledge the importance of the Secretariat's role in crisis management and as a conduit to prevent disputes between the two governments escalating. Kenneth Bloomfield claims,

> I say this as someone who disliked many aspects of the Agreement, one great advantage that it did have was early and informal communication about controversial issues which could often prevent megaphone diplomacy based on misunderstandings. . . . They [the Irish] certainly had these eyes and ears around the place and if something was picked up that seemed disturbing, you then had a really quite effective high-speed mechanism for getting an explanation, which might, or might not, satisfy people. But in the best of cases would prevent something coming all the way to the Conference table.
>
> (Bloomfield, 19 May 2000)

What changed under the AIA was not that the Irish suddenly had access to information from the ground in nationalist areas in Northern Ireland but the creation of a standing institution that gave the Irish access, at a high level, 24 hours a day, to the British government. For the Irish side the institutionalisation of the 'right' of input was seen as very important, even if, as Hurd seems to suggest, it was not seen as a major change by at least some on the British side. Whereas before the Irish felt consultation was on a 'grace and favour basis' (Dorr, 25 May 2000; Barry, 23 May 2000) by the British, the AIA gave Dublin 'a *right* to put forward proposals and the British had an *obligation* to mediate those problems' (Donlon, 12 April 2000; Donlon's emphasis).

Mediating the problems: Disputes and recriminations

Whilst the mechanism for crisis resolution and better intergovernmental communication may have been created by the AIA it did not follow that disputes between the two governments were either eradicated or even less visible following its signing. The AIA faced a severe test in the first few months of its existence and by the time of its review many early supporters of the Agreement were questioning both its efficacy and worth. Once again some of the areas of dispute between the two states were as a result of outside 'shocks', events that were difficult for the governments to anticipate. But the majority of the problems that arose between the two governments were attributable to the underlying strain in Anglo-Irish relations: agreement on the need to stop the violence but a difference of emphasis or outright disagreement on how this could best be achieved. The Irish government was to become increasingly unhappy with what they felt was British failure to address nationalist alienation by making structural changes to the system of justice in Northern Ireland. The British for their part were frustrated by the Irish government's failure to fulfil obligations London felt it had secured regarding security co-operation and measures to target Republican terrorists.

The administration of justice: Irish concerns

For the Irish Government one of the major problems leading to nationalist alienation from the Northern Ireland state was the structure of the justice and policing system. To this end the Irish sought major changes in the court, policing and detention system in Northern Ireland. Some of these issues had been included in the AIA, but the failure to reach agreement on these changes during the negotiations meant that they were simply listed as areas to be examined by the IGC. This illustrated, once again, that the negotiations and the subsequent AIA had succeeded only in creating a mechanism for Anglo-Irish dialogue and had acknowledged a role for Dublin in Northern Ireland affairs. It had not managed to secure agreement on changing the way justice was administered in Northern Ireland. FitzGerald is candid in acknowledging the shortcomings of the AIA in securing the changes his government wanted to see:

> Our concern was to reduce the negative impact on nationalist opinion of the excessively hard-line security operating in the North. That would be done through three-man courts, which we didn't get. Through the topic of prisoner releases, which was dropped. Through the announcement and promulgation of the code of conduct for the police, which was postponed for three years and then wasn't even promulgated. And [the] absolute constant accompaniment of the army by the civil power, the police, so that all arrests were by the police with the army there to protect them and that was not done in twenty-five per cent of cases. None of the things we wanted done were done.
>
> (FitzGerald, 6 June 2000)

During the negotiations the Irish had raised each of these areas but, for various reasons, the issues were not settled during the negotiations. To prevent the initiative breaking down over these topics it was agreed to mention them in the AIA as areas that would be discussed in the IGC. Whilst this was a formula that allowed the AIA to be signed it did mean that these difficult areas would have to be contested by the two governments in the period after November 1985. This formula virtually guaranteed that there would be disputes between the two governments in the immediate aftermath of the AIA. The reason that the issues could not be resolved in the negotiations was that they were very divisive. From the British point of view fundamental changes in the area of administration of justice in Northern Ireland would be seen as an admission that the existing system in Northern Ireland was not satisfactory. Perhaps even more problematically it could be seen as implicitly criticising the judges, soldiers and police who were responsible for the administration of justice in Northern Ireland. It is this point that seems to account for the failure by the British to agree to changes.

The Courts

The Irish wanted terrorist-related trials in the North to mirror the system used in the South and be heard by three judges, rather than the one judge, no jury (Diplock) courts that were used in the North since 1973. Originally the Irish had wanted such cases heard by mixed courts made up of judges from both the South and North. It is clear that during the negotiations the British were at least willing to consider such a system. In her memoirs Thatcher states that at a meeting with FitzGerald in June 1985 she agreed to consider joint courts but she would 'certainly not . . . give an assurance in advance that they would be established' (Thatcher, 1993, p. 401). The *Index* document confirms that the issue was far from settled as the proposed response to a question on mixed courts was for Thatcher to state, 'We do not exclude the possibility of mixed courts being feasible at some future time but we cannot see any easy or early way round or through the political and other difficulties which would be involved' (*Index* A8 c(ii)). The Irish dropped calls for joint courts after the British told FitzGerald that this would not be possible for quite some time. As a result the Irish pressed for three Northern Ireland judge courts (FitzGerald, 6 June 2000).

Whatever willingness Thatcher may have expressed during the negotiations to review the court system dissipated after the AIA was signed. The reason for this was the outright opposition to any changes to the system by the Lord Chancellor, Lord Hailsham, the Lord Chief Justice of Northern Ireland, Lord Lowry, and, perhaps more surprisingly, the Deputy Prime Minister, Willie Whitelaw (*Irish Times*, 6 November 1986; FitzGerald, 6 June 2000). The opposition centred on the belief that to expand the number of judges sitting at terrorist trials would be a criticism of the existing legal system and the Northern Ireland judiciary. In the face of such high profile opposition to the plans Thatcher was unwilling to countenance change. The failure by the British to agree to changes in the court system had the knock-on effect of leading the Irish to make threatening noises regarding whether they would ratify the European Convention on the Suppression of Terrorism (ECST) (discussed below).

Whilst it is the case that the British had only agreed to consider changes to the courts and had not committed to making changes, the lack of progress on the issue caused problems for the Irish government. Dublin had made no secret of their belief that changes in the way terrorist trials were conducted were necessary to reduce nationalist alienation. The British refusal to make such changes allowed opponents of the Agreement to claim that it was failing to improve the conditions of nationalists in the North: the reason the Irish government had given for its existence. There is some sympathy for the Irish annoyance of this point by Goodall:

> I think Garret was entitled to feel let down about the courts. The courts were a long subject of debate in the negotiations and in the end the final communiqué . . . was intended to mean that the British would look into the idea of reforming the courts if the Irish would promptly ratify the European

Convention . . . [But given the opposition of Hailsham] Margaret Thatcher really had no option, because by then even Tom King was persuaded that we ought to go to three judge courts. So I think that was the great pity and of course things were very slow, getting out the police code of conduct and the Irish did drag their feet about the Suppression of Terrorism. So like everything in political life it was a half success and half failure.

(Goodall, 1999)

Whilst the opposition of the Lord Chancellor may have left Thatcher with no choice, such arguments cut little ice in Dublin. The *Irish Times* argued, 'The British signed an agreement to do certain things. They should not be allowed to dodge their responsibilities by hiding behind the judicial robes of uncooperative judges' (*Irish Times*, 1 December 1986).

FitzGerald required successes in the areas he had highlighted as causing nationalist alienation and these successes to be seen by nationalists as a result of the AIA. On this high profile issue the Irish could not persuade the British to move. The formula of including contentious issues in the Agreement as areas to be discussed later may have allowed the AIA to be signed but it became clear these areas were just as problematic post as pre-Agreement, only now expectations had been raised.

Accompaniment

The other high profile failure, and the most important failure in FitzGerald's eyes (ICBH, 1997), was the inability to secure accompaniment of all army (particularly the Ulster Defence Regiment) patrols by members of the RUC. There is no doubt that the Irish pushed this issue very strongly at IGC meetings. Sir Kenneth Bloomfield gives an indication of the priority and time the Irish forced the IGC to give to the issue when he recalls, 'Something that I remember as taking up an enormous amount of time, and really irritating me, was something they called accompaniment. Dear old accompaniment, I'll go to my grave . . . you know how Mary (Tudor) had 'Calais' on her heart? I'll have 'accompaniment' on my heart' (Bloomfield, 19 May 2000).

The issue was considered at the first IGC meeting on 11 December 1985. The joint communiqué issued after the meeting seemed to suggest that the issue would be resolved satisfactorily as it was considering steps towards ensuring, 'save in the most exceptional circumstances, there is a police presence in all operations which involve direct contact with the community'.

Yet for all the emphasis the Irish placed on the policy they were, as FitzGerald acknowledged, relatively unsuccessful in securing its implementation. The reason for this failure is most likely to have been manpower considerations. There seems to have been little objection in principle from the British side to accompaniment (though they did not share the Irish government's analysis of the need for police accompaniment of the army).

The RUC Code of Conduct

The code of conduct was, for the Irish, another element of trying to make the administration of justice in Northern Ireland more acceptable to nationalists. Once again the joint statement issued at the end of the first IGC seemed to suggest that progress on this aspect of policy might be relatively straightforward. The statement noted that

> The Chief Constable of the RUC advised the Conference that a number of other UK police forces were introducing Codes of Conduct and that, in consultation with the Police Authority, he had for some time been preparing and would introduce as soon as possible in 1986 [a] Code which would include these matters.

Yet the Code was not published until 1988. The main reason for this appears to be the opposition of the Chief Constable, Sir John Hermon, for allowing the Code to be associated with the IGC. Kenneth Bloomfield explains:

> Jack Hermon felt it would be no help at all if it was seen as being dictated by the governments so he was keen that it should be seen as something he and the police authority wanted to do. But he didn't want it presented as an initiative of the Conference. And I would agree with him, because that wouldn't be helpful. The thing that really mattered was getting the . . . thing finalised and making it effective. The cosmetics were less important than doing the right thing. If the cosmetics got in the way of doing the right thing then you were shooting yourself in the foot.
>
> (Bloomfield, 19 May 2000)

The problem was that for the Irish the 'cosmetics' of having the Code associated with the IGC were very important. If the AIA was to be successful in reducing nationalist alienation it not only had to secure changes in the administration of Northern Ireland, it had to be seen to be securing these benefits. The British government at the same time was trying to underplay the role that the IGC was having in Northern Ireland affairs to avoid further antagonising the Unionists. For this reason the British also dropped the commitment the Irish felt they had secured regarding a promise to review prison sentences in the event of an end to the violence. Thatcher told FitzGerald that such an undertaking at a time of such Unionist disquiet 'would be dynamite no, not dynamite, nuclear' (FitzGerald, 1991, p. 571).

Combating terrorism: British concerns

Britain's concerns regarding the workings of the AIA centred upon its failure to deliver in the key areas London believed it had been designed to address. The British reservations were over the failure to improve intergovernmental co-operation in methods to combat terrorism and improve security co-operation.

The visible disputes in this area were over Irish enactment of the ECST, extradition, and claims of a lack of Irish co-operation in cross-border security operations.

ECST and extradition

As already noted the issue of extradition had long been a problematic one in Anglo-Irish relations and the British government wanted the legal mechanism simplified. Irish enactment of the ECST would have made the political motivation defence harder to successfully pursue and so increase the chances of securing extradition for terrorist suspects. Article 1 of the ECST lists offences that cannot be considered political for extradition purposes between states that have ratified the Convention including any offence, 'involving the use of a bomb, grenade, rocket, automatic firearm or letter or parcel bomb if this use endangers persons . . . '. Article 2 of the Convention also allows a State to not regard as political 'a serious offence involving an act of violence' (quoted in Hadden and Boyle, 1989, pp. 59–66).

The Irish Minister for Justice, Alan Dukes, signed the ECST in Strasbourg on 24 February 1986. However, the ECST had to be ratified by the Dáil before it became binding on the Irish. This proved to be a long and acrimonious process. The problems in ratifying the ECST were political rather than legal. The Irish felt that there had been clear linkage between the issues of ratifying the ECST and changes to the administration of justice in Northern Ireland, particularly changes to the Diplock court system. As time went on and it was clear that there were to be no changes to the court system the Irish government seemed to be suggesting that the ECST may not be ratified. In October 1986 Barry said the Irish still intended to enact the ECST when they were satisfied progress had been made on improving nationalist confidence in the judicial system in Northern Ireland. The government entered a bill to ratify the ECST in the first week of December but it was not to come into force until 1 June 1987 when the Dáil would have to approve its enactment. FitzGerald stated, 'We expect that the progress . . . by next June will produce a situation in which the Dáil and Senead will not want to postpone the decision' (*Irish Times*, 7 October 1986).

In between the passing of the ECST by the Dáil and the proposed implementation date there was an election in the Republic and Haughey replaced FitzGerald as Taoiseach. Given that Haughey had opposed the AIA on constitutional grounds, had appeared on several occasions to be threatening to seek its renegotiation when elected, and the poor relations between Thatcher and Haughey in the 1981–82 period, there was concern in some quarters as to what effect his election would have on the Agreement (Donlon, 12 April 2000). FitzGerald claims that Thatcher was deeply concerned when he told her in December 1986 that he would lose the forthcoming election to Haughey (FitzGerald, 6 June 2000). (This was not a concern shared by all in the British establishment. T.E. Utley, who had in the past advised Thatcher, wrote in *The Times* that it would make no difference who was Taoiseach as Ireland's electorate 'do not care a row of beans for Irish unity'. Utley argued that actually Haughey was the best Taoiseach, from the British point of view, as he will continue to keep up the 'song' about unification but actually would not, or indeed could not, do anything about it. Utley urged Thatcher to ignore the Irish government arguing, 'the British Government pays far too much attention to the opinions of prime ministers in the Republic about how Northern Ireland should be governed. They are neither able to threaten us or greatly able to help us. Who they are does not matter much' (*The Times*, 23 February 1987)).

The Irish Dáil did ratify the Convention on 1 December 1987. (The IRA bombing of the Remembrance Day parade at Enniskillen, which killed 11 people and the discovery of 150 tonnes of arms and explosives from Libya destined for the IRA are widely attributed as being instrumental in persuading the Irish government to ratify the ECST) (Owen, 1994. p. 166; Hadden and Boyle, 1989, p. 64). However, the Haughey government also introduced stricter rules in terms of the evidence that the British had to provide and the undertakings the British authorities had to give in order to secure extradition. Thatcher claimed the new system made Britain 'the least favoured nation (in Europe) in this matter' (House of Commons, vol. 123, col. 762, 1 December 1987). According to Thatcher the situation was actually worse than that which existed before as previously neither 'side looked through the warrant; they accepted the warrant and the fact that when a warrant was presented there was evidence and intention to prosecute. I believe that the arrangements now . . . are a step backwards . . . ' (House of Commons, vol. 123, col. 1102, 3 December 1987). The extradition issue continued to be problematic and there were numerous high profile cases over the following years (notably the Patrick Ryan case in 1988 and the refusal of an Irish court to extradite two men to Northern Ireland in March 1990 on the grounds that they would face 'probable risk' of assault by prison officers) (*The Times*, 14 March 1990).

Security co-operation

The other area in which the British felt that the Agreement did not deliver the results they had hoped for was security co-operation. By its very nature this area of intergovernmental co-operation is secretive and as such success or failure is very difficult to ascertain. Thatcher centres most of her subsequent criticism of the Agreement on security co-operation. In her memoirs she is very critical of Irish co-operation in security matters particularly in terms of intelligence reports of the activities of IRA in the Republic. 'Once they crossed the border they were lost. Indeed, we received far better intelligence co-operation from virtually all other European countries than with the Republic.' She also claims that the contribution that the AIA made in the fight against terrorism 'was very limited'. The lack of security co-operation made Thatcher conclude that the Agreement and the British 'concessions alienated the Unionists without gaining the level of security co-operation we had a right to expect' (Thatcher, 1993, pp. 410–415). It is evident that others within the Thatcher government were also unhappy with the security gains that hailed from the Agreement. King frequently spoke of his 'impatience to make faster progress' on security co-operation (*The Times*, 4 September 1986 and 4 November 1986; *Irish Times*, 22 September 1982). (Though King was always careful to stress that the situation was improving and avoided outright criticism of the Irish government on the issue.)

There seems, however, to have been a difference in attitude between politicians and civil servants on the security question. Whilst British politicians are highly critical of the gains in security co-operation as a result of the AIA, some British and Irish civil servants have a different interpretation. These differences are two-fold. First there seems to have been a belief by at least some of those who negotiated the AIA that increasing security co-operation was not a primary aim of the AIA. Secondly others question the belief that the AIA failed to deliver improved security.

Séan Donlon claims that the security issue was actually discussed very little during the negotiations. The reason, according to Donlon, was that structures already existed between the two governments to deal with this issue. 'We had decided long before we went into negotiations of what became the 1985 Anglo-Irish Agreement, we decided that security co-operation should be left outside the door because that was a continuing issue for there were good structures in place.' According to Donlon, 'it was never a topic of dispute. Civil servants on both sides tended to see security co-operation as pretty good, politicians didn't always accept that, particularly on the British side'. Donlon is adamant on this point, claiming that he has a full record of the negotiations of the AIA and was surprised himself when he re-examined the records subsequently at how little the subject of security came up (Donlon, 12 April 2000). Kenneth Bloomfield echoes the idea that the IGC was not the place to deal with security issues and claims, 'some of these things had been going on for a long time before anyone ever thought of an Anglo-Irish Agreement' (Bloomfield, 19 May 2000). This is not, though, to suggest that Bloomfield argues that there was not a problem with security co-operation. He simply appears to share the opinion of Donlon, perhaps for different reasons, that the AIA and IGC were not effective tools for dealing with security issues.

Although some may question whether the purpose of the AIA was to improve security co-operation, one of the key British negotiators of the AIA appears to take issue with the argument that the AIA failed to deliver in security terms. Goodall argues, 'Even the greatest enemy of the Agreement wouldn't have said that there wasn't greatly improved security co-operation as a result of the Agreement' (Goodall, 24 June 1999). It is not the case that there was a completely straightforward politician/civil servant split on how the security issue was viewed. The head of the NIO at the time, Andrew, admits that he was disappointed with the security gains the AIA provided (which may be linked to the intra-departmental differences previously noted) (Andrew, 21 November 2000). So it is unclear to what extent there was true disappointment on the British side regarding security co-operation and how widespread such discontent was.

If Donlon is right and the issue of security played little part in the AIA negotiations it raises the question as to whether the issue was overplayed during the
negotiations by the British officials and politicians such as Armstrong, Goodall
and Howe to persuade Thatcher to sign the Agreement. If it was the case that
the issue of security was not anticipated by the British and Irish negotiators
as one that would be dramatically altered by the AIA but was presented as
the cornerstone of the Agreement to Thatcher, it is perhaps unsurprising that
she felt security co-operation did not improve to the level she 'had a right to
expect'. Similarly there is the question of expectation and perception. Some
British politicians may have had unrealistic expectations as to the level of security
co-operation that would result from the AIA. As such their perception would
be that the AIA had failed to deliver. Civil servants like Goodall may have had
lesser expectations and so may perceive any gains in security co-operation far
more favourably.

The Irish for their part reject the idea that they failed to co-operate in security
matters. FitzGerald claims whilst he was Taoiseach practically every suggestion
that the British made on how to improve security co-operation was implemented.
'They made a number of proposals in 1986 for improving the operation of
our policing system. I eventually, with Michael Lillis, got down to that and
agreed 15 of the 16 proposals and forced them through our Department of
Justice, who weren't all that keen' (FitzGerald, 6 June 2000). When FitzGerald
challenged the former head of the NIO, Andrew, over the claim that there
had been disappointment on the British side over security co-operation Andrew
noted, 'There was a perception that, for example, not as much intelligence as
had been hoped for was coming from the South on the movement of suspected
IRA terrorists, and these things are difficult to point out' (ICBH, 1997, p. 70).

As Andrew notes, successes and failures of security co-operation are indeed
difficult to point out. The problem in terms of Anglo-Irish relations and the
workings of the Agreement once again comes down to different expectations
and priorities. The disappointments of both the Irish and British governments
with the 'fruits' of the AIA in its early days can be explained by not only
their different priorities but their different understandings of what was meant
by security. For the British the focus was on the physical aspects of security:
intelligence gathering, policing the border and arms finds. Whilst the Irish agreed
that all of these aspects were important their focus was slightly different. For the
Irish a major way of improving the security situation was addressing what they
saw as the underlying problems that led to a poor security situation: reducing
nationalist alienation from the security forces. Andrew explains this difference
in understanding of what was meant by security.

> We meant different things [by] security. The British first and foremost meant
> catching terrorists, preferably catching them and if we couldn't catch them
> shooting them. That was security, it was in a physical military sense. The
> Irish side saw security much more in terms of the community in the North
> and gaining its support.

Andrew acknowledges problems arose because the two governments

> thought they'd agreed slightly different things . . . I think the reason why
> this was a continuing source of friction was because we still gave primacy
> to what, for the sake of shorthand, I'll call the military aspect of security
> and we wanted more done there. They gave primacy to the other side and
> wanted more done. So we were disappointed that more was not being done
> on the military side and they were disappointed that more was not being
> done on what one might call the community side . . . . So there was a certain
> amount of disappointment all round.
>
> (Andrew, 21 November 2000)

External shocks: The effect of unanticipated issues on the intergovernmental relationship

Whilst the above areas of dispute all centred around issues that had to some
degree been discussed during the AIA negotiations, in the years following the
AIA the Anglo-Irish relationship was placed under strain by other unforeseen
events. The dispute over the decision to allow an Orange march down the
Garvaghy Road in 1986 led to a visible dispute between Barry and King over
alleged failure to consult the Irish, whether the decision was a policing or political
one and accusations of a failure of the IGC to prevent megaphone diplomacy
(*Irish Times*, 15–17 July 1986). Whilst this episode was comparatively brief, the
first 6 months of 1988 saw a more problematic series of disputes between the
two governments. The most important of these centred on the Stalker–Sampson
inquiry and the cases of the Birmingham 6. These issues demonstrated, once
again, that whilst the AIA had created a mechanism for formalised consultation
between the two governments and an arena where the Republic could raise issues
of concern with the British government, it did not create an arena that could
necessarily solve or even contain disputes.

Stalker–Sampson

The Stalker inquiry originally concerned an investigation by the Deputy Chief
Constable of Manchester, John Stalker, into allegations of an alleged shoot-to-
kill policy by the RUC in 1982. (The West Yorkshire Chief Constable, Colin
Sampson, replaced Stalker in June 1986, when Stalker was suspended due to
allegations that he was associated with 'known criminals' – he was subsequently
cleared and reinstated (Taylor, 1987; Stalker, 1988).) The reason that the Stalker–
Sampson inquiry led to an Anglo-Irish dispute was not so much due to the
events that were investigated, but the decision that, on national interests, there
would be no prosecutions. The Attorney General, Sir Patrick Mayhew, and
the Northern Ireland's Director of Public Prosecutions (DPP), Sir Barry Shaw,
decided not to proceed with prosecutions on the basis that information may
become known that would be damaging to national security (although strictly

speaking the DPP is independent of the government and Mayhew insisted that the decision was Shaw's alone) (House of Commons, vol. 125, col. 22, 25 January 1988).

The Irish government was incensed by the announcement. Haughey told the Dáil that he had not been consulted by Mayhew regarding the decision or informed that it was about to be announced. The Irish cancelled a scheduled meeting between the RUC Chief Constable and the Garda Commissioner in protest. The Irish Minister of Justice, Gerry Collins, was particularly critical of the decision claiming, 'a very serious problem now exists in Anglo-Irish affairs . . . these are damnably serious matters. They destroy the credibility of the RUC.' Collins also made a not too veiled criticism of Mayhew when he remarked that 'anyone who believes there was a conspiracy to pervert the course of justice but that there should be no prosecutions is not fit for public office' (Owen, 1994, p. 182). The British Labour Party was also very critical of the decision (House of Commons, vol. 125, col. 23, 25 January 1988). The British government rejected calls for the publication of the report and refused a request by the Irish government, made via the IGC, to see it (*The Times*, 2 February 1988).

It never rains . . .

Problems over Stalker–Sampson were exacerbated over the next few weeks by a series of bizarre events and decisions. The British Court of Appeal rejected the Birmingham 6 appeal a few days after the Stalker–Sampson announcement. The Irish government had pressed the case of the Birmingham 6 (and Guildford 4) at numerous IGC meetings. Gerry Collins said he was 'amazed and saddened' by the decision. In the same month Private Ian Thain, who in December 1984 had been the first soldier found guilty of murdering a civilian whilst on duty in Northern Ireland, was released from jail and allowed to rejoin his old army regiment. Relations deteriorated further the following month when Haughey announced that he was appointing the Garda's Deputy Chief Commissioner to carry out an investigation into the shooting by the British army of Aiden McAnespie at a border checkpoint in Co Tyrone. The NIO claimed, 'As far as we are concerned the RUC is the competent authority. You could imagine the outcry in the Republic if the RUC was to investigate a shooting incident which took place in County Tipperary' (*The Times*, 23 February 1988).

Further strain was placed on Anglo-Irish relations in March with the killing of three unarmed IRA suspects by the SAS in Gibraltar and the announcement of the decision by the Home Secretary, Douglas Hurd, that the Prevention of Terrorism Act was to be made permanent. As Ellis Owen argued Stalker–Sampson 'triggered off a series of crises, each one serious in its own right, but made much worse by the changed atmosphere after Mayhew's statement. Coincidences became conspiracies' (Owen, 1994, p. 181).

The Irish were not alone in being highly critical of these events. *The Times* argued strongly that the British were making mistakes.

The Agreement is ... threatened by political misjudgement in London and Dublin. Admitting to the existence of evidence that policemen conspired to pervert the course of justice and failing to prosecute is a mistaken view of the public interest. Allowing a convicted murderer back into the same army, which is patrolling in Northern Ireland, is similarly foolish. These misjudgements are not wrong because they fail to take into account the views of the Republic: they are simply wrong. In addition they have serious consequences for public faith in the security forces.

(*The Times*, 24 February 1988)

Although the episodes highlighted the relative inability of the IGC to prevent disputes spilling over into 'megaphone diplomacy', the relationship did weather the storm of 1988. The pattern was emerging whereby areas of dispute would be pursued vigorously by the two governments but if they could not be resolved they would be 'set aside'. This is not to say that they would necessarily be off the agenda, but there would be a tacit agreement to concentrate on other issues where progress may be possible. When relations became particularly fraught, as in the early months of 1988, events on the ground in Northern Ireland seemed to refocus the governments on the problems of terrorism and cause them to recommit to the path of co-operation. So the annoyance over the Stalker–Sampson events and Birmingham 6 were downplayed somewhat after the killings of three mourners at the funerals of the 'Gibraltar bombers' by Michael Stone and the murder of two British soldiers at the subsequent funeral. At a special IGC to discuss the deteriorating situation in Northern Ireland the two governments appeared to agree to shelve some of their disputes. Tom King noted,

We have faced a number of problems in recent months, a number of difficulties, that have caused problems for the relationship between our countries under the Agreement ... [but] I am absolutely clear of our common determination to make a success of the Agreement to the benefit of all our peoples and to give a new impetus to [the] work and objectives of the Agreement.

(*The Times*, 26 March 1988)

Collins claimed that there was a determination from both governments to ensure the Agreement worked 'irrespective of the difficulties to be overcome' (*The Times*, 26 March 1988).

Some successes of the AIA

Whilst the numerous areas of dispute and disagreement have been documented above there were numerous notable successes that resulted from the AIA. The first time the new mechanism was used to try and deal with an unforeseen crisis in Northern Ireland was the month after it was signed, when three INLA men went on hunger strike. Given the incredibly destabilising effect the 1981 hunger strike had had the Irish were very keen that this hunger strike was resolved as soon as possible. Barry let it be known that he felt the hunger strike was unnecessary and unhelpful, given that there 'is now a method for raising such matters in the future' (*Irish Times*, 30 December 1985). To this end Dublin requested an emergency IGC meeting, which was held on 30 December. At the meeting Barry put forward plans to change the supergrass system, which had led to the three men's conviction. The men called off their strike on 6 January – 3 days after Hume had met them. Hume had announced that their demands were 'perfectly reasonable' but urged them to abandon their fast (*Irish Times*, 4 January 1986).

The importance of the hunger strike incident is not in the event itself, but the fact that it gave the Irish their first opportunity to test the new mechanism. More than this it also was used by Barry to put a marker down regarding the Irish attitude to the new system. Barry felt that it was vital that the Irish demonstrated to the British, from the very start, their determination to use the new system to push issues they felt important. Barry explains, King is 'a decent, honest man, very open. But he had the idea that this was the British government running the North of Ireland still, with my help. . . . That didn't coincide with my view, (I disagreed) that I was there to calm down the nationalists and stop them firing bullets at his soldiers'. So King requested an IGC meeting. 'Obviously he didn't like to be summoned to a meeting by an Irish minister about something inside the United Kingdom. But we did and we defused the situation and it went away.' According to Barry he needed

> to establish the Irish government's rights. We couldn't let ourselves be taken for granted. We weren't there to cover up Tom King. We were there because we signed an agreement, which gave us rights, and we wanted to see that those rights were lived up to. You can see why it would be upsetting for a British government who had since 1800/1801 been doing the opposite.
>
> (Barry, 23 May 2000)

Whilst the suggestion that the AIA was not designed to allow the British to run Northern Ireland with Irish help is very questionable, Barry's comments do offer an interesting insight into how the Irish saw their role. During the early years the Irish were somewhat forthright in their representations at the IGC, especially whilst Barry was co-chair of the Conference. This may, as Barry suggests, have been necessary to establish the Irish role and rights. As the IGC settled down and the two sides became more used to working with each other the atmosphere in the meetings appeared to change, especially when Fianna Fáil's Brian Lenihan replaced Barry. Kenneth Bloomfield claims 'as time went by, interestingly enough (attitudes changed) . . . Fianna Fáil had the reputation of being the Republican party, and the rhetoric is pretty deeply Republican and yet I found Brian Lenihan in particular, much less disposed to make a nonsense of nit-picking tiny issues unlike some other people' (Bloomfield, 19 May 2000). Perhaps by the time Fianna Fáil replaced the coalition government in 1987 Barry had been successful in establishing Dublin's role thus allowing

Lenihan a more conciliatory approach. Alternatively the change may well be simply a result of differences in political styles and outlook between the two men. Whatever the reason it is not the case that post-1987 the IGC saw fewer disputes (as we have seen 1988 was particularly fraught) but there does appear to have been a determination by Dublin in the early months to work the Conference aggressively.

The Irish did periodically exercise their right to call an IGC but they were faced with the problem that this mechanism allowed them to register their views but they could not, as we have seen above, force the British to alter policy. As O'Malley argued, 'ultimately, the resolution of disputes is a matter of good will and faith – British good will and Irish faith . . . ' (O'Malley, 1990b, p. 66). But it would be wrong to suggest that the British simply ignored the Irish. Whilst in many instances the mechanism did not secure the outcome Dublin wished to see, in many areas it did.

In his memoirs Fitzgerald listed what he saw as changes that the AIA had brought about which benefited the nationalist community. These included the repeal of the Flags and Emblems Act; stricter rules regarding routing of contentious marches; strengthening the law on incitement to hatred; improved fair employment guidelines (with legislation subsequently introduced); improvement in Catholic representation on appointed bodies; demolition and rebuilding of three nationalist ghettos (Divis, Unity and Roseville Flats); and the recognition of the use of Irish for place-names. In the security arena FitzGerald cites the establishment of a Police Complaints Commission; *some* progress regarding accompaniment of the UDR by the RUC; a reduction in complaints of harassment of the nationalist community by the security forces; changes in the powers of arrest under the Emergency Powers Act; the reduction of the time suspects could be held by police on their own authority from 72 hours to 48 hours; and he particularly singles out an increased even-handedness by the RUC in dealing with the two communities. Prisoners saw improvements in the arrangements for parole and compassionate leave. In the area of the administration of justice FitzGerald cites a tightening up of the rules on admissibility of the use of confessions as evidence; a person's right to have someone outside informed of their detention; access to a solicitor after 48 hours; and also the appointment of three additional judges which reduced the waiting time for trial. FitzGerald also notes the abandonment of the use of 'supergrass' trials, which he explicitly links to 'representations by the Irish Government through the Conference'. This is indeed an impressive list and FitzGerald claims the achievements of the AIA have 'certainly been underestimated' (FitzGerald, 1991, pp. 573–575).

It may be possible to raise questions regarding how big a change each of the above made to the lives of ordinary people living in Northern Ireland, and the British side would argue that many of the above points are not connected to the AIA but were in preparation pre-Agreement. There is though no doubt that the period after 1985 did see some major changes to the administration of justice in Northern Ireland and alterations in some social and employment legislation. But as a result of the fierce Unionist reaction to the Agreement there was an unwillingness on the part of the British to risk further antagonising Unionism by taking too many reforming measures that could be seen as a result of the Agreement. FitzGerald admits his government

> were persuaded by the British to play down the success of the Agreement, and the various things achieved under it, [so as] not to annoy Unionists more. The result was that nationalists never really understood how much they benefited by the changes made because of the Agreement in the following eighteen months. The nationalists' positive reaction became totally a function of the Unionists' negative reaction. When that all died down nationalists said, 'well, what did we ever get out of it anyway?'.
>
> (FitzGerald, 6 June 2000)

The agreement to downplay the advantages of the AIA to avoid further antagonising Unionists, meant, according to the former Irish diplomat, Eamon Delaney, 'The full institutional impact of the Anglo-Irish Agreement has never been highlighted or documented.' The AIA 'gave the Irish Government a consultative role in all aspects of Northern Irish life . . . there was not a hospital closure, fisheries initiative or cultural programme that the Irish Government didn't have a 'view' on'. The British also consulted Dublin on certain public appointments. Whilst Delaney conceded, 'Dublin was not always heeded and many parts of the Agreement went unimplemented' he sums up the psychological importance of the AIA to the Irish government well by arguing, 'the very fact that the facility existed was almost as important as its effectiveness' (Delaney, 2001, pp. 289–290).

The Irish pressed (with varying degrees of success) for further changes in Northern Ireland policy and governance. There seems to have been a feeling at least amongst some in the Irish government that the Unionists were Britain's problem and the British needed to deal with that problem, without any suggestion of backtracking from what the Irish believed they had secured at Hillsborough. Peter Barry is forceful on this point arguing it was Britain's failure to prepare the Unionists for the changes that were the problem.

> They hadn't educated the Unionist Party, but frankly, what was it? 'Gone With The Wind?', frankly 'we didn't give a damn'. We had made a probe, we had driven a wedge in and we were going to follow it. No matter what the opposition was we had legal backing for what we were doing.
>
> (Barry, 23 May 2000)

The net result of all of this was something of a confused and confusing picture regarding the effectiveness and outcome of the Agreement in the years following its signing. As FitzGerald's list shows there were numerous changes in Northern Ireland that can be viewed as designed to address the problem of nationalist alienation. That the workings of the Conference and the new role for the Republic's government were not given the credit for these changes may well be, as FitzGerald suggests, the result of a presentational decision rather than a failure of the Conference itself. (Even those who were unhappy with the rate of change regarding areas of nationalist grievance in the North, such as the SDLP's Seamus Mallon, defended the psychological importance of the Agreement (*Irish Times*, 15 May 1986).)

If a major aim of the Agreement, for the Irish government at least, was to halt the rise of Sinn Féin then in this area it can claim some marked success (at least in the medium term). In the four seats contested by the SDLP and Sinn Féin in the 1986 by-elections, caused by the resignation of all 13 Unionist MPs in protest against the AIA, Sinn Féin's vote dropped by 5.4 per cent and the SDLP vote rose by 6 per cent (with Seamus Mallon winning the seat of Newry and Armagh from the UUP for the SDLP). Similarly in the 1987 general election the SDLP's vote rose 3.2 per cent (to 21.1 per cent) compared to the 1983 Westminster election and the vote of Sinn Féin fell by 2 per cent (to 11.4 per cent) (Flackes and Elliot, 1989, pp. 353–355). The SDLP also increased their share of the vote in the local and European elections in 1989 (Bew and Gillespie, 1999, pp. 224–225).

As the suggested reasons of the British in signing the Agreement centred on security issues it is far harder to compile a 'list' of gains the British made from the Agreement. However, despite the remarks in her memoirs Thatcher did at times suggest that the Agreement was delivering improvements in this area. In January 1988 she told the House of Commons, 'The Anglo-Irish Agreement has led to greatly increased co-operation on security, which is to the advantage of people in Northern Ireland and in the Republic of Ireland' (House of Commons, vol. 125, col. 168, 26 January 1988). The Agreement did also mean that it was harder for the Irish to criticise Britain's Northern Ireland policy internationally. For Douglas Hurd the securing of acceptance by the Irish of the principle of consent, via the signing of the Agreement, was of paramount importance. So the AIA certainly went some way in meeting the varied reasons that have been identified as persuading the Thatcher government to institutionalise Anglo-Irish co-operation in 1985.

Conclusion

Academic opinion on the effectiveness of the Agreement has been relatively critical. In the conclusion to his study of the working of the Agreement during its first 3 years Arwell Ellis Owen is somewhat dismissive of Ireland's influence as a result of the Agreement. Ellis Owen claims, 'The Irish played a secondary role in the first 3 years of the Agreement.' Owen appears to base this claim on the failure of the Irish to secure widespread political changes via the IGC. According to his analysis, 'Ireland failed to develop the Anglo-Irish Agreement into a political forum; it remained a security initiative, as the British had intended' (Owen, 1994, p. 252). If Ellis Owen is right then not only did the Agreement fail from the Irish point of view but it must have failed from the British point of view given the disappointments, noted above, regarding security co-operation. Neumann argues the AIA failed to deliver from Britain's perspective due to

Dublin's 'lack of vigour *vis-à-vis* security co-operation'. According to Neumann this was a result of an inability to mobilise support in the Republic for security co-operation as the state did not face 'a similar threat' to that faced by Britain (Neumann, 2003, p. 133).

Neumann also argues that the AIA did not achieve wider British objectives beyond security co-operation. 'As it turned out, none of London's aims could be realised.' The AIA failed to increase nationalists' support for the institutions of Northern Ireland, was rejected by the Unionist community, and 'instead of reducing the tensions between the two governments, Dublin's public criticism of London appeared to have increased'. As a result from 'a strategic point of view, the AIA had therefore been a failure' (Neumann, 2003, p. 146).

Even writers who have generally defended the Agreement, such as O'Leary and McGarry, claim that 'the emergent consensus of commentators was that the AIA had merely created a new stalemate; coercive consociationalism had run up against the limits of entrenched antagonisms' (O'Leary and McGarry, 1993, p. 274). W.H. Cox has argued that any evaluation taken 5 years after the Agreement was signed would have had to conclude that it had been a failure (Cox, 1996, p. 185). Arthur Aughey in his highly critical analysis of the Agreement concludes, 'One must start by acknowledging the dramatic failure of the Agreement to achieve its stated objectives' (Aughey, 1989, p. 204).

Yet to attach the label of 'failure' or 'success' is a somewhat fraught exercise. Given the ambiguity of the Agreement itself and the difficulty in identifying the purposes of what the two governments signed at Hillsborough it is difficult to agree on a yardstick against which to measure success and failure. Ellis Owen sees the Agreement as operating primarily as a security initiative and as such labels it a failure from the Irish point of view. Ellis Owen is correct in so far as it is possible to identify high profile changes to the administration of justice in Northern Ireland that the Irish government publicly called for yet failed to secure. In the areas of Diplock courts, accompaniment and prisoner releases, at least in the short term, the Agreement (and the Conference) demonstrably failed the Irish. But Neumann's assertions that the Irish failed to provide an adequate level of security co-operation are counter to FitzGerald's claims, and little evidence is offered for the suggestion that this 'failure' was a result of prevailing public opinion in the South. Similarly perceptions that the Republic was not comparably threatened by the Northern Ireland situation were certainly not shared by policymakers in the Republic.

O'Leary and McGarry correctly point out that the entrenched antagonisms, entrenched even further by the hated Agreement for the Unionists, meant that it was not possible to coerce Unionists into a consociational structure. Cox and Aughey's claim that, 5 years after the Agreement, it was the case that it had failed, based primarily on its inability to create a more peaceful situation in Northern Ireland, is also hard to refute. Yet once again all of the above can be completely rejected if one disagrees with the premise on which they rest: that the author has correctly identified the purpose of the Agreement.

Was it the case that the Agreement failed to provide political change in Northern Ireland, as Ellis Owen suggests? Whilst it is clearly the case that the Agreement certainly did not secure some of the most important changes the Irish wished to see it did secure political change. Although it may be possible to take issue with some of the 'successes' FitzGerald identifies in his list, there is no question that changes were made in the immediate aftermath of the Agreement. Some of these may be comparatively minor; some, it may be claimed, are not connected to the Agreement – but all are real. How many changes are needed on a 'checklist' to cross the threshold from 'failure' to 'success'?

O'Leary and McGarry's assertion regarding the failure to create a consociational structure is, as discussed in the previous chapter, valid only if that was indeed the intention of the Agreement. As was argued there are serious question marks over this interpretation.

The general point made by Cox that the Agreement was a failure is harder to refute as no real grounds are given for this view. Aughey goes further and bases his 'failure' analysis on the inability of the Agreement to achieve 'its stated objectives'. Aughey's *Under Siege* is consistently critical of the Agreement and is in essence a call for integration of Northern Ireland fully into Great Britain. Aughey attributes various objectives to the Agreement. For Britain he sees it as a desire to 'fatally weaken the Union'. For the Republic its purpose was 'to allow it to help settle the long-running sore in Anglo-Irish relations' and to 'regulate an ideological passion'. But the 'immediate purpose' of the Agreement was as 'an exercise in containment and an attempt to cow Unionists' (Aughey, 1989, pp. 58–59). The argument that the AIA is an attempt to weaken the Union by the British and prepare for withdrawal is one that is difficult to substantiate and is not persuasive. Aughey's claim that the Irish wanted to use the AIA to settle the long-running sore in Anglo-Irish relations (that is Northern Ireland) has more validity. To this end the Agreement did not succeed in that Northern Ireland remained an area of intense and visible dispute between the two states after Hillsborough. However, this is not to say that the Agreement was not successful in helping to regulate that dispute. As the IGC developed and the participants became more used to its ways of working it does appear to have been a more successful, if not an infallible, mechanism for regulating contentious areas between the two governments. In terms of attempting to contain and cow the Unionists the Agreement is on shakier ground (if one accepts Aughey's argument that this was indeed its intention, which is open to debate). In the short term the Agreement incensed rather than cowed Unionists but it may well have, in the longer term, changed the parameters of the debate within Unionism.

So is it possible to label the Agreement at all? Perhaps it is more profitable to talk in terms of the effects of the Agreement rather than in terms of its success or failure. In terms of the effect that the Agreement had on Anglo-Irish relations, its contribution was positive and pronounced. The creation of a mechanism for formalised interaction between the two states was beneficial. Although at times it appeared that it had merely created a mechanism through which each side could register their unhappiness at the operation of that mechanism, in the longer term it made a positive contribution to the search for a solution to the Northern Ireland issue. Not only did the Conference and Secretariat structures aid crisis management they also created an arena that allowed frequent, private and rapid exchange of information between the two governments. This was to play an important role in the development of the peace process and the work leading to the Downing Street Declaration and the emerging peace process. The close relationships that built up between British and Irish officials working the new structures were to prove valuable in keeping the relationship steady at times of dispute at the ministerial level.

The effect on the ground in Northern Ireland is less easy to quantify. In the short term there is no doubt that the Agreement ushered in a more violent and more confrontational period on the streets of Northern Ireland. It did not lead to the creation of devolved government nor did it appear to ease inter-communal tensions. Yet this alone does not damn the Agreement. There was no sign that devolution was a short-term possibility even without the Agreement. The violence did increase but not to take action because it may lead to violence in Northern Ireland is to admit that nothing could be done in the region. A distinction between the short and long terms must be made. Whilst its effect on Unionism in the short term was visible and negative, in the longer-term the influence of the Agreement is harder to ascertain. There was a fundamental rethink within Unionism after the Agreement was signed with documents such as *The Way Forward* and *An End to Drift* being produced. The Unionists eventually had to jettison the early stance of not talking to the British government whilst the Agreement was in existence. How far one can attribute the later inter-party talks under Brooke and Mayhew to the existence and survival of the Agreement is a matter for debate. Did the failure to force the abandonment of the Agreement lead Unionists to seek its overthrow by entering into dialogue with nationalists? Even if this is the case were the Unionists more amenable to change or did the Agreement simply put on hold any hope of change in Northern Ireland for a number of years? Similarly what is the relationship between the Agreement and the subsequent peace process and Belfast/Good Friday Agreement? Kenneth Bloomfield sums up these questions well.

> The protagonists of the Agreement would say it was a significant change in direction that, unpopular as it was initially, it really did in time bear in upon Unionist opinion that nationalism and the representatives of nationalism and Irishness would have to be inside the tent, and I wouldn't dissent from that. I think there is something in that. I think my own reaction at the time was partly emotional.... I think it neither delivered the goods the optimists had expected of it, nor the evils that the pessimists had expected of it. Yes you can see it as some kind of a stepping stone, but on the other hand it did condemn us to quite a number of years of tremendous negativity.

> (Bloomfield, 19 May 2000)

By the review in 1989 in which both governments recommitted themselves to the Agreement, and made no notable changes to its provisions or operations, it was clear that the campaign to force the Agreement to be abandoned had failed. The coming years were to see dramatic changes in Northern Ireland with disputes and recriminations between the British and Irish governments never far from the surface. But the Agreement had succeeded in institutionalising Dublin's role in Northern Ireland's affairs and securing the Irish government's position as co, if not equal, sponsor of initiatives regarding Northern Ireland. The Agreement's achievements during the 3 years after its signing may be debated but its place on the political landscape for the foreseeable future had been assured. For good or ill the Unionists had to accept its existence and work around, if not within the parameters it had created.

5   The move to inclusion

The task facing the two governments in the late 1980s and early 1990s was to entice Unionists back into the political arena and restore some momentum to attempts to improve the condition of the North. By the end of the 1980s the AIA had proved to be an enduring structure that no amount of Unionist pressure had managed to threaten. The subsequent re-evaluation by the Unionist leaders of their strategy of opposition to the Agreement in the face of such British obduracy meant that there was an opportunity to re-engage Unionism in seeking new structures for Northern Ireland. This was to prove a long and difficult task. The early 1990s started with the latest variation of the accepted theme of exclusivity that had underpinned British and Irish policy since the Sunningdale period. Exclusivity rested on the premise that if the constitutional centres of Unionism and nationalism could reach agreement then the extremes of loyalism and Republicanism would be isolated and marginalised. The Brooke–Mayhew talks of 1991–92 were the last great hurrah of exclusivity. By 1992 the first tentative steps towards the radical departure of inclusiveness were being taken. The two governments, at different speeds and with different levels of commitment, began to explore the possibility of enticing the extremes into the centre, rather than trying to protect the centre from the extremes.

The early 1990s are a fascinating period in Anglo-Irish relations. What is striking about the period is the difference that the AIA made to the political debate in Northern Ireland. At the time it was negotiated at least some on the British side did not view the role it ceded to the Irish as particularly important – a *de jure* acknowledgement of a *de facto* reality. Yet the result of the AIA was that the whole remit of debate was altered. For the Unionists all political activity was motivated by the need to remove the hated AIA. Yet as it was an internationally registered treaty alterations required the agreement of both signatories. So the Unionists were left with the unpalatable reality that to remove Dublin's influence over the North they would have to convince Dublin to agree to replace the AIA. Not surprisingly Dublin was not about to give up their hard-won recognition cheaply.

The Brooke–Mayhew talks

The series of talks involving the British and the Irish Governments along with the four Northern Irish constitutional parties that took place in 1991–92 did not achieve a breakthrough in terms of reaching a new agreement on how to govern Northern Ireland or on the relationship between the North and the South of Ireland. Yet the exercise was an important marker on the road towards an agreement. The talks developed the three-strand model that was to be the basis of the eventual Good Friday Agreement of 1998. Whilst it is not possible or necessary to examine the initiative in-depth here, the series of talks highlighted interesting differences between the parties on the perceived role for the two governments towards the North and also illustrates the changed status of the Irish government in the post-AIA period (see David Bloomfield, 1997; Arthur, 1992, 1993).

Brooke's perceived role when he was given the Northern Ireland portfolio in 1989 was one of a night watchman. Brooke recalls, 'When the Prime Minister asked me to go she effectively said . . . "We've got the Anglo-Irish Agreement, it's really a case of managing the situation between now and the election, Peter, and it's extremely interesting." Which couldn't . . . be described as an invitation to activity' (Brooke, 21 July 2000). Yet Brooke did seek an active path and attempted, like many Secretaries of State before him, to initiate a round of talks between the constitutional parties in Northern Ireland.

Brooke was very conscious of the problem that the Unionist boycott was causing. 'The Unionists had promoted a tactic into a principle and had marched into a cul de sac . . . (They) were not going to come out unless they were given an honourable laissez-passer.' The new Secretary of State saw it as one of his prime tasks to provide the Unionist leadership with that laissez-passer. The new reality of the situation in Northern Ireland that the AIA had created meant the British would not act unilaterally in relation to the North. Brooke acknowledged this new reality claiming it was 'clear that that laissez-passer would have to be endorsed by the Irish Government since a lot of the conditions that the Unionists were setting out were rooted in their objections to the Anglo-Irish Agreement. So my signature alone wouldn't get them back into open country' (Brooke, 21 July 2000).

On 26 March 1991, Brooke informed the House, 'We are setting out to achieve a new beginning of relationships within Northern Ireland, within the island of Ireland and between the people of these islands' (the three strands) (House of Commons, vol. 188, col. 771, 26 March 1991). It had been difficult for Brooke to get all the parties to agree to enter talks. There were major problems. One stumbling block was at what stage the Irish Government would become involved? Dublin wanted a seat at the Strand 1 Talks discussing the internal government of Northern Ireland, which Brooke refused. Brooke was adamant on this point primarily for the pragmatic reason that the Unionists would not countenance Dublin involvement in Strand 1. Brooke informed Haughey, 'You will never get to Strand 2 if you want to be in Strand 1' (Brooke, 21 July 2000). Another stumbling block was that Unionists wanted the issues of devolved government settled in Strand 1 before discussion moved onto Strand 2. This in turn was unacceptable to the SDLP and Dublin. Brooke stipulated that all strands must start within weeks of each other and the whole process rested on the premise that 'nothing will be finally agreed in any strand until everything is agreed in the talks as a whole' (House of Commons, vol. 188, col. 766, 26 March 1991). The Unionist demands that the AIA be suspended for the duration of the talks was bypassed by being held during a 'gap' in IGC meetings. Finally Unionists' insistence that they would only enter Strand 2 of the talks as part of the UK delegation led to Brooke informing the House that the 'Unionist parties have made it clear that they wish their participation . . . to be formally associated with my presence and that they will regard themselves as members of the United Kingdom team' (House of Commons, vol. 188, col. 766, 26 March 1991). (Brooke does not mention how he regarded them.)

The Brooke talks achieved little in terms of agreement but they managed to overcome many of the procedural difficulties and paved the way for the more substantial phase of talks that occurred under his successor, Mayhew.

The Mayhew strands of the talks process ran for 6 months with the two governments twice agreeing to postpone IGC meetings in order to facilitate the discussions. The talks finally concluded on the 10 November 1992. The talks ostensibly drew to a close as the Irish government wanted an IGC meeting with an election imminent in the Republic. However, it was clear by November that further progress was unlikely in the short term.

Evaluating Brooke–Mayhew

At one level the Brooke–Mayhew Talks were bound to 'fail'. The Unionists entered the talks with the express objective of destroying the AIA. According to the DUP, 'The Anglo-Irish Agreement is a real obstacle to the establishment of good neighbourliness on the island of Ireland between North and South' (7 July 1992 – The Brooke–Mayhew documents were taken from www.cadogan.org, 27 July 2000). For the UUP, 'the replacement of the neo-colonialist Anglo-Irish Agreement with a treaty which addresses the totality of relationships within our islands is absolutely crucial' (7 July 1992). Whilst both governments openly claimed that they were prepared to replace the AIA as a result of the talks it was clear that the Irish would only accept its replacement with an agreement that gave them at least as much influence in Northern Ireland as the AIA. The Irish Government made their thoughts on this explicitly clear in their opening statement to Strand 2.

> We do not feel that the goal of our negotiations should be to dismantle any gains which have been made in the relationships between the two Governments. Its outcome should not undermine their co-operation on a problem, which is clearly of the utmost concern to both. The Agreement . . . is a formal acceptance that the Irish Government have both a concern and a role in

relation to Northern Ireland. We would expect that any broader agreement, which might be reached, would incorporate these elements in full measure. Otherwise something of value would be lost.

(6 July 1992)

The Irish government stuck to this position throughout the process. The British accepted this position and Mayhew told the Talks, 'Whatever the outcome of the Talks, we shall certainly want to preserve and develop the special and friendly relationship between our two countries' (6 July 1992).

The position adopted by the British Government during Strand 2 of the Talks was one of attempting to play a facilitating, almost non-participatory role, while at the same time having to be a participant given their sovereignty over Northern Ireland and the function demanded of them by the Ulster Unionists. This was not an easy stance to adopt. The potential contradictions of the British position are evident in Mayhew's opening statement in Strand 2:

I enter Strand 2 as a participant rather than as Chairman. Yet it continues to be as important to me to facilitate agreement as to argue my own corner. Her Majesty's Government has obligations and responsibilities which are relevant to the Strand 2 discussions. But it has no blueprint of its own for Strand 2. A range of possible outcomes would be acceptable to it, but only provided they were also acceptable to the Talks participants taken together. What we want above all from the proceedings in the Talks as a whole is an outcome on which Talks participants can agree, and which in the final analysis will be acceptable to the people.

(6 July 1992)

Throughout the Talks Mayhew seemed keen to avoid becoming openly involved in the discussions and concentrated more on the facilitator than participant role. This potential conflict was never really resolved and Mayhew seemed to still be wrestling with it when the talks wound up. During the exchanges in the House of Commons when he announced the ending of the talks, Mayhew was urged to 'move from the role of umpire to that of protagonist'. Mayhew's response shows the difficulties faced by the British government when dealing with Northern Ireland. He argued, 'I do not think I am an umpire, but certainly an umpire does not get drawn into supporting one side or the other in a conflict, and I do not propose to do so' (House of Commons, vol. 213, cols 884 and 891, 11 November 1992). This attempt to play facilitator rather than participant was an underlying cause of Unionist distrust of the British government. The Unionists found themselves as 'members' of a UK team, the captain of which seemed to see himself as a non-participant. Indeed the Irish government also found British periodic statements of neutrality unacceptable. Dick Spring has asserted that the British government 'is a key protagonist, whose decisions are crucial in shaping the environment both of the problem, and of any possible solution. It is not a disengaged referee floating above the fray' (Spring, 1996, p. 137).

The importance of the talks should not though be underestimated. Much of the discussions that took place and the structures that were adopted later resurfaced and underpinned the negotiations that led to the GFA. The UUP leader, James Molyneaux, went to Dublin for the first time to discuss North–South relations with the Irish Government. The talks were yet another important staging post in the search for the solution. As Mayhew himself noted, 'Progress has been made; it is not enough. It has taken six months, but six months in the history of Ireland is but an evening gone' (House of Commons, vol. 213, col. 881). Whilst he pledged to attempt to restart the talks after conducting further bilateral discussions with all the parties, the exercise never resumed in the same form. Intergovernmental relations and the search for progress on the Northern Ireland question was about to move in a new direction with the advent of the peace process and the shift from exclusiveness to inclusiveness.

The Peace Process: From exclusion to inclusion

The main thrust of intergovernmental activity in the early 1990s was aimed at enticing the IRA to abandon violence and enter the political process. This attempt to engage the Republican movement and persuade them to pursue a purely non-violent campaign became known as the peace process. Was this actually a shift in governmental policy? Neumann correctly notes that it had been Britain's stated position that it was violence that led to Sinn Féin's exclusion, if the violence halted then the bar on their participation would no longer apply; their exclusion was practical not ideological in origin. Neumann therefore challenges the idea that there was a shift in policy in this regard (Neumann, 2003, p. 187). But in the early 1990s rather than merely paying lip-service to the idea of possible inclusion, the British began actively seeking to entice the IRA away from violence. As a result there *was* a shift in policy from exclusion to inclusion (O'Kane, 2004). The question is why the two governments followed this path in the early 1990s? What had changed? Why after years of attempting to isolate the IRA and their political wing Sinn Féin did the two governments spend much of the early 1990s trying, both overtly and covertly, to persuade the Republican movement that violence was unnecessary and actually counterproductive? The reasons for this apparent *volte-face* are complex and the result of the interaction of various factors, including changes in government personnel, in Republican thinking, and in how the two governments viewed the IRA.

The departure of Margaret Thatcher in November 1990 and Charles Haughey in February 1992 can be seen as fortuitous. Haughey was greatly mistrusted by Unionists. Thatcher had become a hate figure for Republicans since the hunger strikes, and was distrusted by Unionists since the AIA. Her own opinion of the IRA and Sinn Féin meant it is highly questionable whether progress towards inclusion could have been made whilst she was in office. According to Brooke, 'I don't know whether I would have been able to persuade her but there are a priori grounds for thinking that it wouldn't have worked' (Brooke, 21 July 2000).

The new leaders, John Major and Albert Reynolds, had little 'baggage' and no real record on Northern Ireland. According to Robin Butler, who served as Cabinet Secretary to both Thatcher and Major, Major was 'less conscious of the Unionist past of the Conservative Party' and unlike Thatcher did not have 'emotionally in his political background that link with the Unionists' (Butler, 9 November 2000). Similarly Reynolds did not have the perceived sympathies of his predecessor. As his Press Secretary, Sean Duignan, explained, 'Many, many people in Irish politics have strong beliefs about all this. Reynolds is just a business guy, I don't think he would have a Republican bone in his body and indeed not even a nationalist bone really' (Duignan, 25 May 2000).

The movement towards inclusion was also aided by an apparent re-evaluation within the Republican movement. Sinn Féin's hope of electoral advance in the early 1980s had not materialised, their vote was stagnant at around 11 per cent in Northern Ireland (only around half the vote the SDLP polled) and less than 2 per cent in elections in the Republic. Henry Patterson claims, the 'evident contradiction in the 'armallite and ballot box' strategy, together with the failure to displace the SDLP and political marginalization in the Republic, had begun to generate debate within Republicanism' (Patterson, 1997, p. 218). By the early 1990s the two governments believed that the Republican movement might be amenable to overtures designed to entice them away from violence and towards exclusively political methods. How susceptible and what the overtures should be were though matters of dispute between the two governments.

As a result the British and the Irish governments began reviewing their attitude towards Sinn Féin. From 1989, Brooke was making speeches highlighting the opportunities that would open for Sinn Féin if the violence ceased. In the Whitbread speech of 1990, Brooke specifically addressed Sinn Féin's 1988 document *Towards a Strategy for Peace* when he stated, 'The British Government has no selfish strategic or economic interest in Northern Ireland...' (Mallie and McKittrick, 1996, p. 107). As well as such public overtures the British had reactivated the secret 'back channel' line of communication with Republicans. Brooke suggests that this line of communication was reactivated in 1990 (Brooke, 21 July 2000), Ed Moloney claims it pre-dated this by up to 4 years (Moloney, 2002, p. 247). Whatever the case the exchanges appear to have helped persuade the British that the IRA may well be willing to abandon violence and that this possibility should be pursued (Butler, 9 November 2000; Major, 1999, p. 432).

The Irish government's own periodic clandestine contacts with the IRA were instrumental in convincing Dublin that a policy of inclusion might be productive. Reynolds authorised his advisor, Martin Mansergh, to renew contact with Sinn Féin when he took over from Haughey in 1992. (Mansergh had held meeting with Sinn Féin in 1988 but these were aborted as it was not believed that the IRA were seriously contemplating an end to violence at that stage.) Haughey had floated the idea of a joint declaration to Major in December 1991 and work had begun on a text. The result of the Mansergh–Sinn Féin contacts and the reports coming from Hume of his own meetings with Adams were instrumental in Reynolds' decision to push hard for a joint declaration designed to persuade the IRA to abandon violence.

It is not the case though that by the early 1990s the two governments were united in their belief that the IRA was seriously contemplating an end to violence and therefore an inclusion-based policy was the way to proceed. The British government, in particular, were cautious. London said a message was received from the IRA in February 1993 stating, 'The conflict is over but we need your advice on how to bring it to a close' (Major, 1999, p. 431). Sinn Féin denied this message was sent (Sinn Féin, 1993, p. 7). Butler notes the mixed reactions that the message caused:

> Was this a trap? Was this a way of trying to draw us into direct contact with the IRA which they would then publicise and use it to try and embarrass the government? On the other hand [there was] the recognition that this was a tremendous opportunity and if genuine then of course we did want to help the IRA to bring the armed conflict to an end and to proper political life.
>
> (Butler, 9 November 2000)

Whilst this apparent movement by Republicans offered opportunities that needed to be pursued by intergovernmental co-operation, other factors conspired to make such co-operation difficult. The differing analysis of the two governments regarding the intentions of Republicans, personal rivalries between key individuals as well as the demands on each government from their client community in the North were to place intergovernmental co-operation under severe pressure throughout 1993.

Negotiating the joint declaration

Although it was the stated objective of both governments to resume the talks process after the Mayhew round had ended, divisions emerged between London and Dublin over the advisability of this approach. The Irish decided that the joint declaration route needed to be prioritised over reviving exclusion-based talks. The British were more sceptical of the approach and continued to seek to restart the talks, a difference that was 'argued out at meeting after meeting' (Finlay, 1998, p. 190). The subsequent agreement by the British to focus on the joint declaration was in part a result of SDLP and Dublin disinterest in talks. However, it also reflected a growing interest amongst some British policymakers in whether the IRA might be considering ending the violence. But negotiating a joint declaration was to prove highly problematic.

The genesis and development of the joint declaration, which became the Downing Street Declaration (DSD) signed in London on 15 December 1993, is complex. The existing analysis of the formulation of the DSD rightly portrays it as an Irish inspired initiative but underestimates the input of the British side into the document portraying the British side as too passive in the process.

Mallie and McKittrick claim, 'the Declaration was in effect the culmination of a line of documents which had an input not only from Dublin but also from Hume, the army council of the IRA, loyalist paramilitary groups and Protestant clergymen'. The glaring omission from this list is the British Government. Mallie and McKittrick do quote a British source prior to this claiming that the declaration 'came about through a genuine process of two sides putting in their own ideas and eventually hammering out a deal' (Mallie and McKittrick, 1996, p. 271). Yet there is a tendency in their work to portray the DSD (and by implication the peace process) as not just being the idea of Irish nationalists but the result of Irish nationalists domination of the negotiating process.

Neumann has argued the converse of this claiming, that the DSD was the result of the whole political spectrum uniting

> behind the British agenda for an agreed settlement based upon the principle of consent, limited constitutional change and Nationalist–Unionist co-operation in a devolved system of government. Most significantly in doing so, it compelled the IRA to declare an indefinite cessation of violence without having obtained any privileges, assurances or concessions.
>
> (Neumann, 2003, p. 186)

Both schools of thought ascribe too much influence and 'success' to one government.

To gain a more realistic understanding of the emergence of the peace process and why the DSD was signed, the negotiation of the document needs to be contextualised and the constraints operating on the two governments need to be examined. An analysis of the earlier drafts of the agreement compared to the eventual DSD illustrates a larger input for the British than Mallie and McKittrick suggest. Contextualising the negotiations also illustrates the problems in characterising the agenda as a British one and arguing that the IRA were 'compelled' to declare a ceasefire.

The origins of the joint declaration

In January 1992 the Irish gave the British government a draft version of a joint declaration. This was a reworking of a draft Hume had given to Haughey in October 1991 by Haughey's advisor, Martin Mansergh, Cabinet Secretary, Dermot Nally, and Head of the Anglo-Irish division of Department of Foreign Affairs, Sean O'Huiginn. The draft had been shown to Adams by Hume and eventually presented to the British Government (Mallie and McKittrick, 1996, p. 123). From the British point of view this draft and an alternative one given to the British Government the following month by Hume were unacceptable. According to Major, 'They were utterly one-sided, so heavily skewed towards the presumption of a united Ireland that they had no merit as a basis for negotiations' (Major, 1999, p. 447).

The document included the statement that 'The British Government acknowledge it is the wish of the people of Britain to see the people of Ireland live together in unity and harmony . . . '. Unsurprisingly the British Government was unwilling to agree a document in which they endorsed Irish unity. But the acknowledgement by the Irish that the 'agreement and consent of the people of Northern Ireland' was necessary for unity was seen as a helpful statement (Reproduced in Mallie and McKittrick, 1996, pp. 371–373). A subsequent draft that Sinn Féin sent back to Hume and the Irish government (and the one that Major suggests Hume passed on to London) in February 1992 went even further. 'The British government, consequently, commits itself to such unity (within a period to be agreed) and to use all its influence and energy to win consent for this policy'. This draft repeated the Republican movement's traditional demand for a timetable for withdrawal and saw the British as becoming persuaders for unity, a role the British were completely unwilling to consider. However, both Hume and Dublin saw the statement that the Irish government should state that the 'democratic right of self-determination by the people of Ireland as a whole would be best achieved with the agreement and consent of the people of Northern Ireland . . .' as an encouraging advance by Sinn Féin. Whilst in this draft agreement the consent of a majority in the North was not a prerequisite to unity, Sinn Féin did appear to be factoring Unionist opinion into the equation (Mallie and McKittrick, 1996, pp. 373–374 for text, analysis p. 150).

However, Mallie and McKittrick claim by June 1992 Sinn Féin had apparently accepted that the status of Northern Ireland could not be changed without the consent of the people of Northern Ireland. The next draft stated, 'the democratic right of self-determination by the people of Ireland as a whole must be achieved and exercised with the agreement of the people of Northern Ireland' (Mallie and McKittrick, 1996, p. 150). This suggested an advance of sorts in Republican analysis as it seemed to implicitly acknowledge the 'Unionist veto' that they had so long denied. (The statement is perhaps more ambiguous than Mallie and McKittrick suggest as it does not stipulate that the agreement of a *majority* of the people of Northern Ireland is needed, nor does it identify how such agreement will be measured.) The draft also indicated a willingness on the part of the Republican movement to accept 'exclusively . . . peaceful political means' (Finlay, 1998, p. 188). Dublin and Hume saw this as a breakthrough.

The intergovernmental negotiations

The intergovernmental redrafting began in earnest in June 1993 when Reynolds gave Robin Butler, a new draft. There is a certain amount of confusion as to what exactly the document that Reynolds gave Butler was. Sinn Féin passed a draft document to Dublin via Hume in the first half of 1993. Fergus Finlay suggests that the document Reynolds gave to Butler was basically the one that Sinn Féin had sent to Dublin. 'The document was sent to the British government a few weeks later as an Irish government draft – which it was since it had originated from Martin Mansergh in the first place' (Finlay, 1998, p. 189). Reynolds himself is a little ambiguous on this point. He notes that the document was 'a mixture of everything' but also suggests that it was basically the document provided by Sinn Féin. Reynolds recalls, 'That document in June that was given to Robin Butler was basically the Republican's side, the Republican case. I was asked to put that forward in that shape and that form and I did but I said it's not going to run, there's no balance in it from a Unionist point of view' (Reynolds, 26 May 2000). However, Nally is adamant that the document Reynolds passed to Butler was indeed an Irish draft that had been reworked from the Sinn Féin version. He recalls Hume gave a draft to the Irish government that 'he had been working on with Adams. It was taken apart and put together again by the Taoiseach's Department. In other words it was almost completely redrafted and then in a very much refined form it was handed over by Reynolds (to Butler) in June 1993' (Nally, 2 November 2000).

The parentage of the document was important. The British were unwilling to be seen to be negotiating on the basis of any document that could be linked to the Hume–Adams dialogue (although they were secretly talking to Sinn Féin at this time). Reynolds recalls that Major was firm on this point. He told Major that he had indirect contacts with the Republicans. 'John said, 'Anything I get from you, I want it to be coming from the Irish Government'. I said, 'Fine, I'll stand over that. Anything you get from me will be (from the) Irish Government' (Reynolds, 26 May 2000).

Whatever Reynolds agreed with Major regarding the status of any documents he would pass to London it is clear that Sinn Féin heavily influenced this Irish draft. Mansergh describes how the Republican's stance on three key issues caused problems for the Irish Government. These points were the desire for 'a definite timescale for agreement'; the issue of how the right of Irish self-determination would be applied; and the desire that Britain became persuaders for unity (Mansergh, 1995, p. 154). These were the issues that became the focus of the intergovernmental stage of the negotiations and on each issue the Republican demands were not met. Dublin was, according to Mansergh, 'determined not to subscribe to anything that would clearly be at variance with its international obligations, principally the Anglo-Irish Agreement'. However, Mansergh acknowledges that the draft Reynolds gave to Butler in June 1993 'went to the outer-limits of what was acceptable' (Mansergh, 1995, p. 154). Mansergh, along with Nally, suggests that the Irish government fundamentally redrafted the document but it was done as a result of ongoing consultations with the Republican movement. This is hardly surprising. The whole purpose of the joint declaration was designed to create a situation that would persuade the IRA to abandon violence. Therefore it was essential that those drafting the declaration should ascertain from Republicans what was necessary to achieve this end. This is not though, as the final form of the Downing Street Declaration illustrates, the same as surrendering the initiative to Republicans. There is an element of careful management here. The British knew that the Irish were in contact with Republicans but could not be seen to be negotiating, even at second or third hand, with Republicans. At the same time the British had secretly been in contact with Republicans themselves to ascertain under what conditions the IRA would abandon violence.

The end of the joint declaration initiative?

By late September 1993 the British appeared to have decided that the initiative was not a worthwhile option. Four inter-related reasons seem to account for this decision: the effect of the Hume–Adams declaration; Westminster arithmetic; opposition within the British cabinet and Molyneaux's objections to the draft.

Although the joint declaration idea had originated from Hume and the Hume–Adams dialogue, the two governments were keen to disassociate their joint declaration negotiations from Hume and (especially) Adams after June 1993. The problem for the governments was that Hume continued his dialogue with Adams and was unwilling to allow the two governments to take the initiative. Hume was increasingly frustrated at what he saw as British reticence on the issue and believed that without his pressure the British government may drop the initiative. Those close to the Reynolds' government also believe that personal rivalry between Hume and Reynolds was a factor. As Séan Duignan put it:

> I think the Hume–Reynolds thing is basic personal jealousy. John Hume would see himself . . . as the man who started it all, with Adams. He took huge risks, he ran it and he wasn't about to let Reynolds take the lion share of the credit. . . . These guys were ankle-tapping one another on the way to Oslo for the [Nobel] peace-prize. It wasn't pleasant to watch but that's politics, that's the way it works . . . they didn't trust one another.
>
> (Duignan, 25 May 2000)

In late September, Hume and Adams announced that they had concluded their discussions and were passing on their findings to Dublin. No document was actually passed to Dublin by Hume at this stage. The annoyance that this caused for the Irish government is recalled by Duignan who claims, '(Martin) Mansergh used to say to me that Hume–Adams didn't exist. It was somewhere on the back of an envelope that Hume jotted down . . . You could never pin it down, they could never get their hands on the damn thing' (Duignan, 25 May 2000). But the damage was done; as Major recalled, it meant the 'ball was placed publicly in our court; and yet the prospect of securing Unionist agreement to anything emanating from Adams and Hume was nil' (Major, 1999, p. 450). The British government's demands that anything they got from Dublin was Irish not Hume–Adams inspired were undermined by the announcement. The British, already sceptical about the initiative, were even more reticent a result of Hume and Adams 'disconcertingly upping the ante' (Duignan, 1995, p. 104). The British made it clear to Dublin that 'they would have no truck whatever with any document that had Gerry Adams' fingerprints on it' (Finlay, 1998, p. 194).

This fear of alienating Unionists was also heightened by Westminster arithmetic. Major's Conservative Party had a slender majority in the House of Commons. In July 1993 the Major government was in a precarious position, facing a vote of confidence over the Social Chapter part of the Maastricht Treaty, an issue that had deeply divided his parliamentary party. The 9 UUP MPs supported the government on the vote and rumours abounded of a deal between the government and Molyneaux's party. Speculation centred on a phone call that Major had made to Molyneaux before the vote, and an hour and a half meeting between Mayhew and an Ulster Unionist MP – and future leader – David Trimble. 'Senior Conservatives' were quoted as saying Unionists 'can have anything they want, short of the Anglo-Irish Agreement, which they know we cannot abandon . . .'. Both the government and the Unionists denied that any deal had been done to secure the UUP's support over Maastricht but Molyneaux told journalists that he expected the AIA to 'wither' and the Conservative Party's organisation in Northern Ireland to collapse. Rumours of an agreement to set up a select committee for Northern Ireland legislation at Westminster, a long held Unionist desire, further incensed nationalists (*The Independent*, 24 July 1993 and 28 July 1993). Whatever the reality of the situation, the suspicion of a deal was enough to strain Anglo-Irish relations.

The third related factor that led the British to back away from the joint declaration initiative was unease within the British cabinet over the direction of inclusiveness and the joint declaration. Around this time Major widened the number of people in the cabinet who knew of the initiative and whilst they agreed on 'bottom-line negotiating objectives' Major notes, 'many of my senior colleagues were very sceptical of our chances of achieving them and concerned at the risk of a failed negotiation' (Major, 1999, p. 450). Butler acknowledged the need for Major to proceed cautiously as 'there were elements in his cabinet and certainly in the party that were profoundly sceptical of all this, felt that it was a conspiracy to edge Britain into abandoning the Unionists. They had to be reassured all the time' (Butler, 9 November 2000).

The fourth and highly influential factor was the opposition of Molyneaux to the draft declaration. A striking difference between the negotiating of the Downing Street Declaration and the AIA is the fact that in 1993 the main Unionist leader was informed and consulted over the process in a way that he had not been in 1985. This was a conscious decision by the British Government who had learnt from the AIA period. The British Government was determined that any agreement between the two governments in 1993 would be broadly acceptable to the UUP (though Ian Paisley of the more hardline DUP was deliberately excluded). Although there was a broad acceptance within British (and Irish) circles that Unionism needed to be consulted, there was great anguish regarding at what stage this consultation should be carried out and great trepidation as to what Molyneaux's reaction was likely to be. Butler claims 'someone who should take tremendous credit from this is Jim Molyneaux'. After he was shown the draft declaration, 'Molyneaux gave us some advice and at one point on the basis of Jim Molyneaux's advice the British Government decided the joint declaration had no future' (Butler, 9 November 2000).

Molyneaux's reaction, along with the scepticism of members of his cabinet, were the key reasons that Major sent Butler to inform Dublin that 'Downing Street is not interested' (Duignan, 1995, p. 105). Major states, 'I wanted Albert Reynolds to understand that the Joint Declaration, in its existing form, had no hope of winning British or Unionist acceptance, and suggested that we should look at other ways of moving forward' (Major, 1999, p. 450).

Moving in the right direction: The effect of Irish–Unionist consultation and physical violence

Butler went to see Reynolds with Major's 'deliberately discouraging message' (Major, 1999, p. 450) on 19 October 1993. This appears to have had the effect the British desired. As noted above one of the key concerns for the British was that any declaration, although primarily designed to entice the Republicans away from violence, must be acceptable to the Unionists. Reynolds told the British Cabinet Secretary 'OK, let me just talk to one or two Unionist friends of mine in the North and see what they think of it and see if they can suggest some ways forward' (Butler, 9 November 2000). Again this is a striking change to the 1985 period. Dublin as well as London was conscious of the need to keep the Unionists on side in 1993 and both governments consulted widely within the Unionist community. To this end Reynolds met regularly with Church of Ireland Archbishop, Robin Eames, and officials (such as Finlay and Mansergh) met with representative of loyalist paramilitaries. Another important contact was the Presbyterian minister, Rev Roy Magee who liaised with loyalist paramilitaries (Reynolds, 26 May 2000; Finlay, 1998, pp. 199–201). Reynolds asked Roy Magee to get the loyalists to 'set out to me what they were fighting for, what they wanted protecting in any new movement' (Reynolds, 26 May 2000). As a result the loyalists set out six principles and these principles were put into what eventually became the DSD. (The principles are contained at the end of paragraph 4 and represent a mini bill of rights. The six are the rights to free political thought; freedom of expression of religion; freedom to pursue political aspirations; freedom to seek constitutional change by political means; freedom to live where one chooses; and equal opportunity in social and economic activity.) The Irish government incorporated these points in a new draft that was forwarded to London. Butler notes that the inclusion of these points 'made the document much more acceptable. When we next saw it and showed it to Molyneaux, Molyneaux said: 'This is beginning to move in the right direction' ' (Butler, 9 November 2000).

By this stage the draft declaration was beginning to become more balanced, noting the obligations that would be on the Irish, as well as the British, as part of any overall settlement. It was moving away from being a 'Nationalist manifesto'. Although the drafting process was continuing at the intergovernmental level, the whole initiative was shaken by a marked escalation of violence in October. The catalyst for this was an IRA bomb explosion in a Shankill Road fish shop on 23 October, which killed ten people including one of the bombers, Thomas Begley. The IRA claimed that the bomb was intended for the UFF who they believed were meeting in a UDA office above the shop. No such meeting was taking place at the time and the dead were Saturday shoppers. This bombing caused a wave of tit-for-tat violence. A week after the Shankill bombing, two UFF gunmen murdered seven people in a pub in Greysteel, Co. Londonderry, claiming the attack was on the 'nationalist electorate' in revenge for the Shankill bomb. The sight of Adams carrying Begley's coffin increased denunciations of both Adams and Hume in the British and Irish parliaments. Hume broke down at the funeral of a Greysteel victim under the pressure and complained to friends that he was being 'hung out to dry' and elements of the Irish government began to suspect the Hume was near to a breakdown (Duignan, 1995, p. 105; Nally, 2 November 2000).

Perhaps surprisingly the increase in violence at this late stage in the negotiations contributed to the joint declaration process. In fact Major claims that the whole initiative 'would have broken down had not the Shankill and Greysteel tragedies intervened'. Major argues that, 'In the wave of revulsion that followed the Shankill bomb, the Irish Government took a more critical attitude to the Hume–Adams process' (Major, 1999, p. 450). Major is correct in his evaluation that the events of October shocked the Irish Government. The incident, according to a Dublin source, left Reynolds and Mansergh 'at a complete loss. They didn't know what to do next, or how to proceed . . . '. Reynolds sent a message to Sinn Féin saying, 'If I am to continue with this process this thing has got to stop'. Reynolds also appreciated the problems that the Shankill bomb and Adams' carrying of the coffin caused for Major. 'He was put in an extremely difficult and delicate position. I was really annoyed with it – to be honest I thought for some time that it would probably blow the whole thing sky high' (Mallie and McKittrick, 1996, pp. 202–203). (Though Reynolds appreciated that Adams had no choice but to carry the coffin if he was to retain any credibility and influence within Republican circles.)

The Brussels summit: Get off the pitch

Major's claim that the escalation in violence caused the Irish Government to take a more critical line towards Hume–Adams is only accurate in presentational terms. By October the Irish Government was frustrated by Hume's public pronouncements and was seeking to repackage the initiative in more intergovernmental terms. What the Shankill bombing secured was a willingness on the part of Reynolds to publicly distance himself from Hume. At a meeting on the fringes of a European summit in Brussels, on the 29 October, the two leaders issued a strongly worded joint statement. The purpose of the Brussels summit communiqué was to distance the two governments from the Hume–Adams dialogue.

The Prime Minister and Taoiseach agreed that any initiative can only be taken by the two Governments, and that there could be no question of their adopting or endorsing the report of the dialogue which was recently given to the Taoiseach [by John Hume] and which had not been passed on to the British Government. They agreed that the two Governments must continue to work together in their own terms on a framework for peace, stability and reconciliation.

(quoted in Mallie and McKittrick, 1996, p. 209)

Séan Duignan summed up the summit as 'Hume and Adams told to get off the pitch!' (Duignan, 1995, p. 106). Reynolds continued this theme at his party's Ard Fheis, trying to walk the difficult line of distancing himself from the hugely popular figure of Hume without damaging his standing with the party rank and file. Reynolds told praised Hume's contribution but argued, 'The creation of that peace must ultimately be the responsibility of the Irish and British governments' (*Irish Times*, 8 November 1993).

Although outwardly the Brussels statement seemed to mark a convergence of the two Government's attitudes towards the Hume–Adams dialogue, behind the scenes there was confusion as to what the Brussels summit actually meant. One of the main problems was that the term 'Hume–Adams' had become synonymous with the idea of a joint declaration rather than simply meaning the talks Hume and Adams were having separate from intergovernmental negotiations. From the Irish point of view, Brussels was about trying to separate the two strands, getting Hume's and (especially) Adams's fingerprints off the process. In so far as the concept of a joint declaration, which had unhelpfully gained the tag Hume–Adams, was concerned, the Irish felt that they had got agreement from Major to pursue this course. By this analysis the significance of Brussels was slightly different. After a discussion with Reynolds over the statement, Séan Duignan recorded in his diary, 'He tells me Hume–Adams was still alive and kicking after Brussels, that Major actually accepted this, insisting that he just couldn't publicly wear it. Albert says Major and he reasoned it out together: 'Hume–Adams was being declared dead, in order to keep it alive . . . '' (Duignan, 1995, p. 106).

Unfortunately Major and the British Government had a different evaluation of the Brussels position. After the summit Major informed the House of Commons, 'The joint statement with the Irish Prime Minister provides a clear basis for progress. Both Governments are committed to the talks process . . . . The Government will now intensify their efforts to find a basis for the constitutional parties in Northern Ireland to carry on the talks progress' (House of Commons, vol. 231, col. 21, 1November 1993).

Major therefore portrayed the Brussels statement as an acceptance by the Irish and the British that the joint initiative idea had been dropped and the two governments were seeking to restart the inter-party talks framework. When challenged by Hume as to why he had rejected the Hume–Adams proposals without having spoken to him about them, Major continued to portray the Brussels summit in the same light. Major, whilst praising the efforts of Hume, told the House:

> I had to make a judgement on whether I thought that the proposals reached by the hon. Gentleman, at this time, and in the fashion that he proposed them, would actually lead to progress and to a settlement. I reached the conclusion . . . that that was not the right way to proceed, and for that reason I said earlier today that I believe the way forward is the way set out in the joint statement that the Taoiseach and I issued on Friday.
>
> (House of Commons, vol. 231, col. 21, 1 November 1993)

This interpretation greatly annoyed Albert Reynolds who felt that Major was misrepresenting his position Reynolds 'resented the Prime Minister's repeated harping on the theme that he (Reynolds) was totally in support of his rejection of Hume–Adams' (Duignan, 1995, p. 118).

How then could the two sides place such a different interpretation on what was agreed at Brussels? According to Mallie and McKittrick, 'The crucial point about the Brussels summit was that the two governments came away with completely different versions of what had been agreed.' The reason for this could be because 'one or both prime ministers misunderstood what was being conveyed' (Mallie and McKittrick, 1996, p. 211). An alternative and perhaps simpler explanation is that after the summit both Reynolds and Major had to represent their position in the best light possible to their domestic audience. The Irish, irked by Hume's 'upping the ante', understood the need to create distance between the joint declaration initiative and the Hume–Adams dialogue. This needed to be done in such a way as to create the impression that the reason this was being done was because the two governments were working on a bigger stage and a bigger project. For the British there was the need to distance themselves from anything with Adams' fingerprints on it and the need to reassure backbench Tories and the UUP that the Union was not being undermined. The problem was that it seemed that the two governments were claiming contradictory things: they had agreed to discuss the joint declaration idea but only at an intergovernmental level; they had dropped the joint declaration idea and were re-launching the inter-party talks.

Reynolds' frustration spilled over into the public domain in the so-called 'Houston Declaration'. Speaking to two journalists outside a Whitney Houston concert on the 10 November Reynolds stated, 'If it comes to it, I will walk away from John Major, and put forward a set of proposals myself . . . I am not prepared to let this opportunity pass' (Duignan, 1995, p. 119). Reynolds claims that he would have considered making a unilateral Irish declaration to try and entice the Republicans away from violence. The problem with a unilateral declaration is that it would have been too unbalanced. One of the potential advantages of intergovernmental co-operation is that each government has a stronger relationship with one community in the North, than with the other. Whilst this relationship is often characterised by mistrust, it at least provides some sort of balance. Reynolds noted that a unilateral declaration would have little hope of appealing to the Unionist community. '(It) wouldn't have had the same effect without bringing the British Government along. I mean as I often said to John (Major), "you take responsibility for the Unionists and the loyalists and I'll take responsibility for the nationalists and the Republicans"' (Reynolds, 26 May 2000). Dermot Nally noted that the idea of a unilateral declaration was not something that was seriously considered by the Irish. 'It's silly to be making unilateral declarations on a subject you can do little about' (Nally, 2 November 2000). The incident does, however, serve to highlight the growing frustration within the Irish government at the lack of development over the joint declaration idea.

By the end of November the British appeared to be coming back round to the joint declaration initiative. Dermot Nally recalls, 'It looked as if the whole thing had gone through the floor, like the whole negotiation was being wound up. But Robin Butler phoned me later in the month and said, "Look, despite appearances we're still interested. Can we go ahead with our meetings?"' (Nally, 2 November 2000). So the joint declarations talks were resumed.

Talking to Sinn Féin and telling lies to Paddies

One suggested reason why the British returned to the joint declaration idea was in an attempt to limit the damage caused by the revelation of the existence of the line of communication with Republicans (Dillon, 1996, pp. 333–334). On the 28 November, *The Observer* broke the story of the secret British communications with Sinn Féin and the IRA. What is fascinating about these contacts in the Anglo-Irish context is the fact that the revelation came as a complete surprise to Reynolds and the Irish Government (Reynolds, 26 May 2000). Major had famously told the House of Commons on the 1 November, in reply to a suggestion from Labour MP Dennis Skinner that the British government needed to talk to Republicans, 'If the implication of his remarks is that we should sit down and talk with Mr. Adams and the Provisional IRA, I can say only that that would turn my stomach and those of most hon. Members; we will not do it' (House of Commons, vol. 231, col. 35, 1 November 1993). Strictly speaking Major may have not been misleading the House in so far as he had not met with Republicans, but once the link was revealed this seemed to many a pedantic distinction.

The effect of the revelation on the Irish government was explosive. In his memoirs Major portrays the Irish reaction as unwarranted, noting that they themselves had been in contact with Republicans. 'Sauce for the goose was evidently not supposed to be sauce for the gander' (Major, 1999, p. 452). This is somewhat disingenuous of Major. The problem lay not so much in the fact that the British-Sinn Féin link existed but over the attitude that the British had taken on such contacts when dealing with Dublin. Although there were links between Dublin and Republicans the Irish did not try and hide these links when dealing with the British. Reynolds notes whilst he never told Major the form of the

Dublin–Sinn Féin link he told him that he had indirect contacts with Republicans (Reynolds, 26 May 2000). The anger at the British actions was summed up by the Irish Justice Minister, Marie Geoghan-Quinn, when she recalled how the British continually 'initiated discussions about how much they hated the Provos and how they wouldn't be seen in the same place as them and all the rest of it . . . . They would have been better off not saying anything at all' (Mallie and McKittrick, 1996, p. 260). This perceived duplicity on the part of the British rankled with Reynolds. Duignan claims,

> we discovered that they were forbidding Albert to make contact with them, with the Provos, [yet] they were actually dealing with the Provos themselves, and the British way of operation saw nothing wrong with that. And if they were found out they would shrug. And they would shrug rather arrogantly and look at you and say 'move on, don't bother with that'. They are doing something in the national interest, and if that involves telling lies to Paddies or to anybody, so be it . . . Albert didn't like it.
>
> (Duignan, 25 May 2000)

What Reynolds also did not like was the attempt by the British to steer the joint declaration initiative in a different direction. A few days before the link between the British and Sinn Féin was exposed, Butler flew to see Reynolds and as well as telling him about the forthcoming *Observer* revelations gave him a new British draft of the proposed declaration.

The British draft: Enshrining the essence/treating the Republic like Tongo?

The revelation of the British–Sinn Féin link and the new British draft led to a marked short-term deterioration in Anglo-Irish relations. The new document was a completely new draft drawn up by Major and the cabinet colleagues he had told of the process. Major suggests that the purpose of the new draft was to try to secure concessions from the Irish. According to Major the British realised the Irish 'would not, indeed probably could not, accept an entirely new British draft; but it would demonstrate the width of the gap between us, and would help us to seek the middle ground between us' (Major, 1999, p. 451). Butler questions this interpretation. The former Cabinet Secretary who was involved in framing the new document and who delivered it to Reynolds claims the new draft was an attempt to remove the 'green' language from the process. Butler claims that by this stage in the negotiations the document the two governments had been working on

> was becoming quite turgid. I mean it finished quite turgid but it was becoming extremely turgid. It had all these phrases in it that had deep significance and were argued over . . . . We then produced another document that was meant to enshrine the essence of it . . . . We genuinely thought that this

put what the essence of the document was that we had before but in a more digestible form and without some of the [green language].

(Butler, 9 November 2000)

The Irish reaction was one of unconcealed anger. Nally, who had been involved in the intergovernmental drafting with Butler from the start, was particularly infuriated by the new British draft. Nally told Reynolds, 'It's unforgivable . . . Who do these people think you are – the prime minister of Tongo? They can't be allowed to ignore months of detailed negotiation, and tell us we have to start all over again just because they click their fingers!' (Finlay, 1998, p. 201).

The incident highlights once again the different pressures the two governments faced and the restraint that the relationship with 'their' community in the North placed upon them. The British thought it was reasonable to divest the declaration of some of the 'green language' and the deeply significant phrases. According to Butler, 'the Unionists were very good at identifying (phrases, which) might say something perfectly acceptable but said it in green language and that in itself was a red rag to a bull, or at least a green rag to a bull' (Butler, 9 November 2000). But the Irish Government had been working with Northern nationalists and Republicans for 2 years and believed that a joint declaration containing certain key phrases could lead to an end to violence. To suddenly have a new draft introduced which expunged the significant phrases and attempted to boil the ideas down to their essence was completely unacceptable. For all their protestations that this was an intergovernmental exercise the initiative had grown out of a dialogue with Republicans and was intended to be attractive in some form to them. Nally notes that all sides had been consulted on what was the draft version that the British decided to replace.

You see we had channels for communication with the Unionists and channels for consultation with Sinn Féin and channels of communications with, god knows, everyone in sight. Very secretive, very confidential, but still channels of communication and so these people knew what was in the declaration we had been working on. But they didn't know anything at all about what was in the new draft, which would not have gone down well at all with the people who were most closely involved in all this.

(Nally, 2 November 2000)

There is though another reason why the Irish were so angry at this late British intervention, which offered less than what Dublin felt the British were moving to agree to. The Irish felt that this was a tactic that they had seen before. As Marie Geoghan-Quinn explained, 'What the Brits were trying to do was the same thing the Brits always do – they make an agreement with you and then on the twenty-third hour, they decide they are going to change it in some way' (Mallie and McKittrick, 1996, p. 261. This point was echoed by Michael Lillis, Lillis, 20 October 2000).

Whatever the reason behind the late British draft it definitely rankled with the Irish side. As a result of the draft Major and Reynolds had a bitter phone call on the 29 November. After the call the Irish threatened to contradict the British if the Downing Street press spokesman, Gus O'Donnell, briefed that the call had been friendly and positive (Duignan, 1995, p. 123). The anger over the new draft and the British–Sinn Féin links resulted in a particularly fraught Anglo-Irish meeting held at Dublin Castle on 3 December 1993.

Getting back to the draft and back on track

The meeting in Dublin on the 3 December (which had been downgraded from a 'summit') (*Financial Times*, 3 December 1993) was fraught. From the outset the Irish announced that they would not negotiate on the British document and Reynolds accused the British of bad-faith (at which point the pencil Major was holding snapped in two). When the British insisted that they had the right to table a new draft, Reynolds told Major if that was the case he should leave and, 'We'll go out and tell the journalists that there's no point in talking any more because the British won't do business (Mallie and McKittrick, 1996, p. 262).' Major then suggested that he and Reynolds meet in private. During this meeting the two had a very frank exchange of views with Reynolds castigating Major over the new draft and the secret contacts with Republicans. Major complained to Reynolds about 'the Irish government's deliberate foot-dragging over the three-stranded talks progress' and the number of leaks that were emanating from the Irish side. Major recalls that he 'had the frankest and fiercest exchanges that I had with any fellow leader in my six and a half years as prime minister' (Major, 1999, p. 452). Reynolds makes a similar point if a little more colourfully, 'He chewed the bollix off me, but I took a few lumps out of him!' (Finlay, 1998, p. 203). One of the 'lumps' was that the British draft would be withdrawn. Butler explained, '(we) allowed ourselves to be drawn into discussing the joint declaration again and our document was tacitly dropped' (Butler, 9 November 2000). (The Irish believe that the British have a policy of seeking to disrupt or prolong negotiations as a negotiating tool. O'Huiginn talks of Britain seeking to 'drown you in process' and Finlay of their inability to get 'from A to B without going via Z and all the letters in between'. Lillis makes similar points (O'Huiginn, 9 November 2005; Finlay, 26 January 2006; Lillis, 20 October 2000).)

After the Dublin meeting the two leaders met again at the fringes of an EU meeting in Brussels and officials continued to meet over the next 2 weeks to remove the last existing areas of dispute. The DSD (officially the Joint Declaration on Northern Ireland) was signed on 15 December 1993.

Evaluating the Downing Street Declaration

The DSD is a somewhat tortuously worded 12-paragraph document. At one level it includes little that had not been said before and was indeed 'a document intended to reassure everybody' (McGarry and O'Leary, 1995, p. 414). It was certainly well received by the British and the Irish press and parliaments. The striking thing about the DSD and where it differs markedly from the original drafts that the Irish Government had drawn up in consultation with Hume and Sinn Féin, is its balance. It is possible to identify sections aimed at enticing Republicans away from violence and those designed to reassure nationalists and Unionists.

Enticing the Republicans

From the start of the joint declaration idea the Irish believed that the key to persuading Republicans to abandon violence was for the British to acknowledge the right of the people of Ireland to self-determination. This is included in paragraph 4 of the DSD (the most important paragraph). 'The British Government agree that it is for the people of the island of Ireland alone, by agreement between the two parts respectively, to exercise their right of self-determination on the basis of consent, freely and concurrently given, North and South, to bring about a united Ireland, if that is their wish'. The wording here serves two purposes; first it appears to meet the demand of Sinn Féin that it is for the Irish alone to decide whether to be a united nation. The phrase also though dictates the unit of that decision-making. Unlike in earlier drafts of the declaration the unit of decision-making is not the whole island of Ireland but two units, Northern Ireland and the Republic, must make the decision concurrently. This was a stumbling block during the negotiations with the Irish side pressing for the island to be treated as one unit, removing the 'Unionist veto' (Butler, 9 November 2000). The final phrasing attempts to reassure both sides, the underlying theme of the DSD. (McGarry and O'Leary suggested that although Molyneaux had been shown drafts of the Declaration, he was not shown this phrasing until the day before the signing of the draft and he may have been unhappy with the wording (McGarry and O'Leary, 1995, p. 419.) Butler refutes this. According to Butler the right of the people of Ireland to self-determination had been in all the drafts. (Butler, 9 November 2000).)

The declaration also contains a repetition of British acknowledgement that they have 'no selfish strategic or economic interest in Northern Ireland' again addressing the imperialist analysis that had underpinned the IRA's traditional justification for violence.

The other key demand of Sinn Féin had been for Britain to be persuaders for unity. The wording of the DSD is constructed to suggest a role for the British as facilitators, not for unity – a role the British would not contemplate – but for agreement in Ireland.

[The British Government's] primary interest is to see peace, stability and reconciliation established by agreement among all the people who inhabit the island, and they will work together with the Irish Government to achieve such agreement, which will embrace the totality of relationships. The role of the British will be to encourage, facilitate and enable the achievement of such an agreement . . .

This is very different from meeting the demand to be persuaders for unity. Paragraph 4 also has echoes of the original Irish draft in this regard. In the June 1993 draft the British were to declare, 'it is the wish of the people in Britain to see the people of Ireland live together in unity and harmony . . . '. The final text noted a wish by the people of Britain 'to enable the people of Ireland to reach agreement on how they may live together in harmony and in partnership . . . '. The offending word of 'unity' had been removed. The British were willing to play the role of facilitators for peace and agreement in Ireland but it was up to the people of Ireland to decide what form this agreement would take. If it was to be a united Ireland the British pledged to legislate to this end, but only if it was the wish of 'the people living in Ireland'. The negotiations had kept some of the terminology from the original draft in an attempt to appeal to Republicans but had inserted important caveats and changed the meaning of phrases in an attempt to avoid alienating Unionists.

The document also repeats the earlier invitations to Sinn Féin (though not specifically named) to enter the political process if violence is ended. The two governments confirm that in the event of 'a permanent end to the use of, or support for, paramilitary violence' all 'democratically mandated parties' which have established 'a commitment to exclusively peaceful methods' are 'free to participate fully in democratic politics and join in dialogue . . . '. This was a repetition of the position the two governments had taken when they began to move towards inclusion in the early 1990s.

Reassuring the Unionists

As paragraph 4 spells out the views, obligations and aspirations of Britain towards Northern Ireland, paragraphs 5 and 6 do the same for the Irish government. In paragraph 5 the Irish government acknowledge 'it would be wrong to attempt to impose a united Ireland, in the absence of the freely given consent of a majority of the people of Northern Ireland'. The paragraph also repeats the idea that 'the self-determination by the people of Ireland as a whole must be achieved and exercised within and subject to the agreement and consent of the majority of the people of Northern Ireland . . . '. In paragraph 6 the Taoiseach pledges to examine 'any elements in the democratic life and organization of the Irish State' which can be seen 'as a real and substantial threat' to the Unionist 'way of life and ethos' or which can be 'represented as not being fully consistent with a modern democratic and pluralist society'. The Irish went even further in addressing the most deep-rooted Unionist suspicion of Dublin when it pledged to support changes to articles 2 and 3 of the repeated Irish constitution 'in the event of an overall settlement'.

The DSD therefore unambiguously confirmed the need for the consent of the majority in Northern Ireland for any change in its status; indeed the fact that nothing would be done without the consent of the majority is mentioned five times in the document (Taylor, 1998, p. 342).

And the winner is?

The DSD is an intricately balanced document that attempted to reassure both communities in Northern Ireland. At the end of any such period of negotiations it is tempting to try and identify the winners and losers in the negotiating process. Unsurprisingly each government claims to have secured its objectives as a result of the DSD. The Irish Government's Press Secretary noted in his diary, 'I have a distinct feeling that Albert has got his way on practically everything, expect, perhaps, the British agreeing to be persuaders for Irish unity . . . '. Whilst, according to Major's biographer, 'Nearly all the points insisted upon by Major at Dublin were indeed present in the final document' (Seldon, 1997, p. 429). Could both sides have got almost everything they wanted?

Comparing the DSD with the earlier Irish/Hume/Sinn Féin drafts it is clear that the Irish Government moved a long way during the negotiations. This movement was not so much in what was changed in the document but in what was added. The original drafts had dealt extensively with what the British would pledge themselves to do but had little to say in terms of the Republic's obligations and concessions. The changes from June–December 1993 created a far more balanced document. The Irish agreed to the need for the consent of the majority in Northern Ireland to change; pledged to re-examine the nature of their institutions and society in light of Unionist fears; and to change articles 2 and 3 in the event of an overall settlement. The negotiations from the British (and Unionist points of view) had resulted in a far more acceptable declaration.

The DSD also represented success for Irish diplomats. They had during a long period of negotiation persuaded the British to recognise the right of Irish self-determination, repeat the pledge contained in the AIA, to legislate for a united Ireland in the future if that was the wish of the majority in the North and effectively proclaim their neutrality on Northern Ireland's status. Indeed much of the early comment on the DSD seemed to subscribe to the view that the Irish had gained most from the Declaration. The *Daily Telegraph* argued, 'it is the British who have moved further to create the Declaration' (*Daily Telegraph*, 16 December 1993).

The whole search for winners obviously rests on the presumption that there must be losers. The purpose of the declaration was to construct a set of joint principles which both governments could endorse. Principles that would hope-fully persuade the IRA that it could best pursue its objectives by renouncing violence and reassure Unionists that there was no question that their position was being undermined. Or, as Reynolds told the Dáil, 'It makes it clear that the British Government are in no sense an enemy to the rights of the nationalist tradition, and the Irish Government are in no sense an enemy to the rights of the Unionist tradition' (Dáil Éireann, vol. 437, col. 1229, 17 December 1993). The Declaration demonstrated that by 1993 it was possible for the two governments to lay out, in a single document, an agreed position regarding Northern Ireland.

The language was indeed somewhat tortuous and the meaning at times opaque. But it demonstrated that the objective of securing a peaceful situation in Northern Ireland was pressing enough to unite the two states and more important for each government than any long-term commitment to unity or union. Both sides could indeed claim to have advanced their position and furthered their aims, as the objectives of the two governments in the DSD were not incompatible. The DSD was not a blueprint for Northern Ireland but was, as Major told the House of Commons, 'a framework for peace, a framework that reflects our responsibilities to both communities in a way that is fully compatible with the undertakings that we have both given and with the objectives of the talks process' (House of Commons, vol. 234, col. 1071, 15 December 1993). Ultimately it succeeded in achieving its main aim, persuading the IRA and Loyalists to abandon violence; 'it did turn out to be a catalyst for peace' (Mansergh, 1995, p. 155).

Conclusion

The 1990–93 period is one of the most productive and most fraught periods of intergovernmental co-operation on Northern Ireland in modern times. The various strands and initiatives that were being pursued concurrently make it hard to decide whether the two governments orchestrated an elaborate, and highly speculative, high-wire act that ultimately led to peace in Northern Ireland, or lurched from crisis to crisis, and ended up with peace despite themselves. The truth is probably somewhere between the extremes. The Irish, especially Reynolds, became convinced that a policy of inclusiveness could end the violence in Northern Ireland and spent much of the 1992–93 period trying to convince the British of their analysis. Yet the British are too often portrayed as reluctant participants in this exercise. As Séan Duignan seems to have come to appreciate at the end of the negotiating period, the pressures on Major not to go down the inclusive road were immense. Duignan records,

> as I shook his hand, the thought struck me that he had taken as many risks as Reynolds, Hume and Adams on the way to the accord. It was not that long since IRA mortars exploded in the garden we could see from inside No. 10. As Tory leader he was also taking a considerable risk, not just in terms of his reliance on the Unionists in the Commons, but also in terms of the large pro-Unionist element on the Conservative backbenches.
>
> (Duignan, 1995, p. 127)

The friendship and determination of the two leaders, as well as the close relationship which had built up between British and Irish civil servants over the years, were undoubtedly vital in keeping the negotiations on track. These good relations were not able to prevent periodic crises emerging in the negotiations and suspicion remained on each side as to the tactics and objectives of the other. It is doubtful though that the process would have survived these crises without the element of trust and friendship that many of the key players had for their opposite numbers.

The role of the Hume–Adams dialogue must also be acknowledged. Although this dialogue and the pronouncements of its participants had become an obstacle to agreement by the end of 1993, it is unlikely that the DSD would ever have happened had the dialogue not occurred. Hume's engagement with the leader of Sinn Féin and his subsequent dialogue with the Irish government convinced many in Dublin that the Provisionals were at least contemplating a re-evaluation of their traditional ideology and tactics. Despite the pronouncements of the two governments that the DSD had no connection to the Hume–Adams dialogue, the fact that so much of its language seeks to address the issues and terminology of the June 1993 draft questions this. The DSD is certainly not the direct descendant of the earlier intra-Irish drafts; there is a balance in the DSD that is clearly absent from the earlier documents. Yet it is possible to trace part of the DSD to Hume–Adams dialogue, just as it is possible to identify the input of the loyalists, Molyneaux, and British and Irish officials.

The DSD is the culmination of numerous inter-related dialogues, re-evaluations and concessions. It changed the debate on and in Northern Ireland from exclusion to inclusion. But it was not, by any means, a panacea. It obviously did not resolve the conflict; it was simply another stage in the long process of seeking a resolution. Nor did the joint declaration signal the convergence of British and Irish policy on Northern Ireland. Intergovernmental disputes were still commonplace, mistrust still evident and acrimony never far from the surface. Goodall noted the DSD was 'a tribute to (the British and Irish) officials who, by skilful drafting and an abundant use of coded language, have laid a veneer of unanimity over what are still divergent and in some respects directly conflicting interests. The result is a minor diplomatic masterpiece' (Goodall, 1993/1994). The DSD was an impressive intergovernmental achievement, indeed one commentator actually proclaimed it, 'possibly the most remarkable political achievement of the entire 1969–98 period' (Neumann, 2003, p. 186). It highlighted the values and objectives that united the two governments in relation to Northern Ireland and, as all good Anglo-Irish documents have done, glossed over those that divide them. Both governments deserve credit for the decision to abandon exclusiveness in favour of inclusiveness and the fact that it managed to keep most of the main players in Northern Ireland on board was no mean achievement. The challenge was to succeed in creating the peaceful environment in Northern Ireland that would allow truly inclusive all-party talks. Once again differences over how to bring about this shared objective, and at what speed, severely strained intergovernmental relations in the coming years.

6 The fledgling peace process

The immediate ending of violence that some had hoped would result from the DSD was not forthcoming. Whilst an *Irish Independent* opinion poll demonstrated that 97 per cent of people in the Republic believed that the IRA should now end the violence, the IRA's actions led many to question whether this was likely. The launching of three mortar attacks on Heathrow airport over 4 days in March 1994 seemed to signal a rejection of the terms of the DSD, although some hope was taken from the fact that the mortars failed to detonate. The announcement of a 3-day ceasefire by the IRA over Easter 1994 was not welcomed as a positive step by the two governments, a fact that perhaps reflected a feeling of exasperation and impatience in London and Dublin. This impatience was particularly evident in Dublin, which had placed great hopes on the DSD and had moved quickly to deal with questions and demands for clarifications from Sinn Féin. Reynolds was reported to be 'dismayed' and Dick Spring went on radio and TV to publicise the Irish unhappiness with the announcement of the time-limited cessation. 'We have been working with the British Government in the context of the Downing Street Declaration to establish a permanent cessation of violence in Northern Ireland. That hasn't happened and it is disappointing' (*The Times*, 1 April 1994). An Irish official went a little further stating, 'To say we're disappointed is a huge understatement' (*The Independent*, 1 April 1994).

Adams immediately called for parts of the DSD to be clarified. The British interpreted this as a delaying tactic or an attempt to seek its renegotiation and refused. Although Dublin favoured offering clarifications, interestingly, Reynolds refused to support Hume's call for the British to meet Sinn Féin in order to clarify the DSD. An Irish official illustrated the annoyance of Reynolds with the IRA around the time of the Easter ceasefire. 'The feeling has been growing that if we or the British give them one more concession they will just demand more.' The official stressed the Taoiseach was not attempting to persuade the British to meet Sinn Féin, stating 'John Hume speaks for himself on this one' (*The Times*, 3 April 1994). Although the refusal to meet Sinn Féin to discuss the DSD whilst the violence continued was understandable, the general point of refusing to clarify the document was tactically questionable from the British perspective, handing Sinn Féin something of a propaganda coup for apparently little benefit. Sinn Féin's line was that it was unreasonable to expect them to respond to a document that was ambiguous. The refusal to clarify this document allowed Sinn Féin to call into question how serious Britain was in its quest for peace. The cost for Britain in responding to written questions from Sinn Féin was comparatively slight, and they took this action in May 1994, 'to call Adams' bluff on the Declaration' (Major, 1999, p. 457). The government issued answers to 20 questions that the Irish government had passed onto them from Sinn Féin, which the NIO Minister, Michael Ancram, called the 'the non-clarification clarification document' (Ancram, 19 October 2005). There were no major surprises in the answers (some questions were deemed to be attempts at renegotiation rather than clarification and the British refused to deal with these). Interesting points included further details on the conditions for Sinn Féin entry into talks. In response to a request as to what the call for Sinn Féin to renounce violence meant the British stated that

> There has to be a permanent end to the use of, or support for, paramilitary, violence. For Sinn Féin and the IRA this would involve a public and permanent renunciation of violence as a means of achieving political ends, and commitment to peaceful and democratic means alone. Within three months, as has already been publicly made clear, the British government would in these circumstances begin exploratory dialogue with Sinn Féin.
>
> (*The Guardian*, 20 May 1994).

(The inclusion of the call for a 'permanent' end to violence prefigured a dispute between Dublin and London after the announcement of the ceasefire 3 months later. As did the assertion in the document that such discussions with Sinn Féin would also 'examine the practical consequences of the ending of violence', which the British would later claim was a clear reference to the need for decommissioning, but was not widely interpreted as such at the time.)

The 'clarification' ended with what was to become a common tactic used by the British government throughout the peace process; the assertion that the process would not wait for Sinn Féin and that they risked isolating themselves by their continued use of violence.

> The democratic path leads to a meaningful role in the political process: a process in which, as has been explained, all issues are open for discussion and negotiation. The alternative is isolation – standing on the outside while those committed to democracy shape the agreement, structures and institutions that will determine the relationships between the peoples of these islands.
>
> (*The Guardian*, 20 May 1994)

This attempt to put pressure on Republicans, although widely used, was only likely to be successful if all other parties to the conflict were willing to restart inter-party talks, in a similar vein to the Brooke–Mayhew initiative, without Sinn Féin's involvement. But it was clear that by 1994 the peace process was primarily concerned with bringing Sinn Féin in and neither Reynolds nor Hume appeared to have much interest in reverting to a Brooke–Mayhew type initiative.

The focus of the Irish government was primarily on how to get the IRA to call a ceasefire. Whilst there would be a move to inter-party talks without Sinn Féin after the breakdown of the ceasefire in 1996, in the immediate post-DSD period the chances of such a move were negligible. Whilst Sinn Féin could not come into the process on any terms, the purpose of the process was to include Sinn Féin and that meant that ways had to be found of convincing the IRA to end the violence. The chances of restarting a talks process, which was favoured by the British government, had been further undermined by the UUP's statement at the end of February that they would not talk to Dublin before an Assembly had been created in Northern Ireland, echoing a stance that the DUP had previously announced (*The Independent*, 1 March 1994).

The British clarification of the DSD increased pressure upon the IRA to call a ceasefire, though there was still little to suggest that one was imminent. The failure of Sinn Féin to endorse the DSD at a conference in Letterkenny in July led to speculation that chances of a ceasefire were slight, and once again prompted anger in London and Dublin. The journalist, Andrew Marr, summed up the general mood when he wrote,

> The republicans had their moment of history, and they blew it. The failure of Sinn Féin to grasp the opportunity given by the Downing Street Declaration sends the province back to the mire of murder and hopelessness. No one died at Letterkenny, but plenty more people will die, Unionist and republican, because of the collective political cowardice of the 500 delegates who met there.
>
> (*The Independent*, 26 July 1994)

The feeling that perhaps the IRA were not moving towards abandoning violence even permeated the Irish Cabinet with the Justice Minister, Marie Geoghan–Quinn, recalling, 'It's fair to say at that stage the Taoiseach was the only one sitting around the Cabinet table who believed that this could be pulled off after Letterkenny' (Mallie and McKittrick, 1996, p. 330). The reason for Reynolds' apparent belief that the negative tones emanating from Letterkenny did not indicate the rejection of a possible ceasefire by the IRA was information that his advisor, Martin Mansergh, had from Republicans prior to Letterkenny. This in turn was relayed to the British by the Irish government before the Ard Fheis (Finlay, 1998, p. 236). Whatever the information that Mansergh had been given there remains a belief that even Reynolds 'had serious doubts' at that stage (Mallie and McKittrick, 1996, p. 299). These doubts were perhaps compounded by the widespread perception in the media that the embryonic peace process had effectively petered out in the face of IRA intransigence and rejectionism.

Not for the first or last time in the peace process though, the public statements and stance of Sinn Féin had belied what the IRA's trajectory was, and the long-awaited ceasefire was called a month later on 31 August 1994.

Ceasefire

The IRA statement declared that there would be a 'complete' end to violence and was greeted by joy in Dublin, but in a more muted manner in London. The reason for the British restraint was the absence of the word 'permanent' in the declaration. This insistence that the IRA unequivocally state that they had permanently ended their armed campaign immediately led to vocal differences between the two governments. Reynolds had lauded the announcement of the ceasefire and treated it as a historic move from the IRA. Major though, whilst welcoming the announcement, claimed:

> We need to be sure that the cessation of violence is not temporary that it is not one week or one month but permanent. Once we have that we can move forward. I do not mind how it is expressed. I don't mind if it is said that the armed conflict is over, that the days of violence are gone for good. But I do need to know that violence is ended for good and that it is not a temporary ceasefire.
>
> (*The Times*, 1 September 1994)

For the Irish government though such a stance was inexplicable and potentially destabilising. Reynolds asked, 'Why get hung up on a word? It does not worry me in the least. It is a total end to violence. That's enough for me' (*The Times*, 1 September 1994). This difference in stance can of course be explained in terms of domestic pressures and audiences, as well as ideological considerations. The British were fully aware that the IRA announcement and the visible sense of jubilation with which it was greeted in Republican areas of Northern Ireland had unnerved Unionists, who were suspicious that some sort of secret deal had been done between the British and the IRA that would be detrimental to their interests. Similarly the caution reflected a continuing suspicion within British government circles of the IRA, its motives and tactics, again understandable after the sustained and bloody campaign that had lasted for over a quarter of a century. For the Irish government though, this was seen far more as a vindication of the peace process and the DSD. It represented the chance to claim that the government had been instrumental in ending, once and for all, IRA violence, was a precursor to a period of peaceful dialogue in Northern Ireland and, hopefully, was an important marker on the road to ending the conflict on the island of Ireland. These sentiments were not only politically very attractive but seem to have reflected the views of the government, who *were* inclined to view the announcement as an historic achievement.

This difference in how to respond to events was to be repeated at various junctures during the coming years. The Irish were frustrated by what they viewed as the foot-dragging of the British. The British suspected that the Irish were too concerned with making concessions to the IRA and did not show enough sensitivity to Unionist concerns and sensibilities. According to Reynolds' Press Secretary, Duignan, increasingly the Taoiseach's reaction was fury that the British hung around after the peace. I mean he really, really felt bitter about it. He felt that they fucked it up and they started entering caveats, saying 'we won't do this'. And the Provos started to say 'what is going wrong?' Reynolds, rightly or wrongly, was furious. He castigated them every way he could, privately, behind the scenes . . . As far as Reynolds was concerned the British seemed to be losing their nerve. Having got the peace it was, 'But they're still terrorists' and Reynolds said 'you must move, you must keep the impetus up, keep it going'. And he felt very very bitter, again rightly or wrongly. He was very dismissive of the British. He refused to see it from the British point of view.

(Duignan, 25 May 2000)

As time would show Irish exasperation with the pace of British response during the peace process was not confined to Reynolds. But on this particular point British tactics can be questioned. The British had a tendency to portray demands for further movement from others, usually the IRA, as fundamentals that were non-negotiable and suggest that all future developments were contingent upon movement on this particular point. The problem was that when movement was not forthcoming, in many cases, it transpired that future developments were, on reflection, not contingent on these issues after all. Such adaptability on the one hand can be viewed as welcome pragmatism by the British government, but it served to blur the line between what actually was fundamental and what merely desirable. This point was clearly expressed by one of the key players on the British side, Quentin Thomas, a senior British civil servant in the NIO since the late 1980s. According to Thomas the British had a 'bad tendency to declare something an issue of principle and then act in a way that shows that it can't really have been because we fudged it' (Thomas, 14 September 2005). The issue of a declaration of permanency in relation to the ceasefire was allowed to be elevated to such a status before it was suddenly dispensed with by Major in his announcement on 21 October that he had made a 'working assumption that the ceasefire was intended to be permanent' and that would allow exploratory talks to begin with Sinn Féin before the end of the year (Major, 1999, p. 460). Such shifts could be read by the IRA as indicating that if they did not move, perhaps the British would. The issue also strained relations between the two governments. In this particular case, the British would have been better served to seize on an apparent concession offered by Adams and McGuinness to British pressure in the days following the ceasefire. The day after the ceasefire was announced Dick Spring said, 'We're now trying to make a distinction between complete and permanent, but our interpretation certainly is that there is a complete end to the violent campaign of the IRA.' In an *Irish Times* article the same day Adams had asserted that the interpretation of the Irish government that the ceasefire was permanent was 'correct'. Martin McGuinness also told the BBC the ceasefire would apply 'under all circumstances' (*The Times*, 2 September 1994). If the British had announced that they took this as confirmation of their demand for clarification and stressed that it needed to be backed by IRA (in)actions during the 3 months period they had already stated would be needed before they would enter into dialogue with Sinn Féin, then it would have appeared to have been Republicans that had responded to pressure. By continuing to insist upon a further statement the British fuelled suspicions in Dublin that they were not fully committed to achieving peace and allowed a propaganda opportunity to Sinn Féin, who claimed the British were placing new obstacles to their entry into the political process. The problem was not the objectives of the British; achieving a transparent commitment by the IRA to the end of violence was highly desirable, but lay in their tactics in raising the stakes to such a visible level only to suddenly switch tack and reverse their position.

Whilst a strong case can be made that the British needed to be seen taking a firm stance in relation to the IRA in order to keep Unionists in the process, it seems, at least in part, the immediate response to the ceasefire by the British government was a result of British unease in dealing with the IRA. Quentin Thomas acknowledges this when he notes that before the ceasefire was declared the British line was that if a ceasefire was called Republicans would be surprised at how imaginative the British response would be. However,

> when they announced they were having a ceasefire, there was a strange psychological flip and ministers, I'm talking specifically about the Prime Minister, John Major, wanted to show that he was not a patsy and that he couldn't be conned that easily, so he started to say, 'well you haven't said permanent, have you?' Now, you couldn't say that any of that was wrong, but it may, if I may respectfully suggest, it may have been tactically inept, because what it amounted to was looking at a gift horse in the mouth, and of course they couldn't then say permanent because they don't do things like that, if you ask for it that's the last thing they'll say. So we were then slightly stuck and they were slightly stuck.
>
> (Thomas, 14 September 2005)

This tactical ineptitude at times led the British government to make too much of comparatively minor issues and somewhat detracted from the stance they rightly took in relation to the IRA and Sinn Féin on issues that were matters of principle. The need to keep Unionists on board was equally important in the longer term if a successful peace process was to be created and the British did have a legitimate argument at times when they accused the Irish of failing to appreciate the concerns of Unionism in this respect. But it was a case of strategically prioritising issues and ascertaining which ones were important and when.

The Framework Documents

Whatever the differences between the two governments over how to respond to the moves of the IRA, they continued to see intergovernmental co-operation as a key to advancing towards a peaceful and stable Northern Ireland. In early 1994 the two governments agreed to work on a joint document, which would be 'an illustrative draft of a possible outcome of the process' (Major, 1999, p. 462). The two governments drawing up documents for the parties to consider (and usually reject) was to become a staple of the process. The governments felt that they were forced into this role as the parties themselves were not willing to perform this function and so such intergovernmental documents at least gave the parties something to discuss (or more often attack). Such documents provided a focus for discussions but they were not easy ones for the two governments to produce. Drawing up agreed joint documents forced London and Dublin to confront issues that divided them. Whilst the governments were united by their objectives of creating a peaceful and stable Northern Ireland, joint proposals had to take account of both governments' wider constituencies and commitments. As a result they needed not only to appeal to (or at least not completely alienate) the parties within Northern Ireland, but also be publicly defensible to the wider British and Irish publics.

A major reason for the length of the negotiations that led to the document *A New Framework for Agreement*, commonly known as the 'Framework Document' (FWD), was the fall of the Irish government with the resignation of Reynolds as Taoiseach in November 1994. This was seen in British circles as occurring 'at the worst possible time' (Major, 1999, p. 465) and was an unhelpful development for several reasons. Most obviously it meant that talks on the joint document would have to be postponed whilst a new government was formed and it would be up to the next Irish government to decide whether to continue the exercise. The document itself was close to completion at that stage, indeed the intergovernmental meeting to finalise the document occurred on the very day that Dick Spring's Labour Party walked out of the Irish Cabinet. As a result the FWD was put back by several months.

The loss of Reynolds was considered unwelcome as, although the British may at times have doubted his command of the nuances of the process and believed he failed to take enough account of Unionism's position, no one doubted his commitment or his willingness to take risks for peace. The Reynolds–Major relationship had also been an important dynamic. In theory the change in government might have been viewed as creating conditions more favourable to progress. The new Taoiseach, the leader of Fine Gael, John Bruton (who formed a coalition government with the Labour Party and the smaller Democratic Left), was potentially a more obvious partner for Britain to work with. Bruton was believed to be more sensitive to Unionist concerns, and likely to exert more pressure on the IRA. Bruton himself suggests he had misgivings about the process when he took office.

> My general view was that it was up and running and that I ought to give it a fair opportunity to yield the potential that it had, not withstanding my concerns about the very difficult ambiguities involved in the peace process, both as to whether Sinn Féin and the IRA had really complied with the terms of the Downing Street Declaration, which looked to a permanent end

to violence, and as to the difficulties for Irish democracy of mixing parties who had no means of physical coercion available to them with a party that did have means of physical coercion available to it.

(Bruton, 6 December 2006)

This was an attitude that was different to Reynolds', who had a far more pragmatic view of dealing with Sinn Féin and the IRA. The continuation of the Labour leader, Dick Spring, as Minister of Foreign Affairs and Tanaiste provided some continuity from the outgoing government. The British were, however, aware that in opposition Fianna Fail tended to be more Republican in outlook and that the Fianna Fail-led coalition headed by Reynolds might be more appealing to Republicans in the North than a Fine Gael-led coalition headed by Bruton. The activities of Fianna Fail in opposition in the past, not least in relation to the AIA, seemed to illustrate the potential damage of having them on the sidelines rather than centre stage. As one British source explained, 'It is far better to have Mr Reynolds in the tent pissing out, than outside the tent pissing in' (*The Guardian*, 17 November 1994).

The new Irish government did though commit itself to the initiative and work resumed on the FWD. On 1 February 1995 *The Times* published a leaked draft of the document. The article opened with the statement, 'The British and Irish Governments have drawn up a document that brings the prospect of a united Ireland closer than it has been at any time since partition in 1920' (*The Times*, 1 February 1995). Major informed Conservative MPs of the impending leak at a hastily convened late night meeting at Westminster on 31 January warning, 'There are black works going on at the crossroads of peace' (Brandeth, 2000, p. 309). The seriousness of the leak is illustrated by the fact that Major felt it necessary to make a televised statement on 1 February to reassure the public. The FWDs were published to a less than receptive audience on 22 February 1995.

For the British the big 'success' of the FWD was the commitment by the Irish 'as part of an agreement' to drop the constitutional claim to Northern Ireland enshrined in articles 2 and 3 of the constitution. According to Ancram the commitment to remove the offending articles was very important as 'that is what we were selling the Framework Document on, that we had the Irish government signing up to something that had been a constitutional anathema to them since de Valera rewrote the constitution, and that was a major gain for the Unionists'. Ancram acknowledges though that the Unionists were not as reassured by this or as unthreatened by the rest of the FWD as the British hoped they would be. 'I kept saying to the Unionists, 'What are you going on about? You have for the first time got an Irish government that has not got a constitutional imperative to get rid of the Union'. But, Northern Ireland politics being what it was, you never saw things quite as succinctly as that' (Ancram, 19 October 2005).

There was a perception on the British side that some Irish negotiators had real reservations about amending the constitution on ideological grounds. According to Ancram, the FWD caused real problems for O'Huiginn, who saw it as 'the giving up of something that the Irish should never have given up' (Ancram, 19 October 2005). O'Huiginn, perhaps unsurprisingly, has a different take on this stating,

> it's not like we stayed awake at night wondering what de Valera would have thought of the removal of these articles? It was more that it had to be part of the package. It was the difference between having a potentially problematic referendum in isolation or a referendum that sailed through as part of a package. So we were careful in putting that card on the table, and rightly so from my viewpoint, but to be honest I think there was never any doubt that it would have to be part of the package and indeed Albert Reynolds more or less said so in the Downing Street Declaration.
>
> (O'Huiginn, 9 November 2005)

But whilst the Unionists might have welcomed this commitment to alter the Irish constitution, they had long argued that the 'cost' of it should be slight as they viewed the articles as an illegal claim on Northern Ireland. Whatever succour they took from the pledge over articles 2 and 3 was more than offset by other aspects of the FWD. Two main issues antagonised Unionists, the remit and powers of the proposed North–South body and the question of what would happen to the body in the event of the new devolved structure collapsing.

Major presented the FWD to the House of Commons on 22 February 1995 as a pragmatic and unthreatening development. Major stressed that the North–South body 'would not have free-standing authority: it would be accountable to the Northern Ireland Assembly and to the Irish Parliament respectively'. He also sought to scotch any suggestion that this marked a derogation of sovereignty (House of Commons, vol. 255, col. 357, 22 February 1995).

Similarly when presenting the document to the Dáil, Bruton was keen to present it as unthreatening. The Taoiseach also argued that nothing would happen without the agreement of the Northern Irish parties and that he did not 'envisage thousands of civil servants working out uniform arrangements' for the whole island, but thought there would be three Irish and Northern Irish ministers 'sitting down from time to time', doing tasks on a North–South basis 'only where it makes practical common sense' (*The Independent*, 23 February 2005).

Unionists were though far from placated by assertions of the FWD's benign nature. The reason for their concern was in large part the statement that the new North–South body would 'discharge or oversee delegated executive, harmonising or consultative functions'. Unionists claimed the FWD envisaged creating a structure with designated executive powers over aspects of Northern Ireland policy on which they were forced to serve and share power with Dublin. (Under the proposals ministers would have 'duty of service' on the body.) They claimed that the proposed institution had the scope to develop into an all-Ireland government. The counter-argument that nothing could happen without their agreement and that the areas that were flagged up for executive action by the new body were ones that involved 'a natural or physical all-Ireland framework', or in such seemingly innocuous categories as 'marketing and promotion activities abroad' and 'culture and heritage' (FWD, para. 31), was not accepted by Unionists. As the DUP's Peter Robinson argued,

> The process is clear. It is to bring about a United Ireland, incrementally and by stealth. This week's published Framework Document offers no Union – strengthening option. It is entirely a nationalist agenda for bringing about a united Ireland . . . For the Unionist community of Northern Ireland, this document confirms their worst fears – that they are no longer wanted and that their Government no longer has any selfish, strategic or economic interest in them.
>
> (*The Independent*, 24 February 1995).

Robinson's central contention that the FWD had a distinctly all-Ireland focus was widely shared, if not his contention that it was designed to bring about a united Ireland. A poll in the *Irish Independent* recorded that 70 per cent of protestants and 64 per cent of Catholics believed that the current political process is 'moving towards some form of a united Ireland' (*Irish Independent*, 2 February 1995).

The suspicion that the FWD was designed to increase Dublin's role whether Unionists agreed or not was fuelled not only by the proposed structure of the body and its executive powers, but also by the 'default mechanism'. Paragraph 47 of the FWD stated:

> In the event that devolved institutions in Northern Ireland ceased to operate, and direct rule from Westminster was reintroduced, the British Government agree that other arrangements would be made to implement the commitment to promote co-operation at all levels between the people, North and South, representing both traditions in Ireland, as agreed by the two Governments in the Joint Declaration, and to ensure that the co-operation that had been developed through the North/South body be maintained.

This was taken to have sinister implications by Unionists. According to their interpretation, although the body was designed to be accountable to the devolved institution created in Northern Ireland, if that institution collapsed it was not axiomatic that the body would also collapse. According to Dean Godson, this was the major concern for the future UUP leader Trimble. Trimble interpreted this section of the document as meaning that 'if the assembly ever collapsed, the default mechanism would allow the two Governments to continue to operate North–South bodies without any local input. Those bodies would be free-standing and not set up by the Assembly. They could, therefore, easily become the vehicle for creeping, even rolling, unification' (Godson, 2004, p. 125).

Neumann's assertion that 'the bodies' responsibilities were to be transferred to a standing Inter-Governmental Conference if the internal arrangements in Northern Ireland broke down' portrayed Unionist fears as a statement of fact (Neumann, 2003, p. 152). What would happen in such a scenario is far more ambiguous as the key is what would 'other arrangements' actually mean? Neumann himself quotes Ancram as stating that when *The Times* portrayed the mechanism as a sell-out, 'I was absolutely amazed. I knew that document, I was living with it for eighteen months. That nuance had never struck us' (Neumann, 2003, p. 152). The interpretation that the default mechanism meant effective joint sovereignty over Northern Ireland and/or a free-standing all-Ireland body with executive, harmonising and consultative power still rankles with Quentin Thomas. Thomas claims that Neumann had written 'as if the Unionists were quite right' but the statement that 'other arrangements' would be made, according to Thomas, does not warrant this interpretation. Thomas sees this as an unthreatening statement, asking:

> could it have said less? What less could it have said? It's just ridiculous. The whole deal, everything about the North–South Body was locked onto what the representatives of the North agreed to and if they didn't agree it was useless. Their position was totally protected, in my view and their reaction was calculatedly hysterical.

According to Thomas, the Unionist reaction 'was greatly over-done and doesn't bear examination against the text' (Thomas, 14 September 2005).

One fact that underlay the Unionist reaction was that, unlike the DSD, Unionists had not been shown drafts of the text during the negotiations. The extent to which Unionists were aware of the initiative is open to debate. Ancram claims that he liased closely with the Unionist negotiating team, which comprised Reg Empey, Jeffrey Donaldson and Jim Nicholson. Whilst they were not shown a draft of the document, Ancram claims he was 'trying things out on them, what I call "lines in the sand". I was saying, "if we go thus far is that over your line in the sand or not?" and most of what was in the Framework Document had been tested in that way'. Ancram suggests that the heated reaction to the FWD was originally not from those he had been dealing with but 'from the likes of David Trimble at that time and then everyone lost their nerve and so they all went into this huddle and said it was a terrible document, even those who had given me the lines in the sand previously' (Ancram, 19 October 2005).

Why though did the British not consult the UUP and in particular Molyneaux during the negotiating stage, as the two governments had done comparatively successfully during the DSD negotiations? The reason given was that the FWD was a different exercise than the DSD. The purpose of the FWD was to be the basis of subsequent negations, rather than a statement of fundamental principles. By this rationale it would be unfair and unacceptable to 'prenegotiate' it with any one party (Godson, 2004, p. 121). According to Quentin Thomas the decision not to show it to Molyneaux was a political decision, which, Ancram states, was largely taken at the behest of the Irish, who were adamant that the Unionists must not be consulted on the document (Thomas, 14 September 2005; Ancram, 19 October 2005). Whatever the reasons behind the exclusion of the Unionists the effect was in some ways similar to that of the AIA process in that the Unionists were alienated not only by the content of what the two governments had agreed but also by the secrecy and their exclusion from the process that created it. However, unlike the AIA, the FWD was not designed to implement changes to either how Northern Ireland was governed or to the relationship between the British and Irish governments. It was largely a negotiating document and as such it did not alienate Unionists as the AIA had done. The FWD represented the thinking of the two governments at that stage as to the possible form that new North–South and East–West structures might take. The negotiating process that followed it was to lead to an agreement that differed in several ways from that the FWD envisaged. Primarily the differences were that the Executive that was agreed under the GFA was a more comprehensive structure than the rather weak committee system that the FWD outlined and the more contentious aspects of the cross-border bodies were somewhat diluted (though these remained a divisive issue). The FWD did though serve its purpose in that it provided a focus for the parties to engage with or merely attack.

A harder question to answer is whether the FWD was primarily constructed to appeal to Republicans and as such was intentionally unbalanced in their direction. Paul Dixon has argued to this end whilst Neumann has claimed that this was not the case (Neumann, 2003, p. 162). Those who were involved seem to believe that it was an honest attempt to get an outline of what might be acceptable to the parties and realised that the subsequent negotiating process would inevitably alter it. The FWD was of course shaped by the negotiating process that created it and by the context of the time in which it was drawn up. At that stage of the peace process the key was to get the Republicans into the process and to demonstrate what might be available to them. These considerations and the exclusion of the Unionists from the negotiations explain the fact that the FWD was of a greener hue than the Unionists would accept.

Decommissioning

One of the major and most persistent issues that bedevilled the fledgling peace process was decommissioning. Having secured the ceasefire the Irish government were keen to move to all-party talks as soon as possible, not least to try and bind the IRA to the process. However, the British were far more reluctant to move onto all-party negotiations that included Sinn Féin until IRA arms had been dealt with. The issue is clouded with uncertainty in relation to whether it was a 'new' hurdle introduced by the British government post-ceasefire, as Sinn Féin claimed, or was always and evidently going to be an issue that needed to be dealt with, as the British argued. There is evidence to suggest that Republicans were at least aware that the issue represented a potential problem at an early stage of the process. In an interview with *The Irish News* in January 1994, 8 months before the ceasefire, Adams claimed he needed a package that he could take to the IRA to persuade them to end their campaign. Adams claimed, 'I couldn't be expected to go to them to ask them to stop their campaign so that we can be engaged in talks after 12 weeks of 'decontamination'; where we can have exploratory talks with senior British civil servants about how the IRA can hand over its weapons' (*Irish News*, 8 January 1994). There is ambiguity in what Adams meant by this, given his mocking tone, but it illustrates that there was awareness that weapons were a potential issue and demands were likely to be made on the IRA and Sinn Féin in relation to them. Similarly Duignan recorded in his diary that Martin McGuinness told Reynolds at an early meeting, 'we know the guns will have to banjaxed' (Duignan, 1995, p. 151). Such episodes somewhat undermine later assertions by Sinn Féin leaders that

> The demand for the surrender of IRA weapons as a precondition to negotiations was never mentioned by the London government before August 31st. In fact, the British were engaged in intensive contact and dialogue with Sinn Féin for two years prior to the IRA cessation and never at any time was the issue of decommissioning raised.
>
> 'In my view, had a surrender of IRA weapons been imposed as a precondition to peace negotiations prior to the cessation, it is possible that there would have been no IRA cessation on September 1st last year'.
>
> (*Irish Times*, 15 June 1995)

Whilst for strategic reasons the British may not have stressed the issue pre-ceasefire and used ambiguous language, Sinn Féin leaders appear to have been aware that the issue would need to be addressed.

Once the ceasefire was secured British statements on the issue became far less ambiguous, and the stipulation that progress could not be made towards talks until it was resolved led to intergovernmental tension. Major claims that the two governments had originally been in agreement on the necessity of decommissioning and the Irish actually made the running on the issue (Major, 1999, p. 470). There is some validity in this argument, given that Spring had made two very strong statements before the ceasefire explicitly calling for decommissioning. On the day the DSD was signed he informed the Dáil that 'Questions were raised on how to determine a permanent cessation of violence. We are talking about the handing up of arms and are insisting that it would not be simply a temporary cessation of violence to see what the political process offers. There can be no equivocation in relation to the determination of both Governments in that regard' (Dáil Éireann, vol. 437, col. 77, 15 December 1993). In June 1994 Spring appeared to commit the Irish government to a policy of demanding decommissioning as a precondition to Sinn Féin's entry into the talks process. After being pressed hard in the Dáil on whether Sinn Féin could participate in talks 'without clear, unequivocal and demonstrated decommissioning by the IRA', Spring stated it was 'not possible' (Dáil Éireann, vol. 443, cols. 1021–1023, 1 June 1994). These comments caused problems within the Irish government as concerns grew that such an approach was untenable and might lead to the IRA abandoning the peace process in order to avoid a split (Duignan, 1995, p. 136). By the time the ceasefire was announced Dublin's line was that decommissioning was a desirable and necessary objective but should not be a prerequisite to progress.

By early 1995 Dublin was increasingly concerned about the centrality that the British were according to decommissioning and the fact that they were arguing that progress towards talks were contingent upon progress on decommissioning, highlighted in the so-called 'Washington 3' speech made by Mayhew on 7 March.

According to Mayhew,

> we will be pressing to achieve three things; a willingness in principle to disarm progressively; a common practical understanding of the modalities, that is to say, decommissioning – what it would actually entail; and in order to test the practical arrangements and to demonstrate good faith, the actual decommissioning of some arms as a tangible confidence-building measure and to signal the start of a process.
>
> (*The Guardian*, 8 March 1995)

At one level this was seen as a watering down of the previous perception that Sinn Féin could not enter into all-party talks until all IRA weapons had been disarmed. The UUP's Ken Maginnis argued, 'The man must be stark raving mad to suggest that those with a hundred tons of the most sophisticated weapons can only get away with a token gesture' (*The Guardian*, 8 March 1995).

Whilst the stance announced by Mayhew in Washington was indeed perceived as a less strident approach, it did not allay concerns in Dublin. Speaking the week before Mayhew's Washington 3 speech Dick Spring stated that, 'If we take the attitude that nothing will happen unless there's a surrender or decommissioning of arms, then I think that's a formula for disaster' (*The Independent*, 9 March 1995). According to Spring's key advisor, 'we had explained to the British government, again and again, that public demands for [decommissioning] would be seen as tantamount to demanding surrender . . . Demanding decommissioning as a precondition of entry could only have disastrous consequences' (Finlay, 1998, p. 288). Dublin could not force London to drop this stance and Ancram told Sinn Féin in another meeting in May that the British would not allow discussion to move beyond exploratory talks to 'substantive political dialogue' until they had met the Washington 3 criteria (*The Times*, 11 May 1995).

However, what is interesting is that the pressure for decommissioning to occur came largely from London. Although some Unionists, notably Ken Maginnis, were vociferous on the issue, the new leader of the UUP, Trimble, did not take the lead on decommissioning. Indeed when asked about it he pointed out that it was the British government who were pressing the point (Thomas, 14 September 2005). Major actually 'rounded on' Trimble for holding too soft a position on decommissioning in their first meeting after Trimble was elected leader in September 1995 (Godson, 2004, p. 162). Why then did the British elevate the issue of decommissioning to such a height and make progress towards talks contingent upon it? Several factors seem to underlie the decision. On one level the issue was one of concern for Unionists; although their new leader did not make the running on the topic that is not to say that the issue was seen as unimportant. However, Trimble did not have to press for decommissioning precisely because the British were doing so. Some British policymakers understandably saw decommissioning as a major issue. Given the mistrust of Republicans amongst some of the Cabinet they would have wanted significant movement on the issue before allowing Sinn Féin into substantive talks. (This is perhaps understandable given that the IRA had come close to killing the leadership of the Conservative Party in the Brighton bombing just 10 years earlier.) Mayhew has argued that 'we were unable to negotiate with Sinn Féin because there was no decommissioning of weapons. The ceasefire of August 1994 was not accompanied by (a statement that the war was over) nor was it accompanied by any decommissioning. We were unable to have carried the support and confidence of Unionists, let alone our own party, in the absence of that . . . ' (Mayhew, 1 November 2005).

However, some within British policymaking circles have criticised the stress that was placed on the issue. According to Thomas this stand-off over decommissioning led to

> a corruption of the process, because they didn't do it, and arguably they couldn't have done it, and equally we couldn't shut up about it. But we had to keep colluding in fudges, or admit that the game was over, and actually when it came to the crunch no one wanted to admit the game was over, as they thought it was valuable.

Once again Thomas argues this was another example of Britain's 'bad tendency to declare something an issue of principle and then act in a way that shows that it can't really have been because we fudged it. So it entered a corruption and everyone in that process has concluded in postponing and smudging decommissioning'. Thomas argues, 'it did not have to be done that way . . . it was the wrong track, both politically and militarily' (Thomas, 14 September 2005). This point is echoed by Finlay who accepts that there was a need for the British to be convinced the IRA were turning their back on violence and decommissioning would have been an indication of this. Given though the problematic connotations of surrender that the Irish believed were associated with decommissioning for the IRA, Finlay claims there were other ways that this could have been deduced (Finlay, 26 January 2006).

But once the issue had taken on such importance it caused a serious logjam in the peace process. As time went on and there was a realisation that the problem could not be overcome, thoughts turned to how the problem could be got around (or 'fudged'), to enable progress to be made on other issues. The solution was to create a mechanism to 'de-couple' the issue of arms from political talks. This was achieved by delegating consideration of when the IRA should decommission to a third party. This proposal originated in Dublin who proposed the creation of an international body at a summit in June 1995. Somewhat to the surprise of the Irish, Major agreed. According to the architect of the plan, Major largely accepted the proposal as the summit had been somewhat unproductive and this would allow them to report in advance to the media (Finlay, 26 January 2006; Finlay, 1998, p. 289). The International Body on Decommissioning comprised the former American Senator George Mitchell, the Canadian General John de Chastelain and the former Finnish Prime Minister Harri Holkeri, all of whom were to remain key players in the subsequent negotiation of the GFA.

This did not though mark the abandonment of the Washington 3 criteria. The continued insistence by the British that there must be prior decommissioning led to a serious intergovernmental row and the decision by Bruton to cancel an Anglo-Irish summit scheduled for 5 September. The reason for the cancellation was the belief in Dublin that the British were seeking to use the summit to put 'further public pressure on Sinn Féin to begin decommissioning, and a very hard line on their entry into all-party negotiations'. Dublin felt that the British wrongly believed that the Provos 'had nowhere to go' and so pressure was warranted. The Irish position at the time was that 'the stability of the peace process is delicate, and may even be in a dangerous condition'. According to Finlay's analysis the result of this difference was that 'unpalatable as it may seem' the British pressure actually pushed the Irish government closer to Sinn Féin's position (Finlay, 1998, p. 290). The Irish wanted to make progress towards all-party inclusive talks the priority, again to assist Adams in his perceived struggle to keep the Republican movement onboard.

The details of the body and its remit continued to divide the two states until a deal was announced at 10 p.m. the night before President Clinton arrived in London. The governments agreed to create the body on decommissioning which would report by mid-January; to hold 'intensive preparatory' talks in which all parties would be treated equally; and announced that it was the 'firm aim' of both governments that all-party talks would begin by the end of February 1996 (*Irish Times*, 29 November 1995). However, at the press conference announcing the deal Major stated, 'We haven't changed our position on Washington 3. We won't be asking the international body to question that position.' Bruton noted that he was not asking Major to change his position but stated it was the Irish government's position 'that a physical gesture of decommissioning of arms in advance of talks, whilst undoubtedly desirable . . . is not an attainable objective' (*Irish Times*, 29 November 1995).

The purpose of the Mitchell Commission (as the body became known) was to get the British off 'the hook of prior decommissioning' that it 'had gotten itself on' (Mitchell, 1999, pp. 29–30). The expectation of the British was that the Commission would endorse their demand that there must be prior decommissioning before Sinn Féin could enter substantive negotiations. Mitchell makes it clear that the Commission was pressurised by the British to endorse their stance (Mitchell, 1999, p. 30). Mitchell's team were though intending to recommend that parallel decommissioning be the model, as a compromise between the two positions, and not least because the head of the RUC, Hugh Annesley, had told them that he did not believe that Adams could deliver prior decommissioning.

In Mitchell's view the demand for prior decommissioning 'was a political policy and was not related to genuine security needs' (Mitchell, 1999, p. 32).

Whilst the Commission was not willing to bow to British pressure on recommending prior decommissioning they did accommodate the desire to make a reference to an elective process in their report published in January 1996. This demand originated with Trimble. The reference to a possible electoral route into talks was hardly the central plank of the report. Article 56 (of 62) noted if 'it were broadly acceptable, with an appropriate mandate, and within the three-strand structure, an elective process could contribute to the building of confidence'. This aside the main proposal of the report was the recommendation that parallel decommissioning be implemented and outlined what became known as the 'Mitchell Principles' that all sides must sign up to before they could participate in the talks. The reaction of the British government to the report, characterised by an Irish official as throwing it into the bin, led to (yet another) crisis in the intergovernmental relationship (*The Times*, 26 January 1996).

The Mitchell Report and the end of the ceasefire

The refusal of the Commission to endorse Washington 3 created a problem for the British. Mayhew circulated a secret document to his colleagues on the Cabinet's Northern Ireland Committee in which he argued they had three options: reject the report, but this would be 'highly damaging' as the government would be held responsible 'for the continued impasse'; accept the Report's approach, which Mayhew advised against, as he did 'not believe it is the right approach'; or take 'a positive line in response to the Report, in no way abandoning Washington 3, but promote a modified way ahead involving an elective process, as identified by the Report albeit rather faintly . . . ' (Godson, 2004, pp. 196–197). The government decided on the third approach. Hennessey's claim that it was later 'virtually forgotten that the British Government had accepted, not rejected, the Mitchell Report' is very debatable (Hennessey, 2000, p. 101). A more sustainable conclusion is that they claimed to accept it but in reality sidelined it, or, as Mitchell himself noted, Major 'reviewed our report, heaped praise on it, then proceeded to suggest an alternative route to negotiations' (Mitchell, 1999, p. 39).

In his comments on the Report to the House of Commons Major stated:

> The body also records its conclusion, on the basis of its discussions, that the paramilitaries will not decommission any arms prior to all-party negotiations. The House will note that the body did not conclude that they cannot decommission; the body concluded that they will not, and the House will draw its own conclusions.
>
> (House of Commons, vol. 270, col. 353, 24 January 1996)

This was in line with the belief in British government circles that Republicans had simply decided not to begin decommissioning; it was a tactical choice rather than a necessary stance to avoid splitting the IRA and endangering the ceasefire. This was not a view shared in Dublin.

The attitude of Northern nationalists and the Irish government were though far more scathing. Hume referred to the suspicion, held not just amongst Northern nationalists but increasingly by Dublin, that Major was pandering to Unionists due to the parlous state of his parliamentary majority (House of Commons, vol. 270, col. 360, 24 January 1996; *Irish Independent*, 29 January 1996).

When Dick Spring commented on the report to the Dáil on the day it was published there was little sign of the impending intergovernmental row. The Tanaiste praised the report and acknowledged, but seemed to set little store by, the reference to an electoral process. The Irish interpretation suggested that the decision whether to have an electoral process might actually arise out of all-party talks themselves (Dáil Éireann, vol. 420, col. 1107, 24 January 1996). Yet the mood changed after Major's statement effectively stipulating that there *would* be elections before talks. The Irish were furious not only with the decision but with the lack of consultation over it. Irish officials informed the media that the government had only been given an hour's notice of the decision before Major announced it (*The Times*, 26 January 1996).

Speaking years later Bruton claimed that he 'never had a problem' with the decision by the British to take the electoral route. He claims that he could see 'an opportunity to get something that might be beneficial to the nationalists [all-party talks] by a vehicle that had been suggested by the Unionists' and he told Major this 'in private discussion'. Bruton claims, 'I could never understand how democrats could object to elections. I have never yet discovered what the objection of Sinn Féin and the SDLP was to an election to a negotiating body' (Bruton, 6 December 2006). However, this was not the reported position of the Irish government at the time when Bruton stated, 'We cannot have any unilateral decision on a matter of this nature' (*The Times*, 26 January 1996). Dick Spring announced on Irish radio that 'The British know full well how we feel after the last few days. We have made it very clear, and we will not be treated in this manner for the future' (*The Independent*, 29 January 1996). The feelings within the Irish government were not aided by perceptions that the British were briefing that there were divisions within the Irish government itself on whether to oppose the plan. Bruton claimed, 'That's been an old British tactic down through the years. That's not just an Irish experience; we have seen this in many parts of the world. The British set out to divide and conquer. They have made attempts before to divide us and they have not succeeded' (*The Independent*, 29 January 1996).

There is little doubt that the dispute over the route to all-party talks caused a real strain in Anglo-Irish relations. The issue again clearly demonstrated some of the key facets of the relationship illustrating the difficulty in maintaining an intergovernmental approach to an issue when there is a genuine difference of prescription in London and Dublin. The main reasons for these alternative prescriptions were the difference in focus of the two governments and the conflicting pressures they were under. The British, as a result of pressure from Ulster Unionists and a continuing scepticism in London of the good faith of Republicans, stressed the need for further movement by the IRA to demonstrate their rejection of violence. The Irish, as a result of pressure from both Republicans and Northern nationalists, and a fear that the IRA were being pushed too far by the British, stressed the need to move to inclusive talks. Spring registered his objection to the electoral process, noting the 'real danger is that we will send out a message that as soon as we have got over one hurdle we have another one to cross' (*The Guardian*, 26 January 1996). Both positions were logical and justifiable, and a compelling case could be made for each. The problem is that they were inherently incompatible.

The dispute also illustrated when such disputes arose, given the asymmetry in actual power in relation to Northern Ireland. Dublin was not in a position to prevent London from taking actions with which they disagreed. By the mid-1990s the relationship between the two states was such that London largely sought to avoid public spats with Dublin, but at times when the analyses of the two states were so divergent London could act unilaterally, and Dublin could fulminate and protest, but could not actually force London to alter course. Subsequent disputes over issues such as the decision to suspend the institutions of government in Northern Ireland a few years later would illustrate that the Irish government was not in a position to ensure that they would 'not be treated in this manner in the future'.

However, the debate over how to advance the process in early 1996 was transformed by the IRA's announcement, at 6 p.m. on 9 February, that 'with great reluctance' it was ending its ceasefire. The explosion at Canary Wharf in London an hour later killed two people, injured over 100 and caused damage totalling over £100 million (Bew and Gillespie, 1999, p. 321). The IRA blamed the British government for the return to violence. According to an IRA spokesperson the 1994 ceasefire had been based upon 'a clear, unambiguous and shared understanding that inclusive negotiations would rapidly commence to bring about political agreement and a peace settlement'. Rather than these negotiations the Major government had introduced preconditions and sought to remain in power by dealing with the Unionists. The result, the IRA claimed, was 'a year and a half of stalling, prevarication and provocation' (quoted in English, 2003, p. 290).

The end of the ceasefire offered a vindication of each government's reading of the state of the peace process. For the British it illustrated that their scepticism regarding the commitment of the IRA to non-violence was justified. The action surely indicated that the policy had simply been 'no more than a tactic' (Major, 1999, p. 488) that could be abandoned if it did not yield the fruits that they hoped for. It was also used retrospectively to vindicate Britain's earlier insistence that the IRA must declare its ceasefire permanent. Major noted in the House a few days later that 'we never lost sight that the IRA commitment had not been made for good . . . I regret to say that the events of last Friday showed that our caution about the IRA was only too justified' (quoted in Bew and Gillespie, 1999, p. 324). This caution with regard to the IRA's intentions was further justified in British eyes with claims that the bombing was being planned for months (English, 2003, p. 290), perhaps even before the Mitchell Commission was created.

For Dublin though the blast at Canary Wharf could be interpreted as proof that their reading of the situation had been correct. The IRA had been pushed too far, the apparent creation of new barriers at each stage of the process, barriers that had not been (explicitly) evident before the ceasefire had been entered into, had led to the hawks within Republicanism reasserting control. This was not to argue that the bombing was inevitable, and certainly not that it was justified, but it seemed to confirm the fears held by many within Irish government circles that Britain's apparent reluctance to engage with Sinn Féin placed too great a strain on the IRA and jeopardised the process.

However, the result of the ending of the ceasefire was that the two governments managed to overcome their divisions and again work towards constructing a common approach. They were aided in this regard of course by the fact that the IRA's action removed the underlying cause of that particular dispute. The issue of when to grant Sinn Féin access to all-party talks was less pressing in this new post-ceasefire situation. Both governments announced that no progress could be made until the ceasefire was restored and that Ministerial contacts with Sinn Féin would cease, though contacts at official level would continue. The two governments began to attempt to put all the pieces back together again.

Towards all-party talks

The perception of the immediate aftermath of the IRA ceasefire was that 'the British and Irish Governments literally fell over themselves to make preparations for all-party talks' (Hennessey, 2000, p. 101). It became clear that the ending of the ceasefire was not necessarily seen as the end of the peace process. Even the British, for whom the resumption of violence could have been seen as indicative that the IRA and Sinn Féin were not viable partners, did not reject their future participation out of hand. Indeed the noises from both London and Dublin were that there was still a seat at the table for Sinn Féin and they quickly announced when the seat would be available. On 28 February Major reported to the House the outcome of a summit held that day with the Irish government. As a result of which, 'both Governments reaffirm their commitment to all-party negotiations with a comprehensive agenda. These will be convened on 10 June, following a broadly acceptable elective process.' The price of admission for Sinn Féin was a restoration of the ceasefire, signing up to the Mitchell principles and addressing 'at the beginning of the negotiations Senator Mitchell's proposals on decommissioning of weapons' (House of Commons, vol. 272, col. 900, 28 February 1996).

Bruton also addressed his parliament on the same day. It was clear from his statement that the Irish had decided that they would have to accept that an electoral element would precede all-party talks. Bruton asserted that the process 'would have to be broadly acceptable and lead immediately and without further pre-conditions to the convening of all-party negotiations with a comprehensive agenda'. He also seemed to indicate that the price of admission for Sinn Féin was slightly lower than that suggested by the British. 'All that has to happen, for Sinn Féin to become a full participant in the negotiations, is a restoration of the IRA ceasefire of August 1994' (Dáil Éireann, vol. 462, col. 897, 28 February 1996). Bruton did also echo an assertion that Major had made, that decommissioning remained an issue which would need to be addressed early in the process. Major had claimed that the 'first item in the negotiations would be the Mitchell principles in their wider aspect, including the points that need to be dealt with on decommissioning. That would be the lead item in the negotiations, which would begin on 10 June' (House of Common, vol. 272, col. 904, 28 February 1996). Bruton acknowledged that parties had 'serious and genuine concerns' about the existence of 'large arsenals' that 'will need to be addressed in a serious manner at the start of all-party negotiations' (Dáil Éireann, vol. 462, col. 903, 28 February 1996).

Several interesting questions arise from the responses to the ending of the ceasefires in London and Dublin. Why did the two governments not take a harder line with Republicans once the ceasefire had broken down and effectively exclude them from the process, or at the very least make much tougher demands of them as a price for entry into all-party talks? To what extent was the announcement of a date for all-party talks simply a response to IRA bombs; and what compelled the Irish to drop their opposition to the electoral process? The contentious statement made by Fergus Finlay in April 1996 that talks without Sinn Féin were 'not worth a penny candle' perhaps best explains the answer to the first question. Without Sinn Féin participation in talks and an IRA ceasefire there was no peace process. There could be talks between what used to be termed 'constitutional' parties, as had last been tried in 1990–92, but this was not the process that the two governments had been pursuing since at least 1993, and there was little desire to pursue it once again in 1996. Finlay's comments seemed to express a view that many found unacceptable, and the general line throughout the peace process had been, and was to remain, that Republicans could not hold the process to ransom. However, the reality was that as long as the focus of Northern Ireland policy was on securing and maintaining peace as a prelude to negotiating a wider political agreement, Republican participation was essential. If the process was to advance as a peace process then permanently excluding Republicans, either formally or informally, by making prohibitive demands of them for admission to all-party talks, would mean the end of the initiative. This is not the same, of course, as saying that the IRA and Sinn Féin must be included at any price. The two governments never wavered in their insistence that Republicans could only be involved once they had ceased violence. But beyond this all that was demanded of Sinn Féin was that they signed up to the Mitchell principles and that they effectively accepted that decommissioning was an issue that would have to be addressed, at some stage in the process.

The announcement on 28 February of 10 June as the date for the start of all-party negotiations was widely seen as a response to the bombing of Canary Wharf 19 days earlier. According to a leader in *The Independent*:

All of a sudden, the British and Irish Prime Ministers resolve arguments that have dogged the peace process for months. There is a firm date for all-party talks; decommissioning of weapons, which seemed such a giant stumbling block last year, has become something that can be discussed once everybody is at the table. There is no escaping the awful truth, no matter how much the two leaders insist that they were not bombed into a compromise. For 17 months, the guns were silent and the bombers lay low: the peace process moved at a snail's pace. Then a half-ton of fertiliser, 100 injuries, two deaths, £80m of damage: within 19 days, we are within sight of the negotiating table. Why does anybody bother to say that violence must always be resisted, that it will never work? Not since Hiroshima has a single bomb achieved the dramatic political effect of the IRA's strike against the London Docklands.

(The Independent, 3 March 1996)

Whether the progress to inter-party talks was actually incidental to the end of the ceasefire, as both governments claimed (Major, 1999, p. 489; Finlay, 1998, p. 301 it is clear that after the bombing of Canary Wharf, Dublin's objection to the electoral process was dropped). The most likely explanation for this is that the Irish had, given their inability to alter it, accepted that Britain was going to pursue this path. To refuse to endorse it would mean that it would be almost impossible to continue the intergovernmental co-operation that had been so important in creating the peace process. However, the Irish could justify this apparent change in course by the fact that they had secured a definite date for all-party talks, enabling this to be portrayed as a concession by the British (*The Independent*, 1 March 1996).

The end of the ceasefire did cause the two governments to re-evaluate the current state of their relationship. As on occasions in the past, a crisis within Northern Ireland served as the catalyst for a rapprochement between the two governments. The shared acceptance of the importance of co-operation between London and Dublin in the face of renewed IRA activity led the two states to try and shelve their differences. Major claimed that 'Canary Wharf had brought London and Dublin closer together' (Major, 1999, p. 489) and went so far as to tell the House that 'Co-operation between the British and the Irish Governments has never been better than it is at the moment' (House of Commons, vol. 272, col. 901, 28 February 1996) – a view somewhat at odds with the opinion of British–Irish relations widely reported at that time.

The electoral process

After a consultation process with the parties in Northern Ireland Major announced the format of the elections on 21 March (House of Commons, vol. 274, col. 497, 12 March 1996). The system would be based on party lists and was specifically designed to ensure that the smaller parties connected to loyalist paramilitary groups would be represented at the all-party talks; the 'plan was ingenious'

(Mitchell, 1999, p. 44). The elections would result in a 110-strong Forum from which the parties would select their representatives for the negotiations to begin on 10 June. The Forum itself was not to play any direct role in the subsequent talks and really had no purpose beyond the necessity to create the electoral process. The residual anger amongst Northern nationalism at the imposition of the electoral process meant that Sinn Féin never attended the Forum and the SDLP walked out a month after it was set up.

The elections, held on 30 May, produced Sinn Féin's best-ever electoral performance up to that point. They polled 15.5 per cent of the vote and secured 17 seats in the Forum. The SDLP retained their predominant position amongst nationalists with 21.4 per cent (21 seats), and the UUP secured 24.2 per cent (30 seats) against the DUP's 18.8 per cent (24 seats). The strong Sinn Féin performance was interpreted in conflicting ways: as both a demand for the restoration of the ceasefire, or as an endorsement of the hard-line stance (Bew and Gillespie, 1999, p. 329).

Little progress was made at the talks that began on 10 June 1996. The failure of the IRA to restore the ceasefire, and indeed the bombing of the centre of Manchester 5 days after the talks began, ensured the continued exclusion of Sinn Féin. The absence of Sinn Féin was undoubtedly a barrier to progress, but there could be no question of their admittance whilst the IRA remained active. By the summer of 1996 Republican faith in the stewardship of Major and Bruton of the peace process had all but disappeared. Related to this even if a new ceasefire had been called the chances of moving to inclusive all-party talks were minimal. Unionists were unwilling to enter into such talks at that stage. Although the UUP would do so a year later, there was little chance of them providing Paisley with 'an electorally lethal "Trimble's a traitor" slogan' so close to a general election (*The Independent*, 30 November 1996). Major subsequently acknowledged that the process needed an election to restart it (Major, 1999). The election of the Labour Party on 1 May 1997 by a landslide and the ousting a month later of the Bruton government by Bertie Ahern's Fianna Fáil/Progressive Democrats coalition was to give the process a new momentum that would eventually carry it to the heady Good Friday of 1998.

Conclusion

The period between the ceasefires and the fall of the Major and Bruton governments can be depicted as one of disappointment and apparently wasted opportunities due to the failure to make real progress towards a negotiated agreement. Yet such a characterisation would gloss over difficult and pertinent questions. To what extent were these disappointments avoidable? Why was more progress not made in the peace process during the Major–Bruton years? Who, if anyone, was to blame?

Though it would be unfair to claim that Major was in hock to the Ulster Unionists as a result of his perilously small majority in the later days of his premiership, Westminster arithmetic was a consideration for the Tories. It is possible to identify times when the government did take action that was unpopular with Trimble and his colleagues, such as the FWD publication. Yet the perception grew that Major was constrained by his slender majority and polling suggested that he was unlikely to win the next election. As a result it did not really matter whether Major actually *was* increasingly sensitive to Unionist concerns, the mere perception that this was the case meant that his government was not going to make any breakthrough after early 1996. By 1996 there could not be progress under Major as the IRA would not restore their ceasefire and so the process could not progress.

One source from which no discernible pressure was applied to the British government was the British opposition. The Labour Party during the period was firmly supportive of Major's handling of the peace process. The replacement of Kevin McNamara by Mo Mowlam as Northern Ireland spokesperson and abandonment of Labour's commitment to 'unity by consent' policy after Blair became leader in 1994 brought the two main parties in Britain even closer on the issue of Northern Ireland. This bipartisanship was not a new feature in British politics but had been the norm, arguably, since the division of Ireland. The policy served at least two purposes. First it served to help insulate 'British' politics from the 'Irish question', which had loomed so large for much of the late 19th and early 20th centuries. This attitude was illustrated by Herbert Morrison's observation to the Labour Party Conference in 1949 that 'We do not want to interfere with the internal politics of Ireland, and, with great respect, we would like Ireland not to interfere with the internal politics of the United Kingdom' (quoted in Dixon, 1995a, p. 153). The outbreak of the Troubles in Northern Ireland in the late 1960s meant that the issue could no longer be kept off the 'British' agenda. However, the bipartisan approach largely remained in place as it served another purpose. According to Dixon,

> bipartisanship works by the two principal British political parties broadly agreeing on the constitutional principles of their approach to the issue. They can then present a united, British, front to the contending communal groups in Northern Ireland. This prevents those groups from exploiting the political differences between the British parties and playing one off against the other and holding out on agreement.
>
> (Dixon, 1995a, p. 156)

The actions of Labour during the latter years of the Major government certainly fitted this characterisation. Even when their 'sister' party the SDLP were venting their outrage at Major's decision to 'bin' the Mitchell Report, the Labour leadership did not join in the criticism. According to Mowlam,

> The Labour Party has maintained bipartisan support for the Government throughout the Northern Ireland peace process. We want to continue to give the Government as much room for manoeuvre as possible within the

principles set out in the Downing Street Declaration and the Joint Framework Document.

We do not believe that ministers should be dependent on their right wing or on minority parties for support on this issue. Equally, we do not want to give any of the Northern Ireland parties cause to procrastinate or prevaricate in the hope that it can get a better deal if it waits for a Labour government.

(*The Independent*, 17 March 1996)

Labour's policy was seen in Dublin as keeping them 'two safe steps behind Mr Major' (*Irish Times*, 17 March 1996).

The bipartisanship evident in Westminster is in contrast to the situation in Dublin. Northern Ireland has frequently been an area of inter-party competition and criticism in the Republic. The reason for this is that, unlike in Britain, there is a perception that the issue can be used for electoral advantage. These differences often come to the fore in the run up to elections. At the Easter Rising commemoration in 1997 the then opposition leader, Bertie Ahern, claimed the peace process had faltered because, in contrast to the approach of (Fianna Fáil's) Reynolds, there had not been 'the same passionate conviction and firm guidance coming from the new Government in Dublin'. According to Ahern, 'Peace was declared unconditionally by the IRA on the public understanding that after a few months and post Framework Document Sinn Féin would be admitted to talks. The Taoiseach permitted a fatal prevarication by the British on that commitment, using the red herring of decommissioning.' The solution to this problem and the way to restore momentum to the peace process was clear: vote Fianna Fáil. 'Fianna Fáil, as a party that represents nationalist Ireland, is better placed to reach a historic compromise with Unionism, if anyone can' (*Irish Times*, 28 April 1997). He was to get his opportunity shortly afterwards.

If Major's government had had a healthier majority at Westminster, would it have pursued a significantly different approach to the peace process? Such counter-factual questions are of course impossible to answer but a strong case can be made that the British and Irish governments acted in this period, as in those in the run up to the peace process, as a result of a variety of considerations and pressures. The British government's suspicion regarding the motives and intentions of the IRA would have been the same in 1994–97 even if it had had a more substantial majority. The 'psychological flip' was a result of issues beyond Westminster arithmetic. Given such considerations the British government deserve great credit for making the advances they did and taking the chances they took to try to secure peace in Northern Ireland. However, what also needs to be acknowledged is the tactical ineptitude that was all too frequently evident. The tendency to declare things matters of principles, and subsequently act in ways that illustrated that they were not, introduced doubt and ambiguity into a process that needed certainty and clarity.

Domestic issues within the Republic also influenced the process. The fall of the Reynolds' government, which had been so instrumental in bringing about the ceasefires, altered the political picture. Reynolds was a risk-taker who had little compunction about dealing with the IRA. The resignation of Reynolds brought in a Taoiseach of a very different political hue. Finlay claims that it became evident during Labour–Fin Gael talks after Reynolds resigned that Bruton 'was a million miles from where he needed to be for the process. His visceral hatred of the Provos meant that you wondered whether he would be able to cope with the need for a dialogue, at an emotional level.' As a result of these concerns Spring realised he would have to play a different role in the new coalition (Finlay, 26 January 2006). Whereas before Spring was seen as acting as a restraint on Reynolds at certain points, under Bruton, Spring was perceived as being the most nationalist member of the government. Finlay argues that in reality Spring 'kept the straight line', what changed was 'the air around him' when he was in partnership with Bruton rather than Reynolds. Once in government though Bruton was keen to play an active role in the process and, over issues such as the Drumcree march in 1996, the Mitchell Report and the route into all-party talks, at times took a very critical line on British policy and Unionist attitudes. (On Drumcree Bruton was very critical of the British decision to reverse a decision and allow the Orangemen to march along the Garvaghy Road. The Irish were also furious at what they claimed as the lack of notification of the decision (Dáil Éireann, vol. 468, col. 1123, 25July 1996).) The perception remained however that Bruton was more sympathetic to Ulster Unionism, a perception that even led Labour to seek to block a Bruton–Trimble meeting for fear 'that they would see eye-to-eye too much'. The Labour Party feared that close relations between Bruton and Spring at the same time as relations between Bruton and Adams were very negative would be 'bad for the process'. Finlay acknowledges though that the 'net consequences of all that was that Spring became a hate figure for the Unionists' (Finlay, 26 January 2006).

The main reason that more progress was not made in the 1994–97 period was the end of the IRA ceasefire. As a result no real progress in the peace process could be made whilst there was no longer 'peace'. The IRA believed that it could achieve more through non-violence than violence in 1994, it re-evaluated this belief in February 1996. Had the British accepted the ceasefires as permanent at the outset, not set such store by decommissioning and set a firm date for all-party talks much earlier, the IRA might have been far less likely to resume violence. But what would have been the impact on Unionism? If such an approach had been followed then Unionism would have been lost from the process, and it was just as instrumental to achieving an end to the conflict as Republicanism.

A more nuanced and consistent approach was needed by London. Some of the errors were presentational (reaction to the ceasefire), some were substantive (Washington 3). Similarly at times Dublin pushed London too hard to make concessions to Republicans without showing due regard to Unionist concerns and sensibilities. What must be remembered though is that this period was unique and the two governments were largely in uncharted waters post-1994. To criticise certain actions of the Major government after the ceasefires is justified. Also as sovereignty ultimately rests with the British, criticism of the process is likely to be directed more at London than Dublin. Yet it needs to be acknowledged that had the Major government not been willing to take real risks in the period up until 1994 then there would not have been a peace process. As time would show the peace process was not destroyed in the 1994–97 period. But it is evident that whilst Major can claim to be one of the architects of the peace process, he was unable to progress much beyond the planning stage. It took the elections of May and June 1997 to renew the process and create the conditions necessary to move onto the next stage: inclusive all-party negotiations.

7   The Good Friday Agreement and beyond

The end of the conflict?

The election of new governments in both Britain and Ireland offered a real opportunity to re-launch the peace process in mid-1997. A feature of the conflict in Northern Ireland has been that major changes in personnel have often increased the chance of progress and brought renewed dynamism to the intergovernmental relationship. Given the complicated nature of the conflict, the diverse and conflicting demands of and upon the parties, and the frequency of unexpected events that strain the relationship, changes of leadership can be cathartic. Such changes enable a metaphorical line to be drawn under past events, and problems can effectively be attributed to outgoing leaders. The replacement of Thatcher and Haughey by Major and Reynolds had led to advances in the early 1990s. Both were seen as unencumbered by the ideological and historical baggage of their predecessors. By 1997 though Major's own historical baggage was increasingly weighty, particularly as a result of the problems in advancing the peace process after 1994. Whilst Bruton had only been in power for 3 years, his ideological baggage had become an issue and the apparent lack of progress during his time in office meant that relations between his government and Republicans in Northern Ireland were poor. The causes of the problems in the peace process were not solely the result of the actions or ideologies of Major/Bruton or of The Conservative Party/Fine Gael. The issues that caused the problems were not voted out of office in 1997. But the attitudes of the parties in Northern Ireland to the two governments were taken out of the equation (or at least heavily discounted) when new governments came in. Neither was the government elected on a platform of a radically different policy towards Northern Ireland nor was the issue of Northern Ireland of any notable significance in either state's election campaign. But the arrival of two new leaders onto the stage in quick succession and, vitally, the evident intention of both governments to make the issue a priority meant that an opportunity for advance existed in June 1997 in a way that it had not 2 months before.

Blair's commitment to the issue was illustrated by his speech at the Royal Ulster Agricultural Show on 16 May. This was, as Blair pointed out, his first official visit as Prime Minister outside London. The speech he delivered was a carefully balanced but hard-hitting one. Given Labour's previous commitment to a policy of unity by consent, a certain scepticism amongst Unionists towards the new government might have been expected. To address this Blair unequivocally stated that,

> I am committed to the principle of consent. And I am committed to peace . . . My agenda is not a united Ireland . . . Unionists have nothing to fear from a new Labour government. A political settlement is not a slippery slope to a united Ireland. The government will not be persuaders for unity.

He asserted his own Unionism claiming, 'I believe in the United Kingdom. I value the Union' and predicted 'none of us in this hall today, even the youngest, is likely to see Northern Ireland as anything but a part of the United Kingdom'.

Blair also offered words of comfort for nationalists in his speech. He committed his government to the DSD and stated, 'I believe the Joint Framework Document sets out a reasonable basis for future negotiation' (which was not a view that Unionists shared). He acknowledged the importance of the Irish dimension by noting the need for 'sensible arrangements for cooperation with the Republic of Ireland, practical and institutional, which will be significant not only on the ground, but also politically for the nationalist community' and announced that British officials could meet Sinn Féin to explain the British position. But he sought to both entice and pressurise Sinn Féin with the statement that, 'My message to Sinn Féin is clear. The settlement train is leaving. I want you on that train. But it is leaving anyway and I will not allow it to wait for you.'

Although talks between Sinn Féin and British officials were suspended after the IRA killed two RUC officers in Lurgan in mid-June, the attempt to create a sense of urgency was a theme that continued. At the end of June, Blair announced that September would see the start of detailed talks on Northern Ireland's future, with or without Sinn Féin. This was accompanied by the stipulation that the British would evaluate whether Sinn Féin could be admitted to talks 6 weeks after an IRA ceasefire and let it be known that they wanted the talks to be completed by May 1998.

The issue of decommissioning had also been under discussion by the two governments and a new plan was devised to create an independent commission on decommissioning. This meant that no prior decommissioning was necessary by the IRA for Sinn Féin to enter the talks, a point underlined in a letter sent to Sinn Féin by the British on 9 June 1997. The letter noted, 'voluntary and mutual decommissioning can be achieved only in the context of progress in comprehensive and inclusive political dialogue', which explicitly rejected the idea that prior decommissioning was necessary. The letter also stated, 'provided that all participants are acting on the basis of the implementation of all aspects of the Mitchell Report, in good faith, progress should be possible'. The dishonouring of the Mitchell principles was the only basis for exclusion from the talks, and this was to be decided by the governments (*The Independent*, 18 July 1997). As a result the government had directly met demands that Sinn Féin had made in November 1996 for immediate entry to the talks (albeit in 6 weeks), a date for their completion and an undertaking that Unionists would not be allowed to use decommissioning to block negotiations (*Financial Times*, 29 November 1996).

At one level Blair was not actually offering anything radically different to that which Major had appeared to offer in November 1996 (House of Commons, vol. 286, col. 461, 28 November 1996; *Financial Times*, 29 November 1996). The Labour government still demanded a restoration of the ceasefire, a period of time must elapse before they could enter talks, and for Sinn Féin to sign up to the Mitchell principles. But they did provide more clarity and apparent urgency to Republicans (as well as the benefits of a huge parliamentary majority). The combination of clarity on what was necessary for entry into talks, sense of dynamism and the new opportunities offered by new leadership in Britain and the Republic led to the IRA calling a new ceasefire on the 19 July 1997. Sinn Féin signed up to the Mitchell principles on 9 September (although the IRA noted they would have 'problems' with the principles 2 days later) and were admitted to the process that was to lead to the GFA.

Negotiating the Good Friday Agreement

Several accounts exist of the negotiations of the GFA, which provide a fuller examination of both the negotiations and content of the Agreement than is offered here (Godson, 2004; Hennessey, 2000; Dixon, 2001; Tonge, 2004; Wilford, 2001). This section examines the negotiations from the perspective of inter-governmental relations and analyses the impact that intergovernmentalism had on the agreement, and the problems that seeking the agreement caused for the intergovernmental approach.

The entry of Sinn Féin into the negotiating process led to the withdrawal of the DUP and the smaller UKUP. The UUP, however, did not withdraw, Trimble argued, 'Unionism will not be marginalized. Those who walk out leave the Union undefended' (quoted in Aughey, 2006). This stance was largely possible because the two parties associated with loyalist paramilitaries, the UDP and the PUP, also decided to stay at the talks. Indeed George Mitchell claims that the withdrawal of the DUP and the UKUP actually meant that the GFA was possible. 'Reaching agreement without their presence was extremely difficult; it would have been impossible with them in the room' (Mitchell, 1999, p. 110).

A bone to gnaw on: The Heads of Agreement

The structure of the talks was established before Sinn Féin entered the process. The three-strand approach that had been used by the Brooke–Mayhew talks was again adopted. Strand 1 dealt with how Northern Ireland was to be governed and was chaired by the NIO minister, Paul Murphy (the Irish government played no formal part in this strand). Strand 2 dealt with relations between North and South and was chaired by George Mitchell. Strand 3 dealt with wider British–Irish relations and was negotiated directly between the two governments. However, the pace of the talks did not markedly improve once Sinn Féin was admitted.

By December the talks had not even led to agreement on an agenda, much to the frustration of George Mitchell. In an attempt to break the logjam in January 1998 the two governments drew up and distributed to the parties the document, *Propositions on Heads of Agreement* (HOA).

The HOA was a brief document designed 'for debate and discussion' and stated clearly that it was to 'offer only the outline of an acceptable agreement'. Once again the two governments had had to table proposals in an attempt to move the talks forward. Although the document was an intergovernmental one it stressed that the proposals 'derive in a very real sense from the views of all parties' expressed at the talks. The plan was for the British to change section 75 of the Government of Ireland Act and the Irish to alter Articles 2 and 3 of the constitution. A Northern Ireland Assembly was proposed with 'devolved executive and legislative responsibility'; a new British–Irish Agreement to replace the AIA, which would include a new intergovernmental council, to deal with 'the totality of relationships' between Britain and Ireland, including for the first time representatives from a Northern Ireland Assembly and the proposed devolved Welsh and Scottish institutions. There was to be a North–South ministerial council where each side was to 'consult, co-operate and take decisions within the mandate of, and accountable to, the Northern Ireland Assembly and the Oireachtas respectively'. Implementation bodies for policies agreed by North/South Council were to be created. The proposals also dealt with need for protection of rights and noted the need to deal with 'issues such as prisoners, security in all its aspects, policing and decommissioning of weapons'.

The HOA was described by the Irish Foreign Minister, David Andrews, as 'a road map to a new agreement' (*Irish Times*, 13 January 1998) and by a British official as 'a bone for the parties to gnaw on, designed to concentrate minds and get negotiations going in earnest' (*The Guardian*, 13 January 1998). The document was the result of frenetic negotiations between the two governments with 300 telephone calls exchanged in the two days before it was published (Godson, 2004, p. 317). The dividing lines were on whether there *might* or *would* be a Northern Ireland Assembly, the status of the North/South bodies and to whom they would be answerable. The outcome as published on 12 January was widely seen as a victory for Trimble and the Unionists. Indeed Dean Godson claimed it, 'illustrated that the Irish Government would submit to the superior muscle of the British state if the latter ever chose to exert itself' (Godson, 2004, p. 318). This is an over-exaggeration of both the importance of the HOA and the amount that the Irish had moved on the issue. The document did state that there would be an Assembly (Dublin favoured 'might be' reflecting Sinn Féin's reluctance to see the creation of what they argued was a partitionist structure) and North–South bodies were not described as having 'executive' powers, as they had been in the FWD. But the document also noted that the British would alter Section 75 of the Government of Ireland Act, an Irish demand to off-set their alteration of Articles 2 and 3 of their constitution and dealt with rights and the normalisation of society in Northern Ireland.

The document was though more tailored to Unionist sensibilities than those of Sinn Féin. Given that the document was simply a 'bone for the parties to gnaw on', its importance, or those of the apparent concessions by Dublin, should not be over stated. As the negotiating process was to illustrate, concessions and victories were to be claimed at different times by different parties over different documents.

When Sinn Féin reacted negatively to the document, Ahern publicly stated that the North/South bodies would be 'stand alone' and would be 'an executive implementation body'. After meeting with Sinn Féin, Ahern stated he was 'watching and protecting the interests of nationalists' and stressed that he had followed the FWD in negotiating the HOA (*Irish Times*, 14 January 1998). According to Ahern a week later, what the HOA outlined 'is executive bodies. It was then, it still is, and will be next week' (*Irish Times*, 12 January 1998). As so often in the process steps were taken to keep all sides onboard and assuage fears in the immediate aftermath of joint publications, even to the extent of increasing the ambiguity of what had just been proposed.

The 'Mitchell' draft

The document did give the talks a certain momentum, providing a focus for the discussions and marked the start of the serious negotiations leading to the GFA. The negative reaction of Sinn Féin though and the subsequent attempts by the Irish to portray the HOA as in line with the FWD were an indication of the troubles that lay ahead. The next major intergovernmental draft of a possible agreement was that issued by Mitchell late in the night on Monday 6 April, 3 days before the proposed deadline for an agreement. The contentious aspect of this draft was the Strand 2 section, dealing with proposed North–South bodies. Although Mitchell presented the whole document as his work, the two governments had drafted Strand 2 and he was told he could not alter it. Getting agreement between the two governments over Strand 2 was extremely difficult. The sticking point was the status and powers of the North–South bodies. The issue was a source of major disagreement between the SDLP and the UUP at the talks. Nationalists wanted bodies similar to those proposed in the FWD, essentially freestanding bodies with executive powers that were set up by London and Dublin. Unionists wanted any bodies to be effectively consultative, not executive, created by and accountable to the Northern Ireland Assembly. The fear of each side was that the other would be able to 'pocket' the gains they craved and make the structures that they did not support unworkable. Unionists feared that the North–South bodies could become a united Ireland government in embryo and the Assembly be undermined by nationalist non-participation. Nationalists feared the creation of powerless North–South bodies that could be undermined by being reliant upon a Northern Assembly dominated by Unionists to decide their function and powers (see Hennessey, 2000, pp. 126–139 for a fuller discussion of this point). Attempts to resolve these differences were undertaken by the two prime ministers. These talks began with a meeting between Ahern and Blair in

London on 1 April and continued until Mitchell's distribution of the report to the parties on Monday 6 April. The result was that the Northern Ireland party leaders, Mitchell, himself and Mo Mowlam were effectively 'out of the loop' for several days, a cause of some annoyance to the talks' participants (Mitchell, 1999, p. 153).

The divisions between the two governments over the issue spilled over into the public domain when Ahern told reporters before flying to London that there were 'large disagreements that could not be cloaked . . . I don't know whether we can surmount this' (*The Guardian*, 3 April 1998). Again Ahern invoked the FWD arguing that was 'what had to stand' and asserted, 'My compromises are over' (*The Observer*, 5 April 1998). Ahern was again playing the role as defender of nationalists' interests and also aware that, given that he had only a one seat majority in the Dáil, such a hard-line stance might assuage the concerns of the Republican wing of Fianna Fáil.

The document that emerged from the talks and was incorporated into Mitchell's draft agreement can at one level be seen as a victory for the Irish negotiators. It proposed a North–South Council be created by Westminster and the Dáil before the Assembly was up and running and contained three annexes totalling some 50 areas of cross-border cooperation. This seemed to confirm Unionists' fears that the Irish were pushing for, and Britain had agreed to, the creation of a North–South body with an extensive remit that was freestanding of the Assembly (which only had control over further areas for cross-border co-operation, in addition to the 50 proposed in the document). Even though Trimble had spoken to Blair 'all weekend' and made clear to the Prime Minister what his party's position on Strand 2 was, the British government had agreed to proposals with the Irish government that were unacceptable to Unionists (Godson, 2004, p. 328). Again though care needs to be taken not to overstate the importance of apparent gains by one group during the preliminary negotiation. As was quickly apparent if it was a 'victory' for the Irish it was an insubstantial one.

The outline of the cross-border bodies proposed in the Mitchell draft served only to alienate Unionists from the process and there was a fear that they would walk away if the Irish refused to allow it to be changed. John Taylor told the media that he would not touch it 'with a 40-foot barge pole'. The Irish were in a difficult position. They had negotiated a deal with the British government, which they felt reflected the need for a tangible and significant cross-border dimension to any new agreement. The British had agreed to the draft after several days of negotiations led by the Prime Minister and Taoiseach. Bertie Ahern had publicly stated that his compromises were over and had made plain his position that the cross-border structures needed to be in line with the FWD. The Taoiseach could have reasonably taken the stance, which was indeed urged upon him by some of his own advisors, that the deal had been negotiated in good faith with the British and it was up to the British to sell it to the Unionists (Mitchell, 1999, p. 171). Whilst this may well have been the case the result would have been that there would not have been an agreement. George Mitchell told the British officials when he saw the draft that it had to be renegotiated or the talks were over, according to Mitchell, 'Trimble would never, could never, accept this' (Mitchell, 1999, p. 162).

The inclusion of proposals that were evidently unacceptable to Unionists in the draft could have been a result of a failure by those at No. 10 to appreciate the significance of what they had agreed. The fact that these negotiations had taken place in London rather than at Stormont could have resulted in British officials failing to appreciate the nuances of what they had agreed. Dean Godson suggests that Quentin Thomas believes this played a role noting Thomas argued the episode indicated the dangers of operating outside the talks' structure (Godson, 2004, pp. 326, 335). Thomas himself though suggests that too much should not be made of this as although he was not in London for these discussions he did have 'his people' there (Thomas, 14 September 2005). Alternatively a more Machiavellian explanation offered by the (then) UUP MP Jeffrey Donaldson is that the detailed proposals were included in the full knowledge that they would subsequently be removed, to allow Unionists to claim a subsequent victory. The cock-up alternative to such conspiratorial explanations is that they were the result of a somewhat 'messy' negotiating process that was shaped in part by numerous meetings between Blair and Ahern at which no one else was present, as well as meetings between British and Irish officials. There was an awareness of the need to be seen to be flexible and 'give something' to Ahern that he could use to keep Sinn Féin and his own Republican flank within Fianna Fáil onside (Hennessey, 2000, p. 160). There also appears to have been differences within the Irish side with a suggestion that the annexes were a result of the endeavours of an Irish official who was an 'SDLP zealot' and the unacceptability of what was agreed was appreciated by the wider Irish delegation itself (Godson, 2004, pp. 336–338; Mansergh, 25 January 2006).

The impasse that the Mitchell document had led to persuaded the British and Irish Prime Ministers to go to Belfast and immerse themselves personally in the talks. That the two governments were essentially co-sponsors of the process was illustrated by the fact that Blair would only attend the formal negotiations if the Irish leader was also there (Godson, 2004, p. 329), according the Taoiseach a status that it would have been hard to envisage a few years earlier. At that stage it was far from clear that an agreement was likely or even possible. Yet when Ahern returned to the talks at Stormont after the funeral of his mother on 8 April, Wednesday, he agreed that Strand 2 could be renegotiated. This decision was perceived as a victory for the Unionists. Trimble stated, 'I've just witnessed the ritual humiliation of the Irish Prime Minister' (Godson, 2004, p. 333). This was based upon the belief that Ahern had compromised on the issue because Blair threatened to blame the Irish for the breakdown of the talks if they did not adopt the Unionist model for Strand 2 (Hennessey, 2000, pp. 166–167). Godson himself notes that whilst it may be too strong to talk of ritual humiliation it was 'possibly a clear demonstration of the muscle of the British state in a negotiation with its Irish counterpart' (Godson, 2004, p. 333).

There are though problems with this assertion. Strand 2, as it ultimately emerged in the GFA, is certainly closer to the Unionist ideal than that proposed in the Mitchell document; but it still had aspects that Unionists did not favour, such as being created by Westminster and the Dáil rather than by the Assembly (to which though it was answerable). But such accounts are also over-simplistic as they fail to take account of the wider context and concessions that others gave in return. A marked feature of the negotiations was the need to give a quid for every quo. The Irish pragmatism over Strand 2 meant that it was incumbent upon Unionists to display similar pragmatism in Strand 1. Godson himself notes 'to achieve a reduction in Strand II proposals, Unionists paid a massive price in other areas such as Strand I, the RUC and prisoners' (Godson, 2004, p. 334). To suggest that the Irish were simply faced down on Stand 2 is misleading. Leaving aside the fact that it would have been somewhat difficult for the British to lay all the blame at Dublin's door given that what Unionists objected to was an intergovernmental draft; the negotiations were multi-stranded and multi-faceted. Whilst one party's concessions might have heartened another party they also led to a sense of obligation to reciprocate. The obligation that Unionism owed Dublin for conceding on Strand 2 was met with Unionist movement in Strand 1.

Breakthrough on Strand 1

Strand 2 had not been the only sticking point in the negotiations. The parties' suggestions for the internal government of Northern Ireland were also markedly different. Unionists favoured a committee system drawn from the Assembly with chairs and membership allocated in proportion to party strength in the Assembly, which also had the attraction that it would not force them to sit in a cabinet with Sinn Féin. The SDLP though feared a Unionist-dominated Assembly and insisted upon an institutionalised power-sharing cabinet/executive. A highly visible power-sharing cabinet system would serve to institutionalise 'parity of esteem at the very heart of government' (Hennessey, 2000, p. 123). The UUP eventually agreed to the SDLP type package. They did this for a variety of reasons. They were persuaded that presentationally it made sense to have 'Ministers' in charge of 'Departments' rather than 'Chairs' of 'Committees', as the status of the latter would be less in the eyes of those abroad. But the key issue related to the gains they perceived themselves as having made in meeting their Strand 2 objectives. As the UUP negotiator Reg Empey argued, 'We can't push the SDLP to the limit. We'd then be doing to them what the SDLP and the Irish and Whitelaw did to Faulkner [at Sunningdale in 1973]' (Godson, 2004, pp. 338–339).

Another reason that it was possible to get agreement between the SDLP and the UUP over Strand 1 was that Sinn Féin played no effective part in the Strand 1 talks. Sinn Féin's position was that they would not support an Assembly as this represented a partitionist structure. According to Hume,

> new beginnings suggested by the three stranded agenda necessarily includes new institutions in the North as well as well as North–South institutions. The latter cannot be created without the former. A North–South Council could

not exist without new institutions in the North [from] which its Northern membership could be drawn. By suggesting otherwise Sinn Féin is being deliberately obstructive or is failing to face reality.

(Hennessey, 2000, p. 120)

The reality was that if a deal was going to be done it would have to reflect Unionist concerns regarding the North–South council and Nationalist concerns regarding devolved government in Northern Ireland. Sinn Féin's assertions that they were seeking a maximalist cross-border settlement as a step towards a united Ireland, but would not countenance a partitionist structure, was never a realistic option and this was 'a tactical position which they later simply dropped' (Mallie and McKittrick, 2001, p. 266).

'Enter' Sinn Féin

Sinn Féin were unhappy with the proposed Strand 1 and Strand 2 structures, which proposed a North–South body that had less powers than had been laid out in the FWD or the Mitchell draft, and the creation of the 'partitionist' structure in the North. What then did Sinn Féin gain at Castle Buildings that was adequate to persuade them to ultimately back the deal? Much of the negotiation of Strand 1 had been conducted by the UUP and SDLP; Strand 2 by the Irish and the British governments during the construction of the Mitchell draft, and the Irish and the UUP in its subsequent reformulation. Whilst it was the case that the Irish were concerned to negotiate a model that would be acceptable to both the SDLP and the Sinn Féin in Strand 2 talks, Sinn Féin seemed to have played very little part in the negotiations. Any suspicions that Sinn Féin would be the dog that did not bark at the talks were though laid to rest in the early hours of Good Friday morning. Sinn Féin produced a list of 78 points that required clarification, a move that prompted Tony Blair to observe, 'Ah for Jesus' sake . . . this is impossible' (Godson, 2004, p. 347). The Irish delegation worked on the points that Sinn Féin raised and Ahern went through them 'for hours on end' with Adams and McGuinness (Mallie and McKittrick, 2001, p. 272). Of particular concern to Republicans were the issue of prisoners and decommissioning. Sinn Féin's stance was that the prisoners should be released as soon as possible and that decommissioning should not be a barrier to their taking seats in government. As a result of negotiations the British reduced their original plan for a 3-year period for prisoner releases to two. Attempts by Sinn Féin to persuade the two parties associated with Loyalist paramilitaries, the PUP and UDP, to adopt a common stance to push for release of prisoners in a year failed when the Loyalists refused to co-operate (Mallie and McKittrick, 2001, pp. 273–275). Blair enlisted the support of President Clinton on this issue asking him to phone Adams to attempt to persuade him to agree to the 2-year deal.

The issue of decommissioning which had so bedevilled the peace process in the 1994–97 period had been marginalised during the talks themselves as a result of the creation of the independent commission to consider the issue.

It re-emerged, however, in the final days and almost wrecked the chances of agreement. The Unionists were perhaps not as concerned about decommissioning and even the creation of compulsory power-sharing as one might have expected during the talks for the reason that they did not really expect Sinn Féin to agree to what was being proposed. As Trimble later argued, as late as Good Friday itself, he believed 'there was a fair probability that Sinn Féin would reject the Agreement . . . ' (Millar, 2004, p. 67) and as a result the UUP did not necessarily believe that they were signing up to a deal that would inevitably lead them to sit in government with Sinn Féin.

Unionists also believed that they had a commitment from Blair at Chequers 2 weeks before Good Friday that there would be an explicit linkage in any agreement between decommissioning and office-holding (and indeed that the British favoured a committee system rather than a cabinet one) (Godson, 2004, p. 325). Yet when the final draft of the proposed agreement was circulated the linkage between the two was absent. The reason for this was Sinn Féin's unwillingness to agree to what Trimble believed he had settled with Tony Blair. The relevant wording in the GFA stated that all participants,

> reaffirm their commitment to the total disarmament of all paramilitary organizations. They also confirm their intention to continue to work constructively and in good faith with the Independent Commission, and to use any influence they may have, to achieve the decommissioning of all paramilitary arms within two years following endorsement in referendums North and South of the agreement and in the context of the implementation of the overall settlement.

When the Unionists saw the wording in the draft they were horrified and came very close to walking away from the negotiations.

The issue of the impact of how decommissioning was dealt with during the negotiations raises several interesting questions. Why was the link between decommissioning and office not in the agreement? Why did Blair apparently renege on the undertaking he had given Trimble and Donaldson? Why did the Unionists not walk away? And what exactly did the GFA commit the parties to regarding decommission? (A question that led to continuous disagreements and crises in the peace process for years to come.) The first question is perhaps the easiest to deal with. Decommissioning was not made a pre-requisite for office-holding as this was seen as a 'deal breaker' for Sinn Féin. Given that the basis of the peace process was to effectively entice the IRA away from violence, both governments were sensitive to Sinn Féin's demands on this issue. This sensitivity to Sinn Féin and the desire not to take action that might cause them to reject the agreement, and ultimately potentially endanger the ceasefires, also goes some way to answering the second question. Whilst the British and the Irish governments acknowledged that decommissioning was a necessary part of the process there may have been a failure by the British government to appreciate the problems linking the issues of decommissioning to office-holding would cause.

When the difficulties became apparent in the final hours of the negotiations the British may simply have dropped the commitment that Trimble believed he had secured from Blair two weeks before. The problem from a Unionist perspective was they left Chequers with the belief that Blair had agreed to back their demands that decommissioning and office holding be linked. By the time it became clear to the Unionists that the link was missing it was argued by the British that it was too late to alter the draft as it was 'impossible to start unpicking one corner of the agreement without unravelling the whole tapestry' (Rawnsley, 2001, p. 137).

Although the failure of the British to insist upon an explicit link between decommissioning and office holding can be seen as understandable pragmatism given the opposition that Sinn Féin displayed to such a link, others see it in more Machiavellian terms. Trimble himself recognised the possibility that Blair duped him and Donaldson in order to keep them involved in the talks to an extent that it would be more difficult for them to walk away at the last moment and risk the wrath of world opinion. Speaking several years later, Trimble still seemed unsure about the motivations behind the apparent changes between Chequers and Belfast. 'Did Blair sucker us? I don't know, he may very well have been genuine both at Chequers and in the last week' (Millar, 2004, pp. 69–70). Whatever the motivations, given that this was seen as a key issue for the UUP why did they not walk away when the British refused to alter the draft to reflect their demands? Although keeping Sinn Féin onboard was a priority for the British and Irish governments, they could not afford to lose the UUP. If the UUP had walked, then agreement would have been impossible, so in that regard their power was the same as Sinn Féin's. Three things prevented the UUP from bringing down the talks over the decommissioning issue; a belief that Sinn Féin was unlikely to sign up to the GFA, the fear that they would be blamed for the lack of an agreement and, most importantly, the side letter that Tony Blair gave to Trimble on the decommissioning issue. According to Reg Empey the UUP were 5 minutes from walking out when an NIO official gave them Blair's letter (*The Observer*, 12 April 1998). The letter stated that, 'In our view the effect of the decommissioning section of the agreement, with decommissioning schemes coming into effect in June [1998], is that the process of decommissioning should begin straight away.' Trimble claimed this effectively meant that there was an obligation on the IRA to begin decommissioning. As Trimble was told by the British that devolution of power was unlikely to occur before February 1999, he envisaged that the interim period could be used to sort the issue out. It is clear the assurances that Trimble believed he had been given by Blair in the letter were enough, along with the fear of the world blaming the UUP for failing to secure an agreement, to get the UUP to sign up to the GFA (Millar, 2004, pp. 71–76).

Whilst the side letter that Blair gave to Trimble was sufficient to persuade his party to back the deal, it introduced further ambiguity into the decommissioning question. There were two documents relating to decommissioning at the end of the process. The section in the agreement itself seemed to commit all parties to use any influence they had to bring about decommissioning within 2 years. The Prime Minister's letter seemed to suggest that decommissioning must begin immediately. The problem was that different parties focused on different documents to justify the interpretation of the issue they favoured. Sinn Féin pointed to the wording of the GFA to back their claim that decommissioning was not a prerequisite for their entry into office; the UUP invoked Blair's letter to support their subsequent claims that government could not be created in Northern Ireland until there was decommissioning. As the political commentator Jonathan Freedland observed of the letter, 'By that action, Tony Blair may well have made the Good Friday Agreement possible. But with that same gesture he may also have fatally undermined it. For he enabled both sides to agree to different things' (*The Guardian*, 31 March 1999).

Whatever problems and divisions were to occur as a result of the ambiguity surrounding decommissioning the move did indeed make the GFA possible. The two governments had succeeded in effectively co-sponsoring negotiations that led to an agreement that was widely seen as likely to end the conflict in Ireland. It was an incredible achievement.

Implementing the GFA

The two governments and the pro-agreement parties worked hard to convince the people to endorse the deal in simultaneous referenda North and South on 22 May and the people of the South to ratify the amendment of articles 2 and 3 of the Irish constitution.

The doubts that many Unionists had over the agreement did not prevent the deal being approved. Blair himself though acknowledged that the decision to back the GFA had been a difficult one for many when he stated, 'The people of Northern Ireland have shown courage and vision. I know some have voted with deep misgivings. I accept my duty to answer those misgivings' (*The Observer*, 24 May 1998). The cause of this concern was polling which suggested that whilst up to 99 per cent of Catholics had voted in favour of the GFA the protestant community was very divided on the issue with the DUP claiming that a majority had voted against it and Trimble claiming that a narrow majority had backed the deal. The problem for pro-agreement Unionists was that protestant support for the GFA would continue to decline over the coming years ultimately leading to a sea-change in Unionist politics. Ian Paisley and the DUP were widely portrayed as politically irrelevant at the time of the GFA conclusion. According to Ronan Fanning, 'poor Dr Paisley, he resembles nothing so much as a beached whale, a once fearsome Moby Dick who now excites only pity as he thrashes about in the shallows' (*Sunday Independent*, 24 May 1998). Yet by 2003, Paisley would, for the first time, be leader of the largest Unionist party in Northern Ireland and see his UUP opponents hold only a single Westminster seat to the DUP's 9 by 2005.

The reason for the continuing decline in Unionists support for the GFA lay in the ambiguity within the agreement itself and the related implementation problems that stemmed from this ambiguity. The model that had been agreed by the parties was one of all-party power-sharing government, but the issues that had proved so difficult in getting that agreement, particularly decommissioning, had not been resolved at the talks. The 'fudge' on decommissioning along with the creativity in postponing hard decisions on issues, such as policing and the exact composition of North–South bodies, allowed the parties to reach agreement. However, such issues could not be postponed indefinitely and Unionists in particular were unwilling to see the creation of the proposed Executive until the practicalities of these issues had been addressed. Much of the focus of the two governments after 1998 was on seeking to persuade and cajole one or other side to make the first/next move that it was hoped would break the numerous logjams that occurred. Yet very often the two governments could not agree on what that move should be, or who should make it.

Decommissioning (again)

The issue of decommissioning continued to bedvil the peace process after the signing of the GFA. The two governments took the lead in attempts to resolve the dispute. There were two possible ways that the issue could be resolved, or at least made less of an obstacle: the IRA could begin decommissioning, or the Unionists could agree to enter government before this happened. The approach of the two governments was to seek to bring about either of these outcomes. The initial attempts focused on the first option. In January 1999, Blair argued, decommissioning had to take place because 'people have to know if they are sitting down [in the Executive] with people who have given up violence for good' (quoted in Bew and Gillespie, 1999, p. 389). In February, Ahern argued that, 'being part of a government, or part of an executive, [is not possible] without at least a commencement of decommissioning' (*Sunday Times*, 14 February 1999).

In April the governments published the 'Hillsborough Declaration', which attempted to choreograph movement from the two sides. The scheme would have seen the institutions created but power would not have been devolved until the IRA had begun decommissioning. Trimble claimed it had 'the potential to resolve satisfactorily the problems we have encountered' (*The Times*, 2 April 1999). However, Sinn Féin rejected the proposals, apparently due to the reaction from grassroot Republicans (*The Guardian*, 14 April 1999; Godson, 2004, pp. 418–419).

As a result the focus of the two governments changed. In May the governments proposed a plan under which there would be no actual decommissioning before power was devolved, just the assertion by the head of the Decommissioning Body, General John de Chastelain, that progress was being made. Although it originally appeared that Trimble would agree to the proposals he was unable to persuade his fellow UUP MLAs to back the proposals (Godson, 2004, pp. 420–424). In response to the failure to achieve a breakthrough, Blair announced an 'absolute deadline' of 30 June by which time progress was to be made.

The tactic of setting an absolute deadline was one that was periodically employed by the two governments. It is though a highly risky tactic and one that was on occasions invoked too lightly. The deadline set for the completion of the all-party talks that led to the GFA in April 1998 did indeed serve to bring about a sense of urgency, not least because it was feasible that the whole process would break down without agreement and George Mitchell might depart. But once the GFA was signed the imposition of a deadline was a far harder tool to use strategically or successfully. Speaking in mid-June 1999, Blair suggested that he was becoming frustrated by the lack of progress. 'Politicians in Northern Ireland need to take responsibility for this process – It is no good saying they will leave it to the two Governments.' He stressed that he wanted 'people to understand that I am serious about this deadline. Either on 1 July we move this process forward or we will have to look for another way forward.' The problem is such a threat only works if it is perceived as credible. In the very same speech the Prime Minister had announced, 'The Good Friday Agreement is the one chance Northern Ireland has got. I know it. You know it' (Speech at Stranmillis College, 15 June 1999). As a result what was the possible alternative 'way forward'? The constant assertion that there was no alternative to the GFA, no plan B, meant that when deadlines passed little seemed to change. As Mo Mowlam noted, 'We kept setting deadlines to try and concentrate minds and make progress. But there was a growing feeling, as each one passed without agreement, that people were losing faith in them' (Mowlam, 2002, p. 297).

The governments subsequently changed tack and sought primarily to pressure the UUP to change its position. On 3 July, Ahern argued it was only possible to get decommissioning 'in the context of a confidence in functioning demo-cratic institutions' (*Irish Times*, 3 June 1999). As the deadline arrived Sinn Féin announced that against the background of functioning institutions, 'we believe that all of us, as participants acting in good faith, could succeed in persuading those with arms to decommission them in accordance with the agreement'. This was obviously not a commitment to decommission but it was seized upon by Tony Blair as indication of 'historic seismic shifts in the political landscape of Northern Ireland' (quoted in Hauswedell and Brown, 2000, p. 36). Two days after the 30 June deadline had been and gone with no apparent breakthrough an IICD report asserted that Sinn Féin's statement gave 'the basis for believing that decommissioning can be completed in the time prescribed by the Good Friday Agreement'.

The governments used this pronouncement to launch another proposal, *The Way Forward*, on 2 July. This plan was similar to that proposed in May in that it did not propose that decommissioning began before devolution. The govern-ments sought to reassure Unionists by the proposals for a decommissioning timetable and a pledge that if the IRA did not make progress towards decom-missioning the institutions would be suspended. This though was not seen as much of a reassurance by Unionists, not least because they felt this scenario to be inequitable. Unionists believed that suspension of the institutions punished all rather than simply those at fault and wanted an undertaking that if the IRA failed to decommission it would be Sinn Féin that were excluded from the insti-tutions, rather than the institutions that were suspended. The SDLP and the Irish government refused to agree to such an approach, which was seen as attempting to rewrite the GFA. Blair put great pressure on the UUP stating, the 'alternative to this agreement is not decommissioning faster or on different terms, it is no decommissioning at all: ever'. It would give 'Sinn Féin the massive propaganda victory of being able to say: we were never even given the chance to get decommissioning but excluded from the Executive. The blame would fall on Unionists. It would be a tactical own goal of monumental proportions' that would 'hand the whole high ground to the anti-Unionist cause' (*Sunday Times*, 4 July 1999). Ahern argued rejection would lead many to conclude decommissioning had just been used by Unionists 'all along as a plausible excuse for procrastination and exclusion, and that the real difficulty was the principle of inclusive government agreed to on Good Friday . . . ' (*Irish Times*, 13 July 1999). The pressure was not enough to force the UUP to alter its stance though and they stayed away from the Assembly meeting on 15 July (the 'new' deadline for progress) leading to the resignation of Seamus Mallon as First Minister. The governments then put the process into 'review' until the autumn.

The attempts by the two governments in 1999 to overcome the decommissioning logjam were undoubtedly energetic and creative, with Blair apparently spending 40 per cent of his time on the issue (Godson, 2004, p. 499). They were not, however, successful. Neither government saw decommissioning in moral terms, which was how the Unionists sought to portray it, nor as an unfounded precondition to deny Sinn Féin its electorally mandated right, as Republicans sought to portray it. Sinn Féin resisted early pressure to decommission any weapons and so pragmatism dictated that pressure be applied elsewhere. Trimble summed up the governments' approach well complaining, 'They had been spending months trying to push Republicans . . . . It hadn't succeeded. So they said, "Oh well, we can't move them, let's turn around and see if we can move the other people" ' (*Sunday Telegraph*, 18 July 1999). But again to no avail. The deadlines came and went, and the new approach to find a way forward was to review the old approach of trying to implement the GFA.

Given the evident failure to achieve a breakthrough many began to believe that the chances of progress were negligible. As the governments announced that there would be a review, the BBC's Northern Ireland editor, Stephen Grimason, observed, 'The wheel is still turning, but the hamster is dead' (quoted in *The Sunday Times*, 18 July 1999). Yet a breakthrough was achieved along the lines envisaged in *The Way Forward*. What is interesting about the review process that led to the breakthrough from an intergovernmental perspective is that it had very little direct input from the two governments. Mitchell returned to conduct the review and although the governments provided support for it, they did not participate directly in the discussions or seek to dictate the progress. In this regard, Northern Ireland politicians took 'responsibility' to a greater extent. What seems to have been a key factor in making progress was that an element of trust emerged between the UUP and the Sinn Féin during the almost 300 hours of direct negotiation during the review, much of it conducted by Mitchell with no officials present (*Independent on Sunday*, 21 November 1999). On 15 November a carefully choreographed process began. Trimble announced he was willing to sit in an Executive with Sinn Féin, and Sinn Féin accepted that 'decommissioning is an essential part of the process' but one that 'can only come about on a voluntary basis'. On the 18 November the IRA issued a statement that it was 'committed unequivocally to the search for freedom, justice and peace in Ireland', confirmed the appointment of 'a representative to enter into discussions with Gen John de Chastelain' and described the GFA as 'a significant development' (*Irish Times*, 19 November 1999).

Substantially what was agreed was not really any different to that which the two governments pressured Trimble so hard to accept 5 months earlier. There were differences though in process and authorship. The plan was a result of the actions of Adams and McGuinness and was followed by an IRA statement, whereas Ahern and Blair had put the previous one together. Trimble did not argue that the statements committed the IRA to decommissioning (plainly it did not) but seems to have believed that it set in train a chain of events that would force them to do so (*Daily Telegraph*, 19 November 1999). Trimble confirmed he had 'reluctantly accepted that it was not possible to persuade the IRA to lay down its arms prior to setting up an Executive, nor even to do so on the same day' (*The Times*, 24 November 1999). Given this assessment a failure to move by the UUP would have meant no further progress towards devolved government was possible and the GFA could not be implemented. Trimble claimed it represented 'a change of tactics, but one that enables [the UUP] to deliver decommissioning and devolution as we promised' (*Daily Telegraph*, 26 November 1999). They were aided in this by a commitment from the new Secretary of State, Peter Mandelson, who had replaced Unionism's *bete noire*, Mo Mowlam, in October, to collapse the institutions if the IRA failed to deliver. Mandelson stressed the intergovernmental aspect of this commitment when he stated, 'We and the Irish Government will act together, without delay, to suspend the institutions' (Victoria College, Belfast, 25 November 1999). What was unacceptable in July had become acceptable in November, in almost the exact form. The deadlock over decommissioning had largely been broken by persuading the Unionists to 'jump first'.

The last hurdle was overcome when Trimble managed to secure the backing of the party's Ulster Unionist Council, not least as a result of his post-dated letter of resignation, which would be activated in February 2000 if progress had not been made on decommissioning.

Power was devolved to the new Assembly on the 2 December 1999, when the AIA lapsed as the new British–Irish Agreement came into force, articles 2 and 3 were changed and the North–South bodies created. All of which led the former Taoiseach, Reynolds, to write in the *Irish Times* that the date 'will feature prominently in future history books of Ireland and Britain. It will be remembered as the day the conflict ended' (*Irish Times*, 2 December 1999). However, the failure of the IRA to begin decommissioning once power was devolved meant that devolution was brief. The two governments rejected IRA claims that the UUP's deadline of February was an attempt 'to set preconditions on further political progress (that) was not part of this understanding' (*BBC News Online*, 6 January 2000). Ahern noted that the deadline had made things more difficult but saw decommissioning as necessary. 'If there is no decommissioning, it is my view with certainty that the entire thing will fall apart. Whatever happens after that is another question.' Ahern argued that the agreement of the UUP to enter into government with Sinn Féin negated Republican arguments over decommissioning. 'The position is that they are now in a power-sharing executive, the old arguments about surrender are not relevant. . . . How could you say that an organization has surrendered by decommissioning when they already have two senior members inside the cabinet directing policy?' (*Irish Examiner*, 13 January 2000).

Matters were brought to a head by a pessimistic report from the IICD on 31 January. The Commission stated 'we have received no information from the IRA as to when decommissioning will start' and warned that the time was approaching 'beyond which it will be logistically impossible for us to complete our task by 22 May'. Mandelson suspended the institutions on the grounds that the alternative, the collapse of the institutions as a result of the withdrawal of the Unionists, was worse. It is notable that Mandelson stressed to the House that the two governments were united on this and quoted at length comments by Ahern from November 1999 to indicate the Taoiseach's commitment to suspension if decommissioning did not occur. The perceived need by the British to stress a common stance with Dublin over suspension is interesting. Legally speaking it was the British and not the Irish who implemented the suspension, and London did not need Dublin's agreement to do so. The Irish appeared to offer 'very reluctant' support to the British suspension. As a government spokesperson explained,

> we know Trimble can't move anymore, but the suspension creates some more space for the IRA to change position. But the Irish government knows we can't ignore the issue anymore. Whether we like it or not in the Unionist mentality only a start to decommission is the real signal that the IRA's war is over for good. That means there must be decommissioning, that's the Irish position.
>
> (*The Observer*, 6 February 2000)

The mood was hardening towards the IRA in both Britain and Ireland at this stage. The Unionists had gained credit for 'jumping first' and even the SDLP were openly calling for the IRA to move. Writing in the *Washington Times*, Seamus Mallon praised Trimble's decision to jump first and argued that Republicans 'have hidden behind concepts of "seismic shifts" in their attitudes to arms decommissioning and their own interpretation of "jumping together". The time for such rules and strategems is over – we need clarity' (though he argued against the 'collapsing' the institutions) (*Washington Times*, 8 February 2000). A new form of words offered from the IRA on 11 February was not enough to prevent the suspension and served only to strain intergovernmental relations when Dublin urged London to delay the suspension (*Irish Times*, 14 February 2000). (This dispute became public in May when a leaked British memo criticised the Irish Minister of Foreign Affairs, Brian Cowen, claiming he believed 'beyond the constitutional acceptance that Northern Ireland remain part of the UK, there should be no further evidence of Britishness in the governance of Northern Ireland'. A view he 'presented with all the subtlety and open-mindedness that one would expect from a member of Sinn Féin'. Mandelson apparently believed 'that Cowen has no feel for, or understanding of, Unionist concerns, and can usually be reliably counted on to tack to the green at every opportunity' (*The Independent*, 5 May 2000). Despite attempts to limit the damage London continued to believe that Cowen had failed to exert sufficient pressure on Sinn Féin (*The Guardian*, 4 July 2000).)

Why did the IRA fail to decommission by the end of January and why did others appear to believe they would? These two issues are closely linked. The most persuasive answer to both lies in the explanation that perhaps the IRA never intended to decommission by the end of January but equally never believed that Britain would act upon its apparent commitment to suspend a functioning Executive during a continuing ceasefire as a result of the absence of decommissioning. So Republicans went along with the process that led to Unionists jumping, without giving a commitment to decommission. Other parties took Republicans' lack of clarity on the issue not as a signal that they would not decommission but as an indication that they were likely to do so. When the IRA proved resistant to pressure it became clear that both camps had misinterpreted the other's positions and the first brief foray into devolved government came to an abrupt end. As Frank Millar noted as the recriminations flew between London and Dublin, 'perhaps the real angst behind the apparent confusion is the painful awareness that the biggest failure of all may have been to understand where the Republicans were coming from on the issue of decommissioning' (*Irish Times*, 19 February 2000).

Whatever the underlying cause of the problems that manifested themselves in February 2000 the IRA's last minute statement served primarily to cause a rift between London and Dublin and illustrate again the conditional nature of the united front between the two governments on how best to advance the peace process.

The dispute over policing

Whilst decommissioning remained the major cause of stalemate in the process, several other issues became obstacles to creating sustainable devolution. These were grouped under the headings: policing; stability of the institutions; security normalisation and decommissioning. However, these were inter-linked and decommissioning never lost its centrality. Security normalisation referred to what was also known as demilitarisation, and primarily focused upon the dismantling of military observation posts and bases in Republican areas of Northern Ireland. This was a matter that could only be addressed by the British government.

The British line was that these were simply a result of the security situation in Northern Ireland and when that improved they would no longer be necessary. The stability of the institutions was linked to the claim by Sinn Féin, the SDLP and less directly the Irish government, that it was not acceptable that the new institutions in Northern Ireland could be brought down by Unionist boycotts and threats or by unilateral action by the British in response to such threats. Again though this can be linked to decommissioning, the Unionists' actions in this respect was related on each occasion to the failure of the IRA to decommission. Policing though was a more substantive issue.

The GFA had stipulated an 'independent Commission will be established to make recommendations for future policing arrangements in Northern Ireland, including means of encouraging widespread community support for these arrangements . . .'. Chris Patten, who had been an NIO minister in the 1980s, headed the Commission. *A New Beginning: Policing in Northern Ireland*, known as the Patten report, was published in September 1999. The Report was a substantial document, running to over 130 pages, and contained 175 specific proposals, some of which were highly contentious for Unionism. Unionist objection to Patten centred around the symbolic changes that were proposed, notably the changing of the RUC's name (although the Report claimed that the 'RUC should not be disbanded') and badge; the stipulation that the Union flag should no longer be flown from police stations; and a variety of further measures to ensure that the new Northern Ireland Police Service's symbols should be 'free from associations with the British or Irish states'. The Report also recommended the creation of a new policing board and reduction of the size of the force to 7500 (from the then 13,500). The composition of the force was also to be fundamentally altered by a stipulation that new recruits should be drawn on a 50/50 basis from the two communities, to offset the overwhelmingly Protestant nature of the existing RUC. The Elements of Unionism were furious at what they took as a slur on the RUC and angered by the move to remove the 'Britishness' of the force. The move further undermined Unionist support for the peace process, and was portrayed by the DUP as a direct consequence of the UUP supported GFA. This interpretation was somewhat endorsed by Patten's reaction to Trimble's attacks on the Report, 'What on earth did they think they were signing up to?' (Godson, 2004, p. 472). A rearguard action to try and prevent the government implementing sections of the Report, notably around the name and badge changes, was largely ineffective. Mandelson announced in January 2000 that almost all of the recommendations were being adopted. In March 2000 the UUC voted to make the retention of the RUC title a pre-condition for involvement in future devolved government, a stance that was not carried through. Nationalists quickly viewed the Report as the minimum acceptable reforms, and although Sinn Féin were cool towards it at the outset, Dublin pressurised London to ensure that it was implemented, and, in particular, there was no move towards allowing the RUC title to be retained in any form. Pressure also came from America on the issue with the House of Representatives unanimously passing a resolution calling upon the British to 'fully and faithfully' implement the Patten Report. The US Vice President and Democratic Party Presidential candidate, Al Gore, also issued a statement urging Britain 'to fully and expeditiously implement these recommendations' (*Irish Times*, 28 September 2000). Although aspects of policing remained a divisive issue in the peace process, Unionism effectively 'lost' the battle. As Christopher Farrington argues, Patten 'seemed to represent a significant defeat for Unionists; with no accompanying pay-off . . . ' (Farrington, 2006, p. 158). Although the issue was a highly emotive one for Unionism, it was never one over which Trimble was willing to risk the wider peace process. Although he reacted angrily to the Report and believed (erroneously) that the British government would water it down, he 'never threatened to bolt over Patten'. Largely this was because his primary objective was 'the return of accountable Government to the Province', and he would not risk this objective to prevent Patten (Godson, 2004, pp. 490–493).

An IRA statement on the 6 May that, in the context of 'the full implementation' by the two governments 'of what they have agreed', the IRA would, 'initiate a process that will completely and verifiably put IRA arms beyond use', provided Trimble with the opportunity to fulfil his objective. According to Trimble it meant 'that the IRA campaign is finally over' (*Sunday Times*, 21 May 2000). Whilst Trimble insisted that decommissioning must still happen, he used the statement as the basis to persuade the UUC to agree to re-enter government.

Unionism's deteriorating opinion of the GFA

Despite the restoration of devolved government in May 2000 the change of attitude within Unionism towards the GFA was posing problems for the peace process. The failure to secure decommissioning, unease over police reform and the perception amongst elements of the majority community that the GFA was not delivering what they had been led to believe it would eroded support for the GFA amongst that community. In 1999, 59 per cent of Protestants believed nationalists had benefited a 'little' or 'a lot' more than Unionists. By 2001 this had risen to 63 per cent (and only 35 per cent of Protestants stated they would vote for the GFA if a vote was held 'today') (*Life and Times Survey*, http://www.ark.ac.uk/nilt/). The two governments at times appeared to have different attitudes to what, if any, actions they should take to attempt to shore up Trimble and the UUP. The ghost of Sunningdale continued to haunt the process and a British official asserted, 'Let's not repeat the mistakes of Sunningdale. We cannot afford to lose moderate Unionism and any who think we can are fooling themselves' (*Irish Times*, 26 September 2000). This was to be a major theme over the coming years (arguably right up until moderate Unionism was 'lost'). The problem was how could moderate Unionism be assuaged and the appeal of rejectionist Unionism reduced? Or indeed was it already too late by that stage as elements of the SDLP and Sinn Féin were apparently advising Dublin (*Irish Times*, 27 September 2000). A key development would have been to secure decommissioning, but this was plainly not in the gift of either government.

Alternatively a move on the policing reforms that addressed some of Unionism's concerns might have helped stabilise Unionist support for the agreement. This, however, was not a step that nationalists would countenance and, as a result, nor would Dublin. The result was that all that could really be done was to continue to try and secure decommissioning, stress the benefits that Unionism had gained from the GFA or threaten Unionism with the spectre of an increased role for Dublin if the GFA collapsed, as Mandelson appeared to do on occasion. None of this succeeded in placating Unionists. Nor indeed did Trimble's refusal to nominate Sinn Féin members to meetings of the NSMC (a move that was opposed by both governments) or his announcement in May 2001 that he would resign as First Minister if the IRA did not act on decommissioning by 1 July. In the General election of 7 June 2001 the UUP lost 3 seats and the DUP gained 3 to take them to within one seat of the UUP. Sinn Féin was far from punished for the IRA's failure to decommission, gaining 2 seats and overtaking the SDLP in both seats at Westminster and numbers of votes polled for the first time.

There was some disquiet in Dublin and London at the highly visible decline in the appeal of pro-agreement Unionism and increased support for the party linked to the IRA. Reporting to the Dáil after an intergovernmental meeting with the leaders of the UUP, Sinn Féin and the SDLP, Ahern's tone was pessimistic and he acknowledged that the elections had put the process back. He noted that as a result of the poll, 'people's positions on all sides have polarised.' Ahern had assumed 'that we would pick up matters after the election and proceed from there' but he admitted that was 'wishful thinking'. He acknowledged the difficult position that Trimble was in and that his hands were 'tied in the absence of some stated progress on decommissioning'. He sought to put pressure on Sinn Féin noting that they were the ones who 'gained in the election' and were 'the only ones with a role when it comes to decommissioning'. Ahern noted that there were issues of concern for nationalists regarding policing and demilitarisation but again stressed decommissioning, 'if we do not get progress on decommissioning, I cannot see us being able to get progress on other issues' (Dáil Éireann, vol. 583, cols. 475–477, 19 June 2001).

The two governments were forced to deal with another crisis in the process when Trimble carried out his threat to resign at the start of July. The then NISS, John Reid (who had replaced Mandelson in January 2001), twice invoked a procedural device implementing a 24-hour suspension of the institutions in order to secure a further 6 weeks each time to attempt to restore the Executive and avoid having to collapse devolution or call new Assembly elections. In August the governments produced a 'final', 'non-negotiable' package (*The Independent*, 15 July 2001; *Irish Times*, 16 July 2001), 'Proposals for the Implementation of the Good Friday Agreement'. A good deal of the package was aimed at appealing to Republicans, notably in the areas of demilitarisation with proposals to demolish security bases if the terrorist threat was reduced and an undertaking not to pursue 'on the runs' ('supporters of organizations now on ceasefire against whom there are outstanding prosecutions'). But it stated that decommissioning was 'indispensable' and 'must be resolved in a manner acceptable to the decommissioning body'. A few days later the IICD reported that the IRA had proposed 'a method for putting IRA arms completely and verifiably beyond use' and the Commission believed 'that this proposal initiates a process that will put IRA arms completely and verifiably beyond use'. Although this move was widely welcomed by the two governments and in the media, it was not enough to persuade the UUP back into government. According to Trimble, this move was a 'step by Republicans but it falls far short of what we need which is to see the decommissioning actually begin' (*The Guardian*, 8 August 2001). The IRA subsequently withdrew the offer.

Yet 2 months later the IRA finally carried out an act of decommissioning. This was widely seen not as a result of actions by the governments or Unionists but was, at least in part, influenced by two unanticipated events: the arrest of three men in Colombia and the September 11 attacks in America. The arrest of three suspected IRA men in Colombia in mid-August 2001 and the suspicion that they had been involved in training FARC guerrillas was a cause of concern for the Bush administration. In October the newly appointed Head of Counter-Terrorism in the United States, Francis Taylor, described the IRA as a 'threat to Americans' (*Irish Independent*, 21 October 2001). Bush's advisor on Northern Ireland, Richard Haass, had told Adams 'If any American, service personnel or civilian, is killed in Colombia by the technology the IRA supplied then you can fuck off' (*The Observer*, 28 October 2001). This meeting coincidentally took place on the day that the attacks on the Twin Towers and Pentagon occurred. The resulting 'war on terrorism' that Bush launched after September 11 changed the climate. As Reid argued, 'after the terrible events in Washington and New York there is a colder wind blowing and a growing intolerance of terrorism' (*Irish Times*, 20 September 2001). The announcement on 22 October that the IRA had carried out an act of decommissioning was widely linked to the pressure from the United States, who had threatened to remove visa and fundraising rights if no decommissioning occurred (*The Observer*, 28 October 2001).

Some caution is needed, however, when evaluating the impact of US pressure on securing decommissioning. The IRA had withstood periods of concerted pressure to decommission before and it is unlikely that the intensification of criticism in the United States after Colombia and the wider war on terror after September 11 alone were enough to secure decommissioning. The importance of these events is more likely to be that they caused the IRA to accelerate a process they were already embarked upon. Ed Moloney made this point persuasively in an article entitled, 'Decommissioning was always going to happen'. Moloney examined the careful language that the IRA had used on decommissioning throughout the peace process and concluded

It grew into a slow but boring strip tease in which the name of the game became about the Provos extracting an extra dollar bill for every piece of flesh that was exposed. But in the end, once the dollar bills dried up, the veil had to fall . . . . The only impact Colombia and September 11th had was to cause decommissioning to happen a lot faster than otherwise might have been the case. But it was always going to happen.

(*Sunday Tribune*, 28 October 2001)

The 'dollar bills' that the IRA attempted to extract were not just the pecuniary kind but also an attempt to use decommissioning as a powerful bargaining chip to secure concessions from the other participants in the process. At some stage the IRA had to decommission if the process was to continue. By October 2001 the process was in crisis, institutions suspended with little prospect that Unionists would 'jump first' again. The act of decommissioning persuaded the UUP to return to government and went some way to reduce pressure on Republicans not only from the United States but also from London and Dublin. This is not to suggest though that the IRA could necessarily have delivered decommissioning at any time it chose, it would appear for a time at least, as Anthony McIntyre suggested, that the rank and file of the IRA acted as a brake on the leadership on the issue (*Sunday Tribune*, 14 November 1999). But the logic of the process was at some point decommissioning would have to either be delivered or dropped as a demand by Unionists. The UUP's withdrawal from government had demonstrated that they were unwilling to drop it (and the June election demonstrated the price that would be paid by Unionists seen as too accommodating to the IRA on the issue). So Moloney's assertion that it was always going to happen, although far from evident before the act occurred, has logic to it.

The restoration of devolved government was, however, to be brief. By September 2002, Trimble was warning that his party would again withdraw from government on 18 January 2003 if the IRA did not demonstrate that they were committed to peace. However, the Assembly would not last that long and was suspended following a police raid on Sinn Féin's offices at Stormont amid allegations that Republicans were operating a spy ring. This crisis provoked one of the toughest speeches from Tony Blair aimed at the IRA. In October he told a Belfast audience, 'The fork in the road has finally come . . . we cannot carry on with the IRA half in, half out of this process. Not just because it isn't right any more. It won't work anymore.' Blair claimed 'the continuing existence of the IRA as an active paramilitary organization is now the best card those whom Republicans call 'rejectionist' Unionists, have in their hand' as it justified 'their refusal to share power; it embarrasses moderate Unionism and pushes wavering Unionists into the hands of those who would just return Northern Ireland to the past'. Blair also suggested it was damaging nationalists as it 'embarrasses the British and Irish Governments' and so made it 'harder for us to respond to nationalist concerns'. This was not another impasse, 'but a turning point' (Speech at the Harbour Commission, Belfast, 17 October 2002).

Whilst the Irish were unhappy about the suspension and highly critical of the way the raid was carried out, they accepted that suspension was inevitable given the UUP's intention to withdraw if Sinn Féin were not expelled from the Executive. What then could the governments do to either facilitate this turning or would they take 'the other road'? The approach post-raid was though remarkably similar to that pursued pre-raid and indeed since the GFA was signed: attempt to broker agreement amongst the parties to return to government, protect what they could of the institutions (including keeping the cross-border bodies functioning, much to the fury of Unionists (*Irish Times*, 13 November 2002)) and put pressure on the IRA to abandon violence and completely disarm. Despite Blair's tough speech, there was still, as far as the governments were concerned, no alternative to the GFA. Although they were frustrated at the turn of events, they were not willing to abandon it. The refusal of the SDLP to accede to Blair's request that they support Sinn Féin's exclusion meant that no real alternative to this approach existed (*Irish Times*, 10 October 2002).

The failure to 'save Dave'

By late 2003, Republicans were arguably even more central to the process and the chances of successfully achieving restoration had been reduced further. The reason for this was the outcome of the Assembly elections of November 2003, which saw the Sinn Féin and the DUP emerge as the two largest parties. This changed the landscape of Northern Ireland's politics and meant that devolution now rested on the agreement of Ian Paisley's party to share power with the political wing of the IRA. This was the scenario that Tony Blair himself had described as 'pie in the sky' a few months before (*The Guardian*, 2 May 2003) and some British officials believed would result in 'five to ten years of ice age' (Godson, 2004, p. 761). Trimble had claimed that if this 'nightmare scenario' transpired 'the whole thing goes pear-shaped and probably it will take you another generation to fix it' (*The Guardian*, 22 July 2002). It was the desire to avoid this scenario that led the British government to postpone Assembly elections in May 2003. There was a belief that there had to be a functioning devolved government and movement towards IRA 'acts of completion' as a backdrop to calling an election in order to give the UUP the best possible chance of retaining their position as the largest Unionist party. (It is interesting that the same importance was not attributed to the SDLP in relation to their status as the largest nationalist party within the Assembly.) The failure to get a sufficiently unambiguous statement from the IRA in April 2003 led to the postponement. There had been an intensive round of talks between the two governments and parties at Hillsborough the previous month, which resulted in a joint declaration by the two governments (also know as a 'shared understanding' between the two governments and the parties). This proposed further demilitarisation (or 'normalisation') including marked troop reduction in Northern Ireland, removal of watch towers, closing some army bases, and removing fortification from police stations. The British also proposed repealing their right to suspend the Assembly and Executive and devolving policing and administration of justice to the Assembly (as the SDLP and Sinn Féin wanted). The declaration though proposed what amounted to the winding up of the IRA with the 'immediate, full and permanent cessation of all paramilitary activity, including military attacks, training, targeting, intelligence gathering, acquisition or development of arms or weapons, other preparations for terrorist campaigns, punishment beatings and attacks and involvement in riots'. The declaration was subsequently published when Tony Blair announced the postponement of the elections. The governments also published proposals for an independent monitoring commission to monitor actions of paramilitary groups, and the British published proposals to effectively grant an amnesty to the OTRs ('on the runs'). Neither of the last two proposals were part of the declaration as the first was not accepted by Sinn Féin, the latter was unacceptable to the UUP.

Given the evident awareness of the problems in preventing the DUP overtaking the UUP, how did precisely the scenario that the British postponed elections to avoid in May 2003 materialise 5 months later? At the most obvious level it can be argued that it was simply another illustration of the inability of London and Dublin to dictate events in Northern Ireland and of a failure to stem the rising tide of Unionist unhappiness with the outcome of the peace process. However, this would gloss over one of the strangest and most poorly handled episodes of the peace process. The failure to create a favourable climate for elections in May did not force the governments to drop the approach but the elections were postponed precisely to give the time deemed necessary to create such a climate. Tony Blair announced the November elections on 21 October as part of what was intended to be a closely choreographed series of announcements. These would include a statement by Adams effectively saying that the war was over, which the IRA would endorse; confirmation from General de Chastelain that a major act of decommissioning had occurred and a statement by Trimble that conditions were now conducive to returning to government. As a result the UUP could enter the elections as the party that had delivered the end of the IRA and there would be the promise of a new era of sustainable devolved government. The electorate, it was hoped, would return the UUP as the largest party and a new era of stable government in Northern Ireland could then indeed be created.

Yet despite months of meetings between the UUP, Sinn Féin and the two governments, the whole choreography collapsed at the last hurdle when Trimble refused to endorse de Chastelain's statement as adequate to enable him to return to government with Sinn Féin. The problem for the UUP was the lack of transparency regarding what the IRA had decommissioned. They wanted at least details of the amounts and types of weapons destroyed, which de Chastelain, as a result of a confidentiality agreement he had with the IRA, was unwilling to release. Thus the day resulted in elections being announced for November but the other parts of the choreography did not go as planned. As Mark Durkan, the leader of the SDLP, observed of the day's events, 'What we had this morning was hope. By this afternoon hype, and now this evening it's a debacle' (http://edition.cnn.com/2003/WORLD/europe/10/22/n.ireland.hold/index.html).

How could such a 'debacle' be allowed to occur? Durkan's colleague, Seamus Mallon, railed against his party's exclusion from the process and asked the key question regarding the day's events.

Did Sinn Féin say in the negotiations that the act of decommissioning would be transparent, and did they renege? Or did the Ulster Unionist Party forget to ask them about the confidentiality clause that this Parliament wrote? Can the Secretary of State answer that simply? Can he confirm that it was Sinn Féin deviousness, or was the UUP simply incompetent?

(House of Commons, vol. 411, col. 644, 22 October 2003)

The fullest account of the episode is given in Godson's book which claims Trimble believed that the UUP had made perfectly clear to all parties the level of transparency needed and was appalled by the lack of detail provided. What is clear though from Godson's account is a commitment was not given to Trimble that this transparency would be forthcoming and indeed that Trimble consciously did not seek assurances from Adams on this point. Trimble did not ask the question of Adams as he did not believe that he would get a useful answer. If he then continued he would be 'settling for ambiguity' and if he broke off he would be 'blamed by London'. So, 'I made (Adams) aware of the need for transparency, so then when they don't live up to their moral obligations, I have freedom of manoeuvre to pull the plug.' This, Trimble claims, was his 'insurance policy' and was backed up by ensuring that his was the last act in the sequence only to be delivered after de Chastelain had made his announcement (Godson, 2004, p. 795). With hindsight though such an approach was highly questionable. The stakes were too high to simply rely on Republicans fulfilling their 'moral obligations'. Given that the UUP knew they would be facing an election a few weeks later, ambiguity and detailed choreography were incompatible. Whatever the moral rights and wrongs of the process and what assurances had and had not been sought and given, the result was that an election was called in circumstances similar to those deemed too risky in April (albeit with a further act of decommissioning having taken place). The UUP subsequently lost its position as largest Unionist party in the Assembly, securing only 27 seats to the DUP's 30. (The UUP position was further eroded shortly afterwards when Trimble's long time UUP critic, Jeffrey Donaldson, along with two other UUP MLAs, defected to the DUP, giving Paisley's party a 33-24 seat advantage over the UUP.)

If the actions of Trimble can be criticised, what of the actions of the two governments? Frank Millar claimed the episode 'was probably one of the greatest failures of Anglo–Irish diplomacy in recent years' (quoted in Godson, 2004, p. 795). Godson argues that there was a belief by the two governments that their attempts to 'micro-manage' the process earlier in the year had been misplaced and so they took the decision to let Trimble and Adams sort it out between them (Godson, 2004, p. 775). But given that the two governments had a central part to play in the process, particularly the British government, which called the election, surely they had as great an interest as Trimble in ensuring that the scripts as well as the choreography were worked out in advance. There were though differences between the two governments on aspects of the process. Dublin was determined that elections should take place, a stance justified in part by the argument that Republicans had been enticed into the peace process by stressing the opportunities that might be open to them via the electoral process. By this rationale it was unwise to continue to postpone elections when the anticipated result may be inconvenient. The Irish also were subject to increased pressure in the Dáil given that Sinn Féin had secured five TDs in the 2002 election. Why though did the British agree to make the announcement of the election at the start of the choreographed process, rather than at the end, at least giving them the option of aborting the process? The answer seems to be that the British had given Republicans an assurance in September that the elections would take place regardless and would not be postponed (Godson, 2004, p. 776). Sinn Féin insisted that this was necessary to get the IRA to agree to the other aspects of the choreography, not least the further decommissioning.

A further possible explanation for the decision to allow elections to go ahead when it was highly likely that they would result in the 'nightmare scenario' was that there was a belief that this was not such a nightmare after all. There had long been suggestions that elements within the Irish government, notably in the Department of Foreign Affairs, had concluded that a campaign to 'save Dave' was doomed to failure (*Irish Times*, 27 September 2000). As a result it was better to allow the inevitable emergence of the DUP as the main Unionist party and then seek to facilitate a DUP–SF deal, which would be more sustainable in the long term. At times it was also reported that this was the belief within sectors of the British civil service and the view held by Richard Haass (See Paul Bew's articles, *Daily Telegraph*, 22 April 2003 and *The Times*, 26 October 2003). Whilst polling could be invoked to support the contention that the DUP was likely to emerge as the largest party in Assembly elections, the grounds for believing that the DUP were likely to be amenable to sharing power with Sinn Féin at this time were far less clear. Such beliefs may have been the result of private soundings of DUP politicians by British and Irish officials, but the public pronouncements of the leadership of the DUP were incompatible with such interpretations. The DUP's electoral growth was the result of continuous castigation of Trimble as too soft in his dealings with Sinn Féin. Although some within the two governments do seem to have believed that a DUP–SF deal was possible, on the most logical reading it was far less probable than a UUP–SF deal. Events in October though ensured that to restore devolution it would be necessary to broker this very DUP–SF deal.

New situation, same 'solution'

According to Ian Paisley Jr, 'It's dead in the water. The Agreement is over – that was the message of this election' (*The Independent on Sunday*, 30 November 2003). The two governments, however, stressed that the majority of people had voted for pro-agreement parties and attempted to continue with the plan of seeking to restore devolved government, but with different parties at the helm. Hope was taken from some more positive comments by members of the DUP, notably Robinson, that although the DUP would talk tough they were eventually pragmatic enough to share power with Sinn Féin. The two governments set about seeking to persuade the DUP to be suitably pragmatic and the IRA to carry out the 'acts of completion' that they hoped would make this possible. After the talks held at Leeds Castle in September 2004 the governments believed they were on the brink of a deal. Robinson stated publicly that he was on 'the optimistic side of this equation' (*BBC News Online*, 20 September 2004) and that the gap between the two parties had narrowed as a result of the talks (*Sunday Times*, 24 October 2004). Ian Paisley himself told Blair, 'I believe that a golden opportunity has been available to realise a stable and entirely peaceful future . . . in some respects we have never been closer to solving the problems that have plagued us for decades' (*Irish Times*, 20 September 2004). Once again the talks were presented as a 'last chance' by the two governments. Tony Blair apparently let his frustration show by swearing at the parties and telling them they could no longer prevaricate as the 'moment of decision' had been reached (*The Independent*, 18 September 2004).

The Leeds Castle talks and the negotiations that continued over the months that followed did not lead to the desired breakthrough. Ultimately the DUP's demands that the IRA allowed photographic evidence of decommissioning as well as problems over their calls for changes in how the Assembly and Executive operated meant no agreement was reached. Problems were further compounded by the IRA's alleged involvement in the £26 million Northern Bank robbery in December 2004 and the murder of Robert McCartney outside a Belfast pub a month later. These actions were presented by the DUP as vindication of their demands for irrefutable evidence that the IRA had ceased to exist before they would enter into government with Sinn Féin. Robinson, whose apparent pragmatism over working with Sinn Féin had given the governments hope of a breakthrough a few months earlier, now argued, 'For progress to be made the Government must come to terms with the reality that Republicans have placed themselves beyond the pale and have demonstrated no desire to conform to peaceful, democratic standards. Let's move on without them' (UTV News, 27 February 2005).

To what extent did the events of late 2004 and early 2005 cause the DUP to abandon its plans to enter into government with Sinn Féin? It does appear that there was widespread hope that a deal was in the offing and more placatory comments than usual were coming from DUP politicians. A DUP delegation led by Ian Paisley and Robinson also travelled to Dublin for the first time in October 2004. Yet there was perhaps too optimistic a gloss put on these comments and gestures by many in the media and government spokespeople. The DUP's success in 2003 was a result of their stated opposition to working with Sinn Féin under anything but the most propitious circumstances. The end of the IRA needed not only to be delivered but also be seen to be delivered. Hopes that the fear of marginalisation would force the DUP to do the deal misunderstood both the nature of the DUP and perhaps the mood within the Unionist community. There were suggestions after the Leeds Castle talks that even the DUP's most hard-line supporters would not forgive them if they failed to deliver a deal (*Irish Independent*, 24 September 2004). The reality was that such analyses would only be correct if the public were desperate for a return to devolved government. This was evidently not the case within the Unionist community. As Henry Patterson noted many Unionists found 'direct rule, even with an Irish input, preferable to devolution with Martin McGuinness as a potential Deputy First Minister' (*Irish Independent*, 14 December 2004). As a result Paisley's demand that the IRA need to wear 'sackcloth and ashes' did not damage his standing within Unionism. Rather than not being forgiven for failing to do a deal in 2004, the 2005 Westminster election saw the DUP all but obliterate the UUP at Westminster with 9 MPs to the UUP's 1. Given that the DUP had pledged during the campaign to 'never enter any government with IRA/Sinn Féin' and Paisley stated afterwards that the GFA had been buried and his party would 'not be talking to the IRA now, tomorrow or ever' (*Irish Independent*, 7 May 2005; *BBC News Online*, 11 May 2005) it was difficult to be optimistic in 2005 about the chances for devolved government. Even the announcement by the IRA in July that it was to end its campaign and the confirmation 2 months later by the IICD that the IRA had decommissioned all its weapons did not break the logjam.

The two governments remained committed to the plan of securing devolution and continued to focus upon that end. However, suggestions of a 'plan B' began to appear around the time of Leeds Castle as an unidentified alternative if the talks failed (*Daily Telegraph*, 20 September 2004). The two governments outlined plan B in April 2006. This was to give the parties until November 2006 to agree to share power, if they failed to do that then attempts to restore devolution would be halted and salaries to MLAs stopped. There would be a radical shake up of local government in Northern Ireland, an increase in rates and the introduction of water rates. Direct rule would continue but it was made clear that co-operation with Dublin would be a key part of this and the government would look to increase 'commonsense North–South partnerships'. The NISS, Peter Hain, spelt plan B out in stark terms and threw down a challenge to the parties; 'If locally elected politicians don't like all this, the solution lies in their hands: (take) their places at Stormont and, for the first time in over three years, (earn) their salaries by exercising self-government' (*The Guardian*, 6 April 2006). Hain was adamant that, this time, the deadline would be adhered to. He acknowledged in the House of Commons that in the past deadlines had been missed with little discernable cost to the parties but,

> if anyone thinks that the Government are going to blink, come midnight on 24 November, they could not be more wrong.... All the parties need to understand that, if midnight on 24 November comes and goes and there is no restoration of the Assembly, the salaries and allowances will stop and the curtain will come down. It would be the parties themselves that had brought the curtain down, not the Government.
>
> (House of Commons, vol. 445, col. 560, 26 April 2006)

Blair also stated, 'This is the last chance for this generation to make the process work . . . . The fact is if we cannot find a way to agreement between the parties for devolved institutions to work we are therefore forced, not because we want to, to go for a Plan B' (*The Guardian*, 27 June 2006).

Finally then 8 years after the signing of the GFA the two governments were forced to develop a plan B, due to their failure to secure sustainable devolved government in Northern Ireland. In October 2006, after 3 days of all-party talks in Scotland the governments published *The St Andrew's Agreement* which proposed some changes to the way the institutions functioned, a new oath for ministers, which included an endorsement of the PSNI, and a commitment to participate in power-sharing. A timetable for compliance was included and again the warning that failure 'to agree to establish the Executive will lead to immediate dissolution of the Assembly, as will failure to agree at any stage, and the Governments will take forward new partnership arrangements on the basis previously announced' (increased intergovernmental co-operation and the collapse of all aspects of devolution). In March 2007 'the pie in the sky' scenario seemed to be achieved with the announcement by Paisley and Adams that they had agreed to form a power-sharing government. Paisley was better placed to take his party into government with Sinn Féin in 2007 than in 2004 as a result of the changes he could claim he had secured at St Andrews, Sinn Féin's decision in January 2007 to support the police and justice system in Northern Ireland and the DUP's increasing domination of Unionist politics. In the Assembly elections on 7 March the DUP secured 36 seats, twice the number of the UUP (Sinn Féin secured 28 seats to the SDLP's 16). Whilst the governments (again) had to be flexible in relation to the 'absolute' deadlines they had previously announced, the agreement to enter into government was warmly welcomed by London and Dublin. Blair claimed, 'In a sense, everything we have done over the last 10 years has been a preparation for this moment' and argued it was 'a very important day for the people of Northern Ireland, but also for the people and the history of these islands'. Ahern described the development as 'unprecedented' and announced, 'We move forward from today in an entirely new spirit and with every expectation of success' (*BBC News Online* 26/3/2007). At the time of writing it is still unclear whether the subsequent restoration of power to the Assembly and Executive on 8 May 2007 will indeed be the point that marked a new and sustained period of devolved government in Northern Ireland. However, even if it is not achieved the objective of insulating British and Irish politics from the Northern Ireland issue will ensure the goal of achieving devolution remains attractive to policymakers in London and Dublin. Events since 1972 have shown that Britain has been willing to pursue direct rule when circumstances dictate, and since 1985 with a green tinge. If St Andrew's fails to deliver then the tinge is indeed likely to darken but suggestions that the objective of devolution will be jettisoned are unconvincing. Having come so close to securing devolved government since 1998 the British and the Irish governments are unlikely to abandon the quest completely and permanently bring down the curtain on devolution.

Conclusion

In some respects the actions by the two governments post-1997 were not radically different to those of their immediate predecessors. The peace process was not created in 1997 and the structure of the talks that led to the GFA and the conditions that needed to be fulfilled for parties to participate in them were largely already decided. The change in governments in 1997 and the opportunity that new leaders offered gave the process a necessary 'kick-start', but the shape of a possible deal was clear long before this. This is not to denigrate what was achieved in April 1998. Although the likely shape of the deal may have long been apparent, the difficulties in getting agreement for this deal had been apparent for just as long. The pragmatism, enthusiasm and commitment illustrated by the two governments post-1997 were instrumental in providing the momentum and persuading the parties to sign up to the GFA. But the GFA was not a comprehensive agreement that represented the resolution of the conflict. Key issues were simply postponed in order to enable an agreement to be reached. In many respects the GFA was an exercise in conflict management and a step towards conflict resolution. The idea of sidelining contentious issues in order to facilitate agreement on other less divisive issues is long established in conflict resolution. However, such issues cannot be sidelined indefinitely and ultimately will have to be dealt with. The theoretical hope is that the momentum generated by the wider agreement and a resulting less conflictual climate will mean that the previously contentious issues lose some of their saliency and are more solvable in the post-agreement period. This did not happen in Northern Ireland. Decommissioning did not lose its saliency, its importance actually increased. The trust that emerged between the largest Unionist party and the leadership of Sinn Féin in the period post-GFA up to 1999 was undermined by the refusal of the IRA to decommission. The two governments tried hard to resolve the conflict but their pragmatic approach ultimately failed to secure a breakthrough in time to prevent Unionist alienation from the GFA. This resulted in the Unionist party that had agreed to do the deal being replaced by the one that had long decried it (as well as the constitutional party that had been the voice of nationalists since the 1970s being replaced by those who had spent those years advocating the use of violence to unite Ireland). As Paul Bew noted, 'We must face up to something about the Good Friday Agreement. James Joyce famously said that he left Ireland because Ireland was the sow that ate its farrow. The Good Friday Agreement is the sow that ate its parents: it ate the SDLP and it ate the Ulster Unionist Party. That is a brutal fact' (Address to the BIIPB, 27 November 2005).

Intergovernmental co-operation was a key factor in creating conditions conducive to negotiating the GFA. However, as so often before, the period demonstrated the limits to what London and Dublin can deliver in Northern Ireland. Although Northern Ireland remained comparatively peaceful in the post-GFA period, the hope for stable devolved government and improved inter-communal relations proved very difficult to achieve. The related longer-term objective of the two governments, insulating the wider British and Irish political life from the Northern Ireland question, was also unobtainable in the years after the GFA was signed, although the issue's influence has been altered. Largely the demands that Northern Ireland makes on the two states now are purely political, neither state is at risk from the type or levels of violence that it faced before the process began.

For Dublin though there has been an unanticipated incursion of Northern Ireland into its 'domestic' politics caused by the growth of Sinn Féin as a significant political party in the South. The prolonged IRA ceasefire as well as intensive efforts by Sinn Féin to re-launch itself as a party of choice, particularly on social issues, in the South, enabled it to secure five seats in the Dáil in 2002. Ahern has found himself having to justify his stance that he would not be willing to sit with Sinn Féin in government South of the border whilst urging Unionists to accept them in the North. The electoral competition that Sinn Féin pose to Fianna Fáil, along with the decreasing likelihood that the Provisional IRA will return to violence, has led to an increased willingness by the Irish government to criticise the IRA and Sinn Féin. Fianna Fáil has looked to protect their 'Republican flank' from this emerging electoral threat. This new electoral consideration may have some influence on Fianna Fáil's relations with London on the Northern Ireland question. Too much should not be made of this, of course, as Sinn Féin has had limited electoral appeal in the South on the basis of the Northern question. The threat of Sinn Féin in the South is based upon its ability to resonate with Southern voters on Southern issues and how successful it will be in this regard remains to be seen. However, this competition with Sinn Féin in the South could actually lead Fianna Fáil to be more critical of Sinn Féin in Northern Ireland. With the Provisional IRA no longer a realistic paramilitary threat, one of the considerations that served as a check upon Dublin's willingness to pressurise Sinn Féin has gone.

Whatever the disappointments that might be felt in London and Dublin over the failure to secure all they hoped for from the GFA in the years immediately after 1998, it is unlikely that the rationale and objectives that underpinned the agreement will be abandoned by either state. Pragmatism will continue to be a hallmark of the intergovernmental approach. Competing pressures from the different communities in Northern Ireland and the asymmetry of power in London and Dublin with regard to Northern Ireland is likely to continue to cause periodic problems between the two states. But intergovernmental co-operation will continue simply because it remains the most logical approach to dealing with the issue, for each state.

8 Conclusion

Anglo-Irish relations have undoubtedly improved since 1980. Yet as has been argued this improvement was not a steady linear one, it was far more cyclical. Keatinge's warning against the fever chart interpretation is an important point, but fever charts are difficult to ignore. This work has largely followed a chronological approach rather than a thematic one. In adopting such an approach there is a danger that the fevers may distract from the themes and that there may be a temptation to plot a median line between the high and the low points of the relationship and conclude that progress has been steady and what has happened over the period was inevitable. As each achievement of the intergovernmental progress appears to be built on the one before it is tempting to underplay the constraints on intergovernmental co-operation. As the chronological development of intergovernmentalism is examined it becomes evident that co-operation was better in the late 1990s/early 2000s than it was in the early 1980s. A corollary of this assessment can be the assumption that the relationship was bound to improve and the two governments were, of course, going to oversee the peace process and a Good Friday-type agreement, eventually. Yet this is far from the case. The purpose of this chapter is to briefly examine the structural constraints and pressures that the two governments faced in seeking to increase co-operation. It will be argued that although the fevers changed over the period they were caused, shaped and alleviated, if not cured by, constraints and pressures that were largely permanent features. Although the path that the intergovernmental relationship followed over the period was not inevitable, these constraints and pressures fixed the parameters of what was possible. These parameters narrowed the options for both the British and the Irish governments when dealing with Northern Ireland.

Constraints and pressures

Numerous constraints and pressures shaped the intergovernmental relationship since 1980. These constraints and pressures were remarkably durable, if not consistent in their influence. The main ones were the demands of 'client' communities within Northern Ireland: international opinion; domestic public opinion; and the ideological slant of each government.

'Client' communities

An important and often determining factor in the intergovernmental relationship has been the demands that each government's 'client' community have made upon them. Each government had for historical, cultural and ideological reasons a closer relationship with one community within Northern Ireland than the other (for a related discussion of this issue, see Cochrane, 1995; Dixon 1995b). These relationships need to be kept in perspective. Neither community were clients of London or Dublin to the extent that they would unquestioningly follow the instructions of 'their' government. However, each community looked to 'their' government as sponsors, to protect and advance their interests. Their sponsors were called on to aid the client *vis-à-vis* the competing community within Northern Ireland and to help them further their wider aims. The governments themselves may not have always accepted the client–sponsor analysis but their actions fitted this framework. The Irish government was perhaps more willing to embrace the role of sponsorship than the British government. Dublin saw the institutionalisation of this role in the 1985 AIA as a major achievement. But Britain did act as the sponsor of Unionism, whether it was keen to acknowledge this role or not. The assertion by Thatcher, Major and Blair during various negotiations that they had to take on board what the Unionists would accept meant they fulfilled the role of sponsorship. The fact that they may have 'misread' or disregarded the views of their clients at various times does not invalidate the relationship. The fact that Unionists turned to London to protect their interests and directed their fury at London when they felt they had been betrayed underlines their view of the British government as their (often perfidious) sponsor.

The client–sponsor relationships have been both an asset and a hindrance to intergovernmental co-operation. The closer relationship that each government had with their clients allowed an element of 'you bring the nationalists, we'll bring the Unionists' to underpin intergovernmental negotiations. This was particularly clear during the negotiating of the DSD and especially seems to have shaped Reynolds' view of the process, but was also apparent during the GFA negotiations. However, whilst Reynolds was right that there has been an element of each side seeking to 'push' the clients where the sponsor wished to go, it has also been the case that the clients have attempted to 'pull' the sponsor where they wish to go. To this end the nationalists, and particularly the SDLP, sought to drag the Republic's government further into the dispute. The Unionists have more often sought to prevent their sponsor from going in the direction they appeared to be set on: intergovernmental co-operation and the ceding of a greater role to the Republic.

It was this struggle between clients and sponsors that largely determined the shape of every intergovernmental initiative in the period. The relationship between client and sponsor was interdependent. The sponsors could not entirely ignore the wishes of their clients, as they could not dictate what the communities within Northern Ireland would accept. The clients could not ignore the desires of the sponsors, as it was the sovereign governments who had the ability to legislate and create the frameworks within which (it was hoped) the clients functioned. Even what appeared to be the clearest example of a sponsor ignoring a client, the AIA, is deceptive. Although the Unionists were excluded from the negotiations the British government attempted to act as the sponsor and scaled back from the original maximalist position on the grounds that Unionism would not accept it. So of all the factors that have shaped the intergovernmental approach over the period the sponsor–client relationship is of primary importance.

International opinion

In recent times there has been an increased interest in the role that international opinion has played in influencing events in Northern Ireland. Much of this has centred on the issues at the end of the Cold War and its impact on Northern Ireland, comparisons with peace processes in the Middle East and South Africa and an apparent increased influence and interest by America (see Cox, Guelke and Stephen, 2006; O'Clery, 1997; Tonge, 2004). Many authors now stress the importance of external factors in influencing the participants to the conflict. Yet the evidence is comparatively scant to suggest that international opinion and pressure was instrumental in determining how the British and Irish governments conducted their policy and pursued co-operation on Northern Ireland since 1980 or indeed post-Cold War (Dixon, 2006). It is true that the British government throughout the period were concerned to preserve the special relationship with the United States and that at times events in Northern Ireland were internationally embarrassing to Britain. It is also true that the Irish-American lobby were influential in the US and that senior Irish-American politicians had both a keen interest in the Northern Ireland question and excellent relations with the Irish government. However, the result of this does not appear to have been an ability by Dublin to use the Washington route to force the British government to adopt a stance more to its liking. Examples have been cited throughout the study of Irish attempts to engage America, and particularly the White House, to advance their cause with mixed results (O'Kane, 2002).

This is not to say that US influence had no bearing on intergovernmental co-operation during the period. Where the US was important was in encouraging the two states to co-operate and supporting them on the direction they had embarked upon. The desire by the British and especially Thatcher to keep America 'on-side' was apparent and it was a consideration in Britain's stance towards co-operation with Dublin. The British desire to keep America happy was not, though, the factor which led them to co-operate with Dublin. The importance of US influence can be overstated and all manner of initiatives and policies attributed to it, leading to assertions that President Carter's statement on Northern Ireland in 1977 'was a potent landmark on the road to Good Friday 1998' (Arthur, 2000, p. 141). Goodall's observation regarding the AIA negotiations that the desire to keep the Americans onboard was a factor, but not a determining one, appears to sum up the British attitude to US influence throughout the period. There was undoubtedly increased visibility to American interest during the peace process (particularly during Clinton's administration) and the direct input of Senator Mitchell was an essential factor in concluding the GFA. However, the US role largely remained one of 'encouragement from the sidelines' and facilitating co-operation between the two governments (Hazleton, 2000, pp. 103–109). It is hard to find examples where US pressure led either government to do something they would otherwise not have done. As a former American Ambassador to London argued, 'so long as relations between Dublin and London remained civil, and so long as the British government continued to put forward negotiable options for the constitutional leaders of the North to discuss, genuine American interests were not affected' (Seitz, 1998, p. 285).

The other area of increased attention has been the impact of Europe on Anglo-Irish relations and the Northern Ireland issue. It has been argued that the joint membership of the European Union has altered the relationship between the two states. What is undoubtedly true is that European membership has reduced Ireland's dependency upon Britain economically and increased the Republic's profile internationally. The advent of the 'Celtic tiger' economy, which has at least in part been due to European Union membership, has boosted Ireland's self confidence and enabled the South to be less preoccupied with her larger neighbouring state. But again the impact of joint European membership can be overstated. As the former NISS and Foreign Secretary, Douglas Hurd, has observed

> some of the Europhiles exaggerate the impact of the joint membership of Europe on Anglo-Irish relations. Of course there's the economic side and that has been helpful, particularly to the Republic, but I've never thought that the fact that we're now both members of the EU . . . was a crucial factor and I don't think that it is now. I think the two governments have come together through quite a different process.
>
> (Hurd, 25 July 1999)

The influence of Europe has, if anything, been less important in terms of persuading one or the other government to change policies or compelling the two to co-operate than the US influence. Where common membership of the EU has been extremely beneficial to the intergovernmental process has been in facilitating closer working contacts between British and Irish officials and politicians. The increased opportunity that EU summits offered during the period for the two sides to get to know each other proved important during later negotiations. EU summits also enabled the leaders and officials to meet in private in an atmosphere far less frenzied and charged with expectation than that which always surrounded Anglo-Irish summits.

So the impact of international opinion is at best mixed. Although the Northern Ireland question is important to both Britain and Ireland, in geo-strategic terms it is of marginal significance. As a result the major international players and forums have been reluctant to become too embroiled in the issue. The US in particular has attempted to play the role of supportive friend to both states rather than side with one side over the other. Whilst international opinion and support has been helpful in shoring up Anglo-Irish intergovernmental co-operation it has not to any great extent dictated or shaped it.

Domestic public opinion in Britain and Ireland

As both the British and the Irish governments are democratically elected it is obviously the case that they are potentially swayed by public opinion within their own jurisdiction. What is surprising in both states is how little importance domestic public opinion placed on the Northern Ireland issue. Polls continually showed that in both Irish and British elections (outside Northern Ireland) voters placed very little emphasis on the Northern Ireland question. At times of exceptional tension within the North, such as the 1981 hunger strike, the North briefly raised its head as an issue. But whilst the low-level intensity conflict continued through most of the period the Irish electorate appeared bored and detached from the issue (Hazelkorn and Patterson, 1994). The old antagonisms in the North seemed out of step with the Republic's increasing view of itself as a pluralist forward-looking European state.

Similarly it may have been expected that the British public would look unfavourably on a conflict that was costing a great deal of money, the lives of their soldiers and embarrassment internationally. Yet again throughout the period it barely registered on the electoral or parliamentary agendas in Britain. The lack of impact is summed up perfectly by the Labour leader John Smith's insouciance over Major's contacts with the IRA on the grounds that there were no votes on the issue in Britain (Major, 1999, p. 432). Douglas Hurd notes, 'since 1969 we've mounted a substantial effort in Northern Ireland, military and financial and this has never been a main cause of dissent or dispute inside governments or between parties and it's really extraordinary' (Hurd, 25 July 1999).

Ideological considerations

It is possible to identify an ideological creed that has, at least nominally, underpinned British and Irish policymaking with regard to the Irish question. From 1937 until 1999 the Irish commitment to a united Ireland was enshrined in the Irish constitution – an outcome that opinion polls throughout the period demonstrated was the favoured option of most people in the South and the stated objective of all Irish governments. Similarly the underpinning tenet of British policy was taken to be a commitment to uphold the Union. When pushed, ministers were willing to make public statements of their personal desire to see Northern Ireland remain part of the United Kingdom. But how important were these ideological considerations in shaping intergovernmental co-operation on Northern Ireland?

Throughout the period under consideration, and arguably for most of the period since partition, the Irish ideological commitment to nationalism and the British attachment to Unionism have been in decline. This is not to say that the Irish government has given up any desire for Irish unity or that the British government wishes to see the Union with Northern Ireland ended. It is just that the traditional ideological viewpoints of the two states became more qualified. Increasingly the Irish would like unity but on terms so favourable that it is highly unlikely to come about unless in the very long term. This is of course closely linked to the observations regarding public opinion made above. The South of Ireland increasingly saw Northern Ireland as a place apart and while a view of the North as part of the Irish nation remained, the South was unwilling to re-embrace the North on any terms that could possibly be destabilising to the newly prosperous Republic. Similarly British opinion has long been at best ambivalent towards Northern Ireland. Even amongst the higher echelons of the most Unionist of British parties, the Conservatives, Unionism as an underlying ideological creed which saw the United Kingdom as part of an indivisible nation seemed to have lost its appeal. (Alan Clark recalled in relation to Ian Gow's concerns in the run up to the AIA, 'Ireland is a ghastly subject. Intractable. Insoluble. For centuries it has blighted English domestic politics, wrecked the careers of good men' (Clark, 1994, p. 117).) This weariness towards Northern Ireland was evident in Mayhew's indiscreet assertion to a German newspaper in 1993 that 'Most people believe we would not want to release Northern Ireland from the United Kingdom. To be entirely honest, we would with pleasure' (quoted in O'Clery, 1999, p. 215).

Such sentiments were also evident during the peace process period. Whilst each NISS has, to some extent, asserted their Unionism, and Tony Blair noted his belief in the Union, when the issue is pursued such observations are more qualified. In an interesting interview with *The Irish Times* in May 2001 the then NISS John Reid refused to advocate that Northern Ireland should remain in the UK but acknowledged that as a Scottish MP he did argue that Scotland should remain in the UK. When he was asked why he did not advocate that Northern Ireland remained in the UK, he replied 'You are asking am I an advocate for the Union of Northern Ireland and I was saying to you no.' At one reading this is simply in line with the British assertion of neutrality, but most of Reid's predecessors had coupled this neutrality with comforting words for Unionists regarding their belief that the Union was beneficial. Quentin Thomas similarly suggests ambivalence of British policymakers towards Northern Ireland's position. According to Thomas any solution that is acceptable to the people of Northern Ireland is acceptable to Britain.

Our central position was, if everyone else is happy so are we. We were like sort of 'good mother'. If all the children can agree to go to the pictures, fine. If they all want to play cricket, fine. What do we care? We had some interests but basically our position was that if everyone would consent to something, if they had consented to the proposition that the moon is made of blue cheese, fine. What do we care?

This reasoning meant that a united Ireland was acceptable to the British. As Thomas stated, 'If they want to go we will hold the door open. We've said it' (Thomas, 14 September 2005).

This dilution of ideological articles of faith was a contributory factor to the increasing willingness of the two states to co-operate at an intergovernmental level on the Northern Ireland issue. The dilution and subsequent co-operation were at one level merely the result of a growing pragmatism within the policymaking echelons of London and Dublin. There was little point in Dublin persisting with the high-minded justification for indolence on the Northern issue on the grounds that unity was inevitable and would out. Experience had shown that unity was in no hurry to out and events in the North forced Dublin to review its policy and ideology. This review resulted in a shift from the pursuit of unity with the North to the pursuit of stability in the North. Irish politicians did not originally sing this shift from the rooftops. Unity was still the stated Irish policy ideal but for practical political purposes efforts were directed towards how to stabilise Northern Ireland and reconcile Northern nationalists to the Northern state. This shift was given more public recognition after the signing of the GFA with the removal of articles 2 and 3 and Ahern's assertion that the constitutional question had been settled.

What has perhaps not been sufficiently acknowledged is the impact that the fear of the North destabilising the South had on Dublin's policy. According to Finlay, 'the central tenet of Northern Ireland policy for every Irish government from 1969 on was: whatever happens don't let it spill over down here' (and Finlay specifically rejects the idea that it was about securing unity, 'it was all about management') (see Finlay, 2006; similar comments were expressed by Sean Donlon). The problems evident during the hunger strikes and Sinn Féin's entry into electoral politics in Northern Ireland in the early 1980s increased this fear of contagion. The fear, to a large extent, led Dublin to try and reconcile nationalists to the North. It also accounts for some of the disputes between Dublin and London.

Dublin believed that the IRA posed a greater threat to the Irish than the British state and were often exasperated with what they saw as Britain's inadequate policies and procrastination in Northern Ireland. Whether this fear was justified, and indeed whether it was at times exaggerated by Dublin as a policy tool when dealing with London, is not particularly relevant here. What is clear is that the fear was real and was a contributory factor in the shifts in both ideological stance and policies pursued by the Republic towards intergovernmentalism during the period.

Similarly the ideological shifts in Britain's attitude towards Northern Ireland allowed London to take a more pragmatic stance towards intergovernmental co-operation. Had Britain stuck to the assertion that Northern Ireland was an issue solely for the people of Northern Ireland, the British government and Westminster, then the AIA, DSD and GFA could never have been negotiated. Of course the ideological shift in Britain's attitude towards Northern Ireland predates Thatcher by many years. What marks the period under consideration out from earlier ones is the acceptance by Britain of the desirability for a sustained and institutionalised role for Dublin regarding Northern Ireland. Sunningdale, which was the previous high point of intergovernmentalism, had proved to be short-lived. Yet the principle that was accepted at Sunningdale, that the only thing preventing a united Ireland was the wishes of the majority in Northern Ireland, made the intellectual justification of intergovernmentalism harder to resist. By acknowledging the legitimacy of a united Ireland in some circumstances it was difficult to deny the Irish had an interest in events in Northern Ireland. The problem was how to co-operate with the Republic towards the shared end of achieving a peaceful stable society in Northern Ireland without appearing to be working to create the united Ireland you have acknowledged may be legitimate.

It is important not to overstate the impact of the decline of Britain's ideological commitment to the Union. Mayhew's 'with pleasure' comment, Thomas's 'what do we care?' question, Reid's refusal to entreat Northern Ireland to remain in the Union should not be taken as indicative of a determination to end the Union. Although the ideological commitment to Unionism may have diminished, this did not mean that Britain had no role in Northern Ireland. London had acknowledged that it had no selfish strategic or economic interest in Northern Ireland but it still had obligations and policy was underpinned by a set of values to which it remained committed. According to Thomas,

> Consent is absolutely fundamental. It was absolutely a matter of principle that would sustain against any challenge to the right of the people of Northern Ireland, or a majority of the people of Northern Ireland to do what they wanted. If they wanted to stay in the Union we would be there. But equally if they ever reached the position that they wanted to join a united Ireland, fine. At various levels we might regret it but we said that we have no strategic interests that would make us want to resist that.

There has been no real suggestion that Britain would renege on this point. Periodic Unionist fears that policymakers were trying to engineer the exit of Northern Ireland from the Union are unconvincing (and often fail to factor in what Dublin's likely reaction to any such move would be). The increased input for Dublin (and the threat of it) has at times been used to try and insulate the British from international criticism, reconcile nationalists to the North, pressurise Unionists to co-operate with nationalists (and later Republicans) to achieve devolution, and in pursuit of improved governance in Northern Ireland in the absence of preferred alternatives. The temptation to see such moves as part of a cunning plan to end the Union needs to be resisted. There is little evidence to support such claims, certainly in the period since 1980. Although ideological changes may have made it more acceptable to co-operate intergovernmentally with Dublin there are limits to how far Britain would agree to alter policy as a result of these ideological changes.

The extent to which the British government were driven towards intergovernmental co-operation by the desire to physically insulate the British state and economy from the Northern Ireland issue also needs to be considered. The degree to which the economic cost of terrorist violence influenced British policymaking is difficult to ascertain. It has been frequently noted that incidents such as the bombing of the Baltic Exchange by the IRA in 1992 – which was estimated to have cost more in financial terms than all the bombs detonated in Northern Ireland throughout the Troubles – and the £1 billion damage caused by a bomb near the Nat West tower in April 1993 were expensive for the British and potentially damaging to London's position as Europe's premier financial market. But such events appeared to have steeled British resolve not to give in to terrorism (Major, 1999, p. 444; Thatcher, 1993, pp. 381–385). Reynolds believed that huge bombs in the centre of London influenced the British and 'the vulnerability of London to such attacks was a factor in subsequent developments' (Duignan, 1995, p. 102). Martin Mansergh disagreed, however, arguing that 'anyone tempted to believe that some future political impasse could be broken by a renewed bombing campaign in the City of London would be disastrously mistaken' (Mansergh, 1995, p. 151). Mansergh's analysis is correct in so far as individual bombs would not result in Britain making concessions to the IRA, and the IRA were wrong in their belief that by bombing economic targets in London they would break the British will to remain in Ireland. Economic considerations were not the primary motivating factors for co-operating intergovernmentally with Dublin, but if as a result of such co-operation the likelihood of bombs aimed at economic targets would be reduced then this was another possible benefit of, and argument for, co-operation.

Working within the constraints: Pursuing the possible

What then was the net result of the constraints identified above? Perhaps the most important effect of the constraints was not in determining what form intergovernmental co-operation took but in prohibiting a variety of policies. The constraints set the parameters within which the two governments operated and importantly these parameters to some extent encouraged/necessitated intergovernmental co-operation.

The constraints taken together meant that certain policies, which had their advocates in both political and academic circles, were to all intents and purposes non-starters. Given that the British government (and perhaps less importantly due to their lack of sovereignty, the Irish) were unwilling to attempt to impose policies by draconian measures, to be a realistic option any policy needed to secure sufficient consent within Northern Ireland. This necessity meant that the options of full integration of Northern Ireland into the UK, repartition, independence, unity without consent and the restoration of majority rule devolution were accepted as unrealistic by the British government throughout the period. Each of these 'solutions' were at times championed by groups within Northern Ireland, integration favoured by the Conservative Party whilst in opposition in the 1970s, and repartition by Thatcher herself in office. Yet each one would have caused more problems than they solved. The negating of these options resulted in only two realistic possibilities remaining: continued direct rule or power-sharing devolution.

Given the inability to secure power-sharing devolution the British were left pursuing their 'temporary' measure of direct rule throughout much of the period. Direct rule was problematic in that it was no group or government's clearly favoured option, yet opinion on the other options were so divided that all attempts to shift from direct rule to devolution failed up until the GFA. To this end, until devolution was restored (sporadically) in 1999 the British had to find ways to make direct rule more palatable and productive. The failure of internal initiatives such as the Atkins Talks and Rolling Devolution in the early 1980s encouraged London to explore co-operation with Dublin. The argument that London looked to Dublin as all other routes were closed has some validity. Similarly failure of the proclaimed desire by Dublin to seek improved relations with Northern Unionists and fears of destabilisation led Dublin to look to London to forward its agenda.

The development of intergovernmental co-operation

Both London and Dublin therefore pursued an intergovernmental agenda for reasons that can be attributed to perceived self-interest. The British did not allow the Irish a say in the affairs of Northern Ireland as a philanthropic neighbourly gesture; the Irish did not get involved out of a sense of obligation to a fellow European state facing a little local difficulty. For the British the rationale was that direct rule was likely to remain the necessary policy for the foreseeable future but it remained deeply problematic. To this end, given the demonstrable lack of progress towards rapprochement between the two traditions within Northern Ireland, and subsequent growing exasperation, London looked towards Dublin for assistance. Fortuitously around the same time the Irish were looking to increase their input on Northern Ireland as a result of the rise of Sinn Féin and nationalist alienation in the North and related fears of destabilisation in the South. The South had of course argued for a greater input into Northern Ireland for many years but the situation under FitzGerald's government in the mid-1980s was slightly different. Under Haughey at the start of the 1980s the calls for an intergovernmental approach to the issue were couched in terms that envisaged the two governments co-operating on how to create the inevitable united Ireland. Under FitzGerald the language changed and whilst the Irish still called for unity they became embroiled in a negotiating progress that was ultimately more to do with stabilising the North than uniting the island.

The perceived self-interests that compelled the two governments towards co-operation did not coincide to the extent that they were united either in their evaluation of the problem or in their prescription for the solution. The desire to create a peaceful society in Northern Ireland united the two states; their analysis of how that could be achieved divided them. It is along this fault line that the periodic Anglo-Irish disputes occurred. This is hardly surprising given that Britain and Ireland are two independent states one of which has, for historical reasons, a deeply ingrained suspicion of the other. However, once the two states had embarked (or re-embarked given the brief earlier Sunningdale foray) on a co-operative approach, certain factors helped if not to overcome then at least to offset the periodic disputes and recriminations.

Factors providing ballast for the intergovernmental relationship

The key factors that have helped to keep the relationship if not on an even keel then at least afloat have been institutional structures, personal relationships and accumulated intellectual capital.

Institutional structures

An interesting and important feature of Anglo-Irish relations since 1980 has been the creation of certain structures that institutionalised or facilitated co-operation. Such structures can be divided between governmental and non-governmental bodies (and further subdivided between formal/standing bodies and informal/ad hoc bodies). For the purpose of this study the most important ones are the governmental bodies. The structures set up under the AIA – the Intergovernmental Conference (effectively replacing the Intergovernmental Council created in 1981) and the Secretariat – were of enormous importance in furthering intergovernmental co-operation. Whilst at times they seemed merely forums for the two governments to air their grievances and castigate one another, their importance was far more pronounced. The institutionalising of direct, regular and permanent contacts between British and Irish officials and ministers helped to provide a forum for resolving differences. It also created a forum for preventing such differences becoming open disputes and enabled the two governments to act in a proactive, rather than simply reactive, manner. It is of course possible, and often useful, to point out the problems that have still arisen despite this structure and question its validity and efficacy. What is harder to deduce is what the status and development of intergovernmental relations would have been over the period had these formal structures not been instituted. That the bodies did not prevent Anglo-Irish disputes does not invalidate them. The inbuilt tension in the relationship assured that disputes would be out. Similarly the institutionalising of negotiations between the two governments and all constitutional parties in Northern Ireland during the Brooke–Mayhew Talks provided another forum for increased contact and ultimately, according to those involved in the process, an increased awareness of the goals and constraints of others.

The level of interaction between the two governments during the Mitchell talks was intense – at times bypassing the formal talks structures. Strand 3 was dealt with by direct intergovernmental negotiation (and was the least problematic), problems in Strand 2 were dealt with in a large part by direct intergovernmental negotiation and even Strand 1, which had no formal Irish governmental input, saw

Dublin becoming embroiled in negotiations in relation to Sinn Féin's objections to proposals. Similarly the crises in the peace process after the signing of the GFA have largely been dealt with intergovernmentally (though this interaction was at times far from harmonious).

Informal meetings, particularly of British and Irish officials, supplemented the formal intergovernmental structures. In the early 1990s the 'Iceberg Committee' was created whereby senior British and Irish officials met in a social context every 3 months to discuss possible problems, not just over Northern Ireland but also matters such as European issues (Butler, 9 November 2000; FitzGerald, 6 June 2000). The crises over achieving and sustaining devolution since 1998 have tended to be dealt with by the two governments directly rather than by utilising formal structures created under the GFA, such as the BIIGC (which did not formally have a summit between 1999 and 2005) (*Irish Independent*, 27 May 2005).

Non-governmental organisations have also played a role in improving general Anglo-Irish relations. Some of these have been created as a result of inter-governmental initiatives, such as the British Irish Inter-parliamentary Body and Anglo-Irish Encounter. Such bodies and others like the British-Irish Association whilst not directly impacting on intergovernmental co-operation have been influential in promoting better relations and understanding between the two states and as such have provided a useful input and backdrop to the process.

Personal relationships

The good relations that emerged between many of the key politicians and officials involved in shaping Northern Ireland policy in London and Dublin are widely cited by those involved as an important factor in the development of intergovern-mental co-operation. Whilst at times personal relations at the political level were strained these problems were to some extent offset by good relations between officials. The considerations that drive politicians are subtly different to those that drive officials. Politicians are of course ultimately constrained by public opinion and what is perceived to be an acceptable and an unacceptable risk. They have what one official termed 'the burden of responsibility' (Chilcott, 20 March 2001). Officials, although of course answerable to their political masters and acting under their instruction, are somewhat freer to explore options and possibilities. Also, given their permanency under both systems they tend to be involved in the process for far longer periods than individual politicians.

Once again there is a need for caution in such an analysis. It would be wrong to suggest that the fact that groups of British and Irish officials had good personal relationships meant that intergovernmental co-operation was assured. Officials may not have 'been burdened by political baggage' and so 'freer in terms of creating possibilities' but these officials are also 'constitutional creatures and unless they can sell their proposition to their constitutional masters it does not even start' (Chilcott, 20 March 2001). (Officials though see politicians' regard for their place in history and the potential of going down in history as the person who solved the 'Irish question' as a motivating factor.) Like most factors good personal relations between politicians and officials were a contributory rather than determining factor. Even the best of relations were at times strained by events on the ground and the responses of each government to them.

Accumulated intellectual capital

When the Troubles broke out it is widely accepted that both London and Dublin were ill-prepared for the situation and had comparatively little understanding of (or interest in) the situation in Northern Ireland. The deteriorating situation in the North forced both governments to review policy and procedure and take an interest in the situation. Somewhat by trial and error and as a result of the constraining factors discussed above, what was feasible and what was impractical became apparent. This analysis and interpretation was not identical in London and Dublin but both sides built up expertise and familiarity on the issue. In the British context the former head of the Northern Ireland Office, John Chilcott, stressed the differences that this expertise made. Chilcott, who had been reviewing Cabinet papers from the 1970s shortly before the interview, commented,

> how confused and incoherent and uncertain British policy was at that time, and indeed relatively ignorant as [there] had been little need to go very deep into Ireland for decades, and then contrasting that with my own experience twenty years afterwards. Twenty years of collective memory, intellectual capital if you like, to draw on and it's a quite different thing.
> (Chilcott, 20 March 2001)

Of course there are those who argue that British policy through the 1980s and 1990s resembled an incoherent crisis-management approach to the issue (for a critique, see Cunningham, 2001, pp. 152–154). Others argue that British governments displayed 'slow learning' and it took the Thatcher/Major governments 'two decades to what Edward Heath mostly understood in 1973' (O'Leary, 1997). Yet what O'Leary terms 'ethno-national policy learning' is perhaps more convincingly explained as working within the parameters of the possible. There is no real evidence that the British government fundamentally altered its view of the Northern Ireland conflict in the period under consideration to accept it as an 'ethno-national' conflict (Dixon, 1998). Arguably the British and Irish governments had, at the outbreak of the Troubles, accepted the rationale behind such an analysis. Events on the ground in Northern Ireland, the demands and expectations of the two communities within Northern Ireland, as well as the domestic and international considerations of the two governments explain the apparent inconsistencies in British and Irish policies in the period. The point that Chilcott makes is important and also applicable to some extent to the Irish government's situation during the period.

The deepening intellectual capital of the two governments improved London and Dublin's ability to work within and have influence upon the constraints they faced. This intellectual capital helped the two governments to decide which outcomes were unrealistic and to attempt to shape policy towards achieving what they believed were realistic ends. For neither government were these ends the ideal, but each accepted that years of intellectual capital had shown them to be the most realistic options.

The capital increased throughout the peace process period. The events of the early 1990s were more difficult to frame by the experience of the Troubles up to that point. The post-ceasefire period saw the two governments attempting to reformulate policy to deal with a situation that was different in many respects to that they had become familiar with. The changed situation and the accompanying debate regarding the extent of the changes and how to respond to them placed a new strain on intergovernmental co-operation throughout much of the 1990s. The differing analyses between (and indeed within) the governments meant that intergovernmental co-operation was more difficult to achieve in the mid-1990s than it had been in the late 1980s and early 1990s.

A process not a master plan

As a result of the factors discussed above it is hard to apply a theoretical model of international relations or inter-state co-operation to Anglo-Irish relations. Indeed attempts to apply an overarching theoretical framework to the co-operation can obfuscate rather than illustrate the relationship. Application of broad-brush explanations concentrating on the 'successes' of co-operation would fail to allow the complexities of the relationship between the two states to be appreciated. Whilst theoretical explanations of the relationship can add to our understanding of intergovernmental relations we must be careful that we do not obscure what we seek to explain by their application. Patrick Keatinge's conclusion in 1982 of the relationship between the two states as 'complex interdependence' is still the best summation of the relationship between Britain and Ireland when dealing with Northern Ireland.

There is little evidence that those involved in policy formation in the two states are particularly troubled or driven by theoretical models and classifications. As one participant noted, 'I find all these academic concepts about consociation and all that thoroughly unhelpful, but I know academics like these things' (Goodall, 24 June 1999). This by itself does not of course invalidate the usefulness of theoretical explanations of international relations. This study has attempted to examine the development of the intergovernmental relationship since 1980 and to explain and contextualise its development in terms of the factors that encouraged and negated British-Irish co-operation. It is the interplay of these numerous, competing and often contradictory factors that have shaped the relationship. Whilst the factors identified above dictated the realm of the possible and set the parameters for the co-operation they did not dictate the exact form that that co-operation *must* take. There is a danger in both overstating and understating the influence of the constraints. If the constraints are seen as too restrictive then the outcome of co-operation appears inevitable and British and Irish policy appears pre-destined to travel from Dublin in 1980 to Belfast in 1998 and St Andrews in 2006, via the exact course and at the exact pace that it did. Or a view of history that FitzGerald characterised as 'a process that converts prospects that seemed at one time inconceivable into what in retrospect appears to have been inevitable' (*Irish Times*, 27 October 2001). If the constraints are under-played the two governments can be appear as omniscient Machiavellian co-conspirators implementing a detailed master-plan concocted between them and imposed on the hapless parties of Northern Ireland. Both scenarios are nonsensical. A better description of the ad hoc and comparatively pragmatic stance pursued by the two governments is given by one of the key players to the process:

> The whole history of the process from 1970/71 onwards is characterised partly by necessary opportunism and underneath supporting that policy of necessary opportunism it is a process, it is dynamic or it is nothing. It is not a conclusion that you simply get to. Therefore movement in any forward direction, however laterally is of itself a good thing, as compared with stasis.
> (Chilcott, 20 March 2001)

This does not mean that the two states were pragmatic to the point of being willing to accept absolutely any proposal that could lead to forward movement in any direction. Each state had to work within the existing constraints and to the existing values that they held. But within those restraints decisions were made as to what policies to pursue and whether to pursue them intergovernmentally or unilaterally.

There is one further danger in a study of this nature. Given its focus it is in danger of overstating the importance of the relationship it seeks to explain and evaluate. British-Irish co-operation since 1980 was responsible for important advances in the search for stability in Northern Ireland but again it needs to be emphasised that the constraints the two governments faced were real and restricting. The two governments could not solve the Northern Ireland problem, if they could it would have been solved long ago. What they can do is try and shape the debate within and on Northern Ireland, co-operate towards creating a more peaceful society and co-sponsor initiatives aimed at bringing a solution to the issue closer. These are important roles which the two states have attempted to fulfil. But given the divided nature of Northern Ireland no amount of British-Irish co-operation by itself can provide the solution. Both states and governments are, whether they like it or not, participants as well as prospective partners in the dispute and as such need to interact with the other participants to try and secure a resolution to the issue.

Bearing in mind these complexities, constraints and the cyclical nature of intergovernmental co-operation since 1980, is it possible to say that the co-operation between London and Dublin has had a positive influence on the issue? The worth of the co-operation is hard to quantify, as is the likely situation that Northern Ireland would have been in if the co-operation had not occurred. However, it is difficult to see how increased co-operation between the two states has been anything but beneficial. The ideological changes that the two states have undergone over many years has led them to adopt a more pragmatic and accommodating approach to each other and each other's interest in Northern Ireland. This in turn has enabled each state to use its relationship with its 'client' community in Northern Ireland to try and address some of the underlying areas of dispute between the two communities in the North. The level of co-operation did indeed deepen between the two states over the period as experience, institutions and co-sponsorship drew them closer together, all of which was beneficial to the situation in Northern Ireland. Yet the co-operation remains driven by pragmatic self-interest on the part of the two states. This self-interest has led the British and Irish governments to institutionalise a level of co-operation on the issue. It has not though led to a uniting of ideals and aims and as such relations over Northern Ireland remain prone to debilitating disputes and fractious recriminations. But the factors that compelled a movement towards co-operation remained strong enough to ensure this co-operation continued and deepened. There were, and remain, theoretical alternatives to intergovernmental co-operation but the constraints and compulsions highlighted in this study mean such alternatives are decreasingly likely to be used. Intergovernmental co-operation, with periodic intergovernmental disputes, will remain a key characteristic of British and Irish policy towards Northern Ireland. But the hope for the two governments is that Northern Ireland will no longer dominate intergovernmental relations (or British and Irish politics) to the extent that it did in the past. As Ahern said in an address to both Houses of the British Parliament in May 2007, 'For decades our relations have been filtered through the prism of conflict. Now, building on the peace and progress of the last decade, we can begin to pay greater attention to the wider partnership of common interests between our two islands'. Whether that turns out to be the case remains to be seen; but the chances of such an achievement and a new evaluation of the 'totality of relationships' between Britain and Ireland have never been greater.

Bibliography

Interviews

Michael Ancram, 19 October 2005.
Sir Robert Andrew, 21 November 2000.
Sir Humphrey Atkins, 26 October 1993.
Peter Barry, 23 May 2000.
Sir Kenneth Bloomfield, 19 May 2000.
Peter Brooke, 21 July 2000.
John Bruton, 6 December 2006
Lord Butler of Brockwell (formerly Sir Robin Butler), 9 November 2000.
Sir John Chilcott, 20 March 2001.
Séan Donlon, 12 April 2000.
Noel Dorr, 25 May 2000.
Séan Duignan, 25 May 2000.
Fergus Finlay, 26 January 2006
Garret FitzGerald, 13 November 1993 and 6 June 2000.
Sir David Goodall, 24 June 1999.
Lord Hurd of Westwell (formerly Douglas Hurd), 25 July 1999.
Michael Lillis, 20 October 2000.
Martin Mansergh, 25 January 2006
Lord Mayhew of Twysden (formerly Sir Patrick Mayhew) 1 November 2005.
Dermot Nally, 2 November 2000.
Sean O'Huiginn, 9 November 2005.
Albert Reynolds, 26 May 2000.
Sir Quentin Thomas, 14 September 2005.

Books, articles and theses

Ahern, B. (1999) *Ireland and Britain. A relationship for a New Millennium*, Speech to The Irish Studies Centre, University of North London, 15 April 1999.
Armstrong, L.R. (1993) 'Ethnicity, the English, and Northern Ireland: Comments and Reflections', in Keogh, D. and Haltzel, M.H. (eds) *Northern Ireland and the Politics of Reconciliation* (Cambridge: Cambridge University Press).
Arnold, B. (1984a) *Margaret Thatcher: A Study in Power* (London: Hamish Hamilton).
Arnold, B. (1984b) *What Kind of Country* (London: Jonathan Cape).
Arnold, B. (1993) *Haughey: His Life and Unlucky Deeds* (London: Jonathan Cape).
Arthur, P. (1983) 'Anglo-Irish Relations since 1968: A "Fever Chart" Interpretation', *Government and Opposition*, Vol. 18, No. 2.

Arthur, P. (1985) 'Anglo-Irish Relations and the Northern Ireland Problem', *Irish Studies in International Affairs*, Vol. 2, No. 1.

Arthur, P. (1986) 'Northern Ireland: the "Unfinished Business" of Anglo-Irish Relations' in Drudy, P.J. (ed.) *Irish Studies 5: Ireland and Britain since 1922* (Cambridge: Cambridge University Press).

Arthur, P. (1989) *Government and Politics of Northern Ireland* (2nd edn) (Harlow: Longman).

Arthur, P. (1992) 'The Brooke Initiative', *Irish Political Studies*, Vol. 7.

Arthur, P. (1993) 'The Mayhew Talks', *Irish Political Studies*, Vol. 8.

Arthur, P. (1996a) 'Anglo-Irish relations', in Aughey, A. and Morrow, D. (eds) *Northern Ireland Politics* (Essex: Longman).

Arthur, P. (1996b) "Time Territory and the Anglo-Irish 'Peace Process' ", *Government and Opposition*, Vol. 31, No. 4.

Arthur, P. (1999) 'Anglo-Irish Relations and Constitutional Policy', in Mitchell, P. and Wilford, R. (eds) *Politics in Northern Ireland* (Oxford: West View Press).

Arthur, P. (2000) *Special Relationships* (Dublin: The Blackstaff Press).

Aughey, A. (1989) *Under Siege* (Belfast: The Blackstaff Press).

Aughey, A. (1995) 'Conservative Party Politics in Northern Ireland', in Barton, B. and Roche, P. (eds) *Northern Ireland: Policies and Perspectives* (Aldershot: Avebury).

Aughey, A. (2006) 'Three Unionist Anxieties', in Cox, M., Guelke, A. and Stephen, F. (eds) *A Farewell to Arms* (2nd edn) (Manchester: Manchester University Press).

Aughey, A. and Morrow, D. (eds) (1996) *Northern Ireland Politics* (Essex: Longman).

Bardon, J. (2001) *A History of Ulster* (Belfast: Blackstaff Press).

Beresford, D. (1987) *Ten Men Dead* (London: Grafton Books).

Bew, P. (1995) *Ian Gow Memorial Lecture*.

Bew, P. and Dixon, P. (1995) 'Labour Party Policy and Northern Ireland', in Barton, B. and Roche, P. (eds) *Northern Ireland: Policies and Perspectives* (Aldershot: Avebury).

Bew, P. and Gillespie, G. (1999) *Northern Ireland: A Chronology of the Troubles 1968–1999* (Dublin: Gill and Macmillan).

Bew, P. and Patterson, H. (1985) *The British State and the Ulster Crisis* (London: Verso).

Bew, P., Gibbon, P. and Patterson, H. (1979) *The State in Northern Ireland 1921–1972* (Manchester: Manchester University Press).

Bew, P., Gibbon, P. and Patterson, H. (1995) *Northern Ireland 1921–1994. Political Forces and Social Classes* (London: Serif).

Bew, P., Hazelkorn, E. and Patterson, H. (1989) *The Dynamics of Irish Politics* (London: Lawrence and Wishart Ltd.).

Bew, P., Patterson, H. and Teague, P. (1997) *Between War and Peace* (London: Lawrence and Wishart Ltd.).

Bishop, P. and Mallie, E. (1992) *The Provisional IRA* (London: Corgi).

Bloomfield, D. (1996) *Peace Making Strategies in Northern Ireland* (London: Macmillan Press).

Bloomfield, D. (1997) *Political Dialogue in Northern Ireland* (London: Macmillan Press).

Bloomfield, K. (1994) *Stormont in Crisis* (Belfast: The Blackstaff Press).

Bowman, J. (1989) *De Valera and the Ulster Question 1917–1973* (Oxford: Oxford University Press).

Boyce, D.G. (1996) *The Irish Question and British Politics 1868–1996* (London: Macmillan Press Ltd.).

Boyle, K. and Hadden, T. (1985) *Ireland: A Positive Proposal* (Harmondsworth: Penguin Books).

Brandeth, G. (2000) *Breaking the Code. Westminster Diaries* (London: Phoenix).

Bruce, S. (1994) *The Edge of the Union* (Oxford: Oxford University Press).

Carroll, J.T. (1975) *Ireland in the War Years 1939–1945* (Newton Abbot: David and Charles).

Catterall, P. and McDougall, S. (eds) (1996) *The Northern Ireland Question in British Politics* (London: Macmillan).

Clark, A. (1994) *Diaries* (London: Phoenix).

Clarke, L. (1987) *Broadening the Battlefield* (Dublin: Gill & Macmillan).

Cochrane, F. (1993) 'Progressive or Regressive? The Anglo-Irish Agreement as a Dynamic in the Northern Ireland Polity', *Irish Political Studies*, Vol. 8.

Cochrane, F. (1994) 'Any Takers? The Isolation of Northern Ireland', *Political Studies*, Vol. XLII, No. 3.

Cochrane, F. (1995) 'The Isolation of Northern Ireland', *Political Studies*, Vol. XLIII, No. 3.

Cochrane, F. (1997) *Unionist Politics and the Politics of Unionism since the Anglo-Irish Agreement* (Cork: Cork University Press).

Cole, J. (1996) *As It Seemed to Me. Political Memoirs* (London: Phoenix).

Connolly, S.J. (ed.) (1998) *The Oxford Companion to Irish History* (Oxford: Oxford University Press).

Coogan, T.P. (1987) *The IRA* (Glasgow: Fontana Paperbacks).

Coughlan, A. (1986) *Fooled Again? The Anglo-Irish Agreement and After* (Cork: Mercier Press).

Cox, M. (1997) 'Bringing in the International; The IRA Ceasefire and the End of the Cold War', *International Affairs*, Vol. 74, No. 4.

Cox, M. (2000) 'Northern Ireland After the Cold War', in Cox, M., Guelke, A. and Stephen, F. (eds) *A Farewell to Arms?* (Manchester: Manchester University Press).

Cox, W.H. (1987) 'Managing Northern Ireland Intergovernmentally', *Parliamentary Affairs*, Vol. 40, No. 1.

Cox, W.H. (1996) 'From Hillsborough to Downing Street and After', in Catterall, P. and McDougall, S. (eds) *The Northern Ireland Question in British Politics* (London: Macmillan).

Cox, M., Guelke, A. and Stephen, F. (eds) (2006) *A Farewell to Arms?* (2nd edn) (Manchester: Manchester University Press).

Cunningham, M. (1991) *British Government Policy in Northern Ireland 1969–1989* (Manchester: Manchester University Press).

Cunningham, M. (2001) *British Government Policy in Northern Ireland 1969–2000* (Manchester: Manchester University Press).

Delaney, E. (2001) *An Accidental Diplomat* (Dublin: New Island).

Devlin, B. (1969) *The Price of my Soul* (London: Pan Books Ltd.).

Dillon, M. (1996) *25 Years of Terror* (London: Bantam Books).

Dixon, P. (1994) ' "The Usual English Doubletalk": The British Political Parties and the Ulster Unionists 1974–1994', *Irish Political Studies*, Vol. 9.

Dixon, P. (1995a) 'A House Divided cannot Stand: Britain, Bipartisanship and Northern Ireland', *Contemporary Record*, Vol. 9, No. 1, Summer.

Dixon, P. (1995b) 'Internationalization and Unionist Isolation: A Response to Feargal Cochrane', *Political Studies*, Vol. XLIII, No. 3.

Dixon, P. (1998) 'Communications', *Political Studies* Vol. XLVI, No. 3.

Dixon, P. (2001) *Northern Ireland: The Politics of War and Peace* (London: Palgrave).

Dixon, P. (2006) 'Rethinking the International and Northern Ireland: A critique', in Cox, M., Guelke, A. and Stephen, F. (eds) *A Farewell to Arms?* (2nd edn) (Manchester: Manchester University Press).

Donoghue, B. (1987) *Prime Minister: The Conduct of policy under Harold Wilson and James Callaghan* (London: Jonathan Cape).

Douglas, R., Harte, L. and O'Hara, J. (1998) *Drawing Conclusions: A Cartoon History of Anglo-Irish Relations 1798–1998* (Belfast: The Blackstaff Press).

Downey, J. (1983) *Them and Us* (Dublin: River Ward Press).

Duggan, J.P. (1989) *Neutral Ireland and the Third Reich* (Dublin: The Lilliput Press).

Duignan, S. (1995) *One Spin On The Merry-Go-Round* (Dublin: Blackwater Press).

Dwyer, T.R. (1987) *Charlie: The Political Biography of Charles J. Haughey* (Dublin: Gill and Macmillan).

English, R. (2003) *Armed Struggle: A History of the IRA* (London: Pan Macmillan).

Fanning, R. (1983) *Independent Ireland* (Dublin: Helicon Ltd.).

Fanning, R. (1984) 'The British Dimension', *Ireland: Dependence and Independence* (Dublin: RTE Books).

Fanning, R. (1985) 'Anglo-Irish Relations: Partition and the British Dimension in Historical Perspective', *Irish Studies in International Affairs*, Vol. 2, No. 1.

Fanning, R. (2001) 'Playing it Cool: The Response of the British and Irish Governments to the Crisis in Northern Ireland, 1968–9', *Irish Studies in International Affairs*, Vol. 12, pp. 57–85.

Farrington, C. (2006) *Ulster Unionism and the Peace Process in Northern Ireland* (Basingstoke: Palgrave Macmillan).

Faulkner, B. (1978) *Memoirs of a Statesman* (London: Weidenfeld and Nicolson).

Finlay, F. (1998) *Snakes and Ladders* (Dublin: New Island Books).

FitzGerald, G. (1991) *All in a Life* (Dublin: Macmillan).

FitzGerald, G. (1993) 'The Origins of the Anglo-Irish Agreement', in Keogh, D. and Haltzel, M.H. (eds) *Northern Ireland and The Politics of Reconciliation* (Cambridge: Cambridge University Press).

Flackes, W. and Elliot, S. (1989) *Northern Ireland: A Political Directory* (Belfast: The Blackstaff Press).

Forde, M. (1995) *Extradition Law in Ireland* (Dublin: Round Hall Sweet and Maxwell).

Foster, R.F. (1993) *Paddy and Mr Punch. Connections in Irish and English History* (London: Allen Lane Penguin Press).

Gallagher, E. (1985) 'Anglo-Irish Relations in the European Community', *Irish Studies in International Affairs*, Vol. 2, No. 1.

Gallagher, T. and O'Connell, J. (eds) (1983) *Contemporary Irish Studies* (Manchester: Manchester University Press).

Gillespie, P. (ed.) (1996) *Britain's European Question* (Dublin: Institute of European Affairs).

Gillespie, P. (2006) 'From Anglo-Irish to British Irish Relations', in Cox, M., Guelke, A. and Stephen, F. (eds) *A Farewell to Arms?* (2nd edn) (Manchester: Manchester University Press).

Girvin, B. (1986) 'The Anglo-Irish Agreement 1985', in Girvin, B. and Sturm, R. (eds) *Politics and Society in Contemporary Ireland* (Aldershot: Gower Publishing).

Godson, D. (2004) *Himself Alone* (London: HarperCollins).

Goodall, D. (1993) 'The Irish Question' *The Ampleforth Journal*, Vol. XCVIII, Part 1, Spring.

Goodall, D. (1993/1994) 'Terrorists on the Spot', *The Tablet*, 25 December 1993/1 January 1994.

Guelke, A. (1988) *Northern Ireland: The International Perspective* (Dublin: Gill and Macmillan).

Guelke, A. (1994) 'The Peace Processes in South Africa, Israel and Northern Ireland: A Farewell to Arms?' *Irish Studies in International Affairs*, Vol. 5.

Hadden, T. and Boyle, K. (1989) *The Anglo-Irish Agreement 1985. Commentary, Text and Official Review* (Andover: Sweet and Maxwell).

Hauswedell, C. and Brown, K. (2000) *Burying the Hatchet. The Decommissioning of Paramilitary Arms in Northern Ireland* (Bonn: BICC/INCORE).

Hayes, B. and McAllister, I. (1996) 'British and Irish Public Opinion Towards the Northern Ireland Problem, *Irish Political Studies*, Vol. 11, pp. 61–82.

Hazelkorn, E. and Patterson, H. (1994) 'The New Politics of the Irish Republic, *New Left Review*, September/October, No. 207.

Hazleton, W. (2000) 'Encouragement from the Sideline: Clinton's Role in the Good Friday Agreement', *Irish Studies in International Affairs*, Vol. 11, pp. 98–112.

Heath, A.F., Breen, R. and Whelan, C.T. (eds) (1999) *Ireland North and South: Perspectives from Social Science* (Oxford: The British Academy/Oxford University Press).

Hennessey, T. (1997) *A History of Northern Ireland 1920–1996* (London: Macmillan).

Hennessey, T. (2000) *The Northern Ireland Peace Process* (Dublin: Gill and Macmillan)

Hermon. J (1997) *Holding the Line. An autobiography* (Dublin: Gill and Macmillan).

Holland, J. (1999) *The American Connection* (Dublin: Roberts Rinehart Publishers).

Howe, G. (1994) *Conflict of Loyalty* (London: Macmillan).

Hurd, D. (2003) *Memoirs* (London: Little Brown).

Hussey, G. (1990) *At the Cutting Edge: Cabinet Diaries 1982–1987* (Dublin: Gill and Macmillan).

Hussey, G. (1995) *Ireland Today: Anatomy of a Changing State* (London: Penguin Books).

ICBH (Institute for Contemporary British History) (1997) *Anglo-Irish Witness Seminar*, 11 June.

Keatinge, P. (1982) 'An Odd Couple? Obstacles and Opportunities in Inter-State Co-operation Between the Republic of Ireland and the United Kingdom', in Rea, D. (ed.) *Political Co-operation in Divided Societies* (Dublin: Gill and Macmillan).

Keatinge, P. (1986) 'Unequal Sovereigns: The Diplomatic Dimension of Anglo-Irish Relations', in Drudy, P.J. (ed.) *Irish Studies 5: Ireland and Britain Since 1922* (Cambridge: Cambridge University Press).

Keatinge, P. (1989) 'Ireland's Foreign Relations', *Irish Studies in International Affairs*, Vol. 3, No. 1.

Kelly, H. (1972) *How Stormont Fell* (Dublin: Gill and Macmillan).

Kennedy, D. (1988) *The Widening Gulf. Northern attitudes to the independent Irish state 1919–1949* (Belfast: The Blackstaff Press).

Kennedy, M. (2000) *Division and Consensus in Ireland* (Dublin: IPA).

Kenny, A. (1986) *The Road to Hillsborough* (Oxford: Oxford University Press).

Keogh, D. and Haltzel, M.H. (eds) (1993) *Northern Ireland and the Politics of Reconciliation* (Cambridge: Cambridge University Press).

Lawson, N. (1992) *The View From Number 11* (London: Transworld Publishers).

Lee, J.J. (1989) *Ireland 1912–1985* (Cambridge: Cambridge University Press).

Lyons, F.S.L. (1985) *Ireland Since the Famine* (London: Fontana Press).

MacDonagh, O. (1983) *States of Mind: A Study of Anglo-Irish Conflict 1780–1980* (London: George Allen & Unwin).

MacManus, F. (ed.) (1978) *The Years of the Great Test* (Dublin: RTE/Mercier Press).

MacQueen, N. (1985) 'The Expedience of Tradition: Ireland, International Organizations and the Falklands Crisis', *Political Studies*, Vol. XXXIII, No. 1.

Mair, P. (1987)'Breaking the Nationalist Mould: The Irish Republic and the Anglo-Irish Agreement', in Teague, P. (ed.) *Beyond the Rhetoric* (London: Lawrence and Wishart).

Major, J. (1999) *John Major: The Autobiography* (London: HarperCollins).

Mallie, E. and McKittrick, D. (1996) *The Fight for Peace* (London: Macmillan).

Mallie, E. and McKittrick, D. (2001) *Endgame in Ireland* (Abingdon: Hodder and Stoughton).

Mansergh, M. (1986) *The Spirit of the Nation* (Cork: Mercier).

Mansergh, M. (1995) 'The Background to the Peace Process', *Irish Political Studies*, Vol. 6, pp. 145–158.

McCann, E. (1993) *War and an Irish Town* (London: Pluto Press).

McGarry, J. and O'Leary, B. (1995) *Explaining Northern Ireland* (Oxford: Blackwell).

McIntyre, A. (1995) 'Modern Irish Republicanism: The Product of British State Strategies', *Irish Political Studies*, Vol. 10.

McKittrick, D. (1996) *The Nervous Peace* (Belfast: The Blackstaff Press).

Millar, F. (2004) *David Trimble. The Price of Peace* (Dublin: Liffey Press).

Mitchell, G. (1999) *Making Peace. The inside story of the making of the Good Friday Agreement* (London: William Heinemann).

Mitchell, P. and Wilford, R. (eds) (1999) *Politics in Northern Ireland* (Oxford: West View Press).

Moloney, E. (2002) *A Secret History of the IRA* (London: Penguin)

Mowlam, M. (2002) *Momentum* (London: Hodder and Stoughton).

Mullin, C. (1990) *Error of Judgement* (Dublin: Poolbeg Press Ltd.).

Needham, R. (1998) *Battling for Peace* (Belfast: The Blackstaff Press).

Neumann, P. (2003) *Britain's Long War* (London: Palgrave).

O'Brien, C.C. (1988) *Passion and Cunning* (London: Paladin Books).

O'Brien, J. (2000) *The Arms Trial* (Dublin: Gill and Macmillan).

O'Clery, C. (1997) *The Greening of the White House* (Dublin: Gill and Macmillan).

O'Clery, C. (1999) *Ireland in Quotes* (Dublin: The O'Brien Press).

O'Halloran, C. (1987) *Partition and the Limits of Irish Nationalism: An ideology under stress* (Dublin: Gill and Macmillan).

O'Kane, E. (2002) 'The Republic of Ireland's Policy Towards Northern Ireland: The international dimension as a policy tool', *Irish Studies in International Affairs*, Vol. 13, pp. 121–133.

O'Kane, E. (2004) 'Anglo-Irish relations and the Northern Ireland Peace process: From exclusion to inclusion', *Contemporary British History*, Vol. 18, No. 1, pp. 79–99.

O'Leary, B. (1987) 'The Anglo-Irish Agreement: Meanings, Explanations, Results and a Defence', in Teague, P. (ed.) *Beyond the Rhetoric* (London: Lawrence and Wishart).

O'Leary, B. (1989) 'Limits to Coercive Consociationalism in Northern Ireland', *Political Studies*, Vol. XXXVIII, No. 4.

O'Leary, B. (1997) 'The Conservative Stewardship of Northern Ireland 1979–97: sound-bottomed contradictions or slow learning?', *Political Studies*, Vol. XLV, No. 4.

O'Leary, B. and McGarry, J. (1993) *The Politics of Antagonism* (London: Athlone Press).

O'Leary, C., Elliot, S. and Wilford, R.A. (1988) *The Northern Ireland Assembly, 1982–1986* (London: Hurst & Co.).

O'Malley, P. (1983) *The Uncivil Wars* (Boston: Beacon Press).

O'Malley, P. (1990a) *Biting at the Grave: The Irish Hunger Strikes and the Politics of Despair* (Belfast: The Blackstaff Press).

O'Malley, P. (1990b) *Northern Ireland, Questions of Nuance* (Belfast: Blackstaff Press).

O'Neill, T. (1972) *The Autobiography of Terence O'Neill* (London: Rupert Hart-Davis).

O'Rawe, R. (2005) *Blanketmen: An Untold Story of the H-Block Hunger Strike* (Dublin: New Island Books).

Owen, E.A. (1994) *The Anglo-Irish Agreement: The First Three Years* (Cardiff: University of Wales Press).

Patterson, H. (1997) *The Politics of Illusion* (London: Serif).

Patterson, H. (1999) 'Séan Lemass and the Ulster Question, 1959–65', *Journal of Contemporary History*, Vol. 34, No. 1.

Peck, J. (1978) *Dublin From Downing Street* (Dublin: Gill and Macmillan).

Prior, J. (1986) *A Balance of Power* (London: Hamilton).

Purdie, B. (1990) *Politics in the Street* (Belfast: The Blackstaff Press).

Rawnsley, A. (2001) *Servants of the People* (London: Penguin).

Rea, D. (ed.) (1982) *Political Co-Operation in Divided Socities* (Dublin: Gill and Macmillan).

Ruane, J. and Todd. J. (1996) *The Dynamics of Conflict in Northern Ireland* (Cambridge: Cambridge University Press).

Salmon, T. (1989) *Unneutral Ireland* (Oxford: Oxford University Press).

Seitz, R. (1998) *Over Here* (London: Phoenix).

Seldon, A. (1997) *Major: A Political Life* (London: Weidenfield & Nicolson).

Sharrock, D. and Davenport, M. (1997) *Man of War, Man of Peace?: The Unauthorised Biography of Gerry Adams* (London: Macmillan).

Shepherd, R. (1997) *Enoch Powell* (Pimlico: Hutchinson).

Sinn Féin (1993) *Setting the Record Straight* (Belfast: Sinn Féin).

Sloan, G.R. (1997) *The Geopolitics of Anglo-Irish Relations* (London: Continuum Publishing).

Spring, D. (1996) 'British-Irish Relations: A New Vision', *Etudes Irlandaises*, Vol. 21, No. 1.

Stalker, J. (1988) *Stalker* (London: Harrap).

Stewart, A.T.Q. (1989) *The Narrow Ground. The Roots of the Conflict in Ulster* (London: Faber and Faber Ltd.).

Stuart, M. (1998) *Douglas Hurd: Public Servant* (Edinburgh: Mainstream Publishing).

Tannam, E. (1999) *Cross Border Cooperation in the Republic of Ireland and Northern Ireland* (London: Macmillan).

Tannam, E. (2001) 'Explaining the Good Friday Agreement: A Learning Process', *Government and Opposition*, Vol. 36, No. 4.

Taylor, N. and Walker, C. (1997) 'The British-Irish parliamentary Body', *Northern Ireland Legal Quarterly*, Vol. 84, No. 4, Winter.

Taylor, P. (1987) *Stalker: The search for the truth* (London: Faber and Faber).

Taylor, P. (1998) *Provos. The IRA and Sinn Féin* (London: Bloomsbury Publishing).

Taylor, P. (1999) *Loyalists* (London: Bloomsbury Publishing Plc.).

Thatcher, M. (1993) *The Downing Street Years* (London: HarperCollins).

Tonge, J. (2004) *The New Northern Irish Politics?* (Basingstoke: Palgrave Macmilan).

Toolis, K. (1995) *Rebel Hearts: Journeys within the IRA's soul* (London: Picador).

Townshend, C. (ed.) (1988) *Consensus in Ireland. Approaches and Recessions* (Oxford: Oxford University Press).

Walsh, D. (1986) *The Party* (Dublin: Gill and Macmillan).

White, B. (1985) *John Hume. Statesman of the Troubles* (Belfast: The Blackstaff Press).

Whitelaw, W. (1989) *The Whitelaw Memoirs* (London: Aurum Press).

Whyte, J. (1991) *Interpreting Northern Ireland* (Oxford: Oxford University Press).

Wilford, R. (ed.) (2001) *Aspects of the Good Friday Agreement* (Oxford: Oxford University Press).

Wright, F. (1989)'Northern Ireland and British-Irish Relations', *Studies*, Vol. 78, Summer.

Index